Inside Narnia

Inside Narnia

A Guide to Exploring
*The Lion, the Witch
and the Wardrobe*

Devin Brown

BakerBooks
Grand Rapids, Michigan

Published by Baker Books
a division of Baker Publishing Group
P.O. Box 6287, Grand Rapids, MI 49516-6287

Printed in the United States of America

ISBN 0-8010-6599-2

Contents

Preface   7
Introduction   10

1. Lucy Looks into a Wardrobe   19
2. What Lucy Found There   45
3. Edmund and the Wardrobe   57
4. Turkish Delight   69
5. Back on This Side of the Door   82
6. Into the Forest   90
7. A Day with the Beavers   103
8. What Happened after Dinner   118
9. In the Witch's House   132
10. The Spell Begins to Break   143
11. Aslan Is Nearer   157
12. Peter's First Battle   166
13. Deep Magic from the Dawn of Time   185
14. The Triumph of the Witch   197
15. Deeper Magic from Before the Dawn of Time   211
16. What Happened about the Statues   225
17. The Hunting of the White Stag   235

Reference List   253

Preface

"The best way to enjoy the Chronicles of Narnia is simply to read them. However, some points might be made towards a fuller appreciation of them."

Walter Hooper, C. S. *Lewis: A Companion and Guide* (1996, 447)

"Why another Lewis book?"

The strongest reason for any new work must be that it (1) takes an approach not taken before or (2) covers ground which has not been covered. I would offer both these reasons for *Inside Narnia: A Guide to Exploring* The Lion, the Witch and the Wardrobe.

While many books have been written about the Narnia stories, most of them take a *devotional* rather than a *literary* approach. In the handful of nondevotional works about the series, each of the Chronicles is typically covered in just a single chapter. By devoting an entire work to *The Lion, the Witch and the Wardrobe*, I hope to provide the kind of close literary analysis it warrants and also supply a good deal of supplemental information from Lewis's life and other writings. In addition, I offer a wide selection of comments and opinions from other scholars, here for the first time collected in a single work. All told, *Inside Narnia* brings together a combination of elements which I believe will add up to the kind of lively, in-depth discussion that Lewis fans old and new will enjoy.

One further characteristic about my book distinguishes it from previous works which often select a single aspect—such as imagination or the arts—and then focus only on sections of the story where that feature is present. My approach is to go through the text from beginning to end, exploring whatever features are found. In this respect my book is more like a running commentary than a collection of formal essays.

My claim is this: although *The Lion, the Witch and the Wardrobe* can be simply read and enjoyed by children, it also can be read seriously by adults because it is a work rich with meaning. Some of this meaning will be discovered just by spending time with the text and paying close attention to what Lewis has written. Further meaning will be seen by drawing connections—connections not only to other passages within the novel but also to other works by Lewis, to the events of Lewis's life, and to the work of other writers who influenced Lewis. The most significant of these other writers is J. R. R. Tolkien, who not only greatly influenced Lewis but also was greatly influenced by him. I contend that this twofold approach—first, a careful reading and then second, adding these kinds of connections—will result in greater enjoyment of an already enjoyable book.

In an essay aptly titled "Sometimes Fairy Stories May Say Best What's to Be Said," Lewis claimed one of the chief reasons he chose to write in the form of a fairy tale was "its inflexible hostility to all analysis, digression, reflections and 'gas'" (1982f, 46). But is a fairy tale really hostile to analysis? Any of my digressions or reflections which shed light on *The Lion, the Witch and the Wardrobe* would serve to contradict Lewis's point. Anytime my comments seem more like just gas, I provide support for his position.

A good general rule is to always read the original work first. My book is intended to be a commentary on Lewis's work, not a substitute for it. I have assumed that my readers have already completed *The Lion, the Witch and the Wardrobe*. My discussion includes numerous "spoilers," where I refer to future events. In order to help readers who may want to switch back and forth between my book and Lewis's, each of my chapters has the same number and name as the corresponding chapter from *The Lion, the Witch and the Wardrobe*. To keep interruptions to a minimum while at the same time allowing those who wish to find a quote the chance to do so, I indicate specific references to *The Lion, the Witch and the Wardrobe* by page number only. If within a paragraph I quote a second time from the same page, I do not give the page number again.

Finally, critics disagree, sometimes quite deeply, on a number of issues raised by *The Lion, the Witch and Wardrobe*. On some of these topics, I make my position clear. For example, I do not see Lewis's decision to include Father Christmas as a flaw, though many Lewis scholars do. On other issues I offer a number of differing viewpoints and allow readers to come to their own conclusions. My goal is not to try to offer the definitive word on any of these subjects, as someone writing an article for an academic journal might try to do. My hope is that my observations here will stimulate further discussion and encourage readers to begin thinking about these issues themselves.

And now with these preliminary remarks out of the way, on to the story.

Introduction

In the summer of 1948, Clive Staples Lewis, like most men his age, must have paused more than once to consider his upcoming fiftieth birthday, just months away. As he looked out from his rooms in Oxford, surely he must have felt that the boy from the suburbs of Belfast, Northern Ireland, born on November 29, 1898, the son of a police court lawyer and an educated rector's daughter, had done pretty well—all things considered.

Those fifty years began well but soon took a turn for the worse. After a somewhat idyllic childhood, Lewis faced the death of his mother when he was nine, and after that came the disastrous series of private schools where bullying often seemed to be more in fashion than learning. But when he was fifteen, his father had allowed him, after a great deal of persuading, to complete his final two years of preparing for university with a wonderful tutor. Those studies resulted in a scholarship to the most prestigious academic institution in the country, perhaps in the world—Oxford University.

Then came six years as a student at Oxford: six because a brief stint in the trenches of France during World War I intervened; six because he had gotten two degrees—one in philosophy and one in literature—with firsts on all his exams, the highest mark possible. Finally on May 20, 1925, at the age of twenty-six, Lewis had been chosen to be a fellow at Magdalen College.

There at Magdalen College, Oxford, Lewis was given his own set of rooms, rooms he had been using for twenty-three years now for student tutorials, for preparing lectures, for meetings with his friends, and, whenever he could squeeze it in, for writing.

Lewis's first two works, extensive book-length poems, had gone nowhere after they were published. No matter how he had tried, he was not a poet, at least not a critically acclaimed one. But his later works had succeeded where these had not, and his writing had taken off in directions he would never have predicted—that no one would have predicted.

Over the past ten years, he had published a science fiction trilogy, a philosophical book on the problem of pain, a satirical novel about the afterlife, a treatise on miracles, and a book of letters from a devil named Screwtape—all successes. In addition, he had broadcast a series of talks on the BBC, had received an honorary Doctor of Divinity degree from St. Andrews, and, to top it all off, had even been featured on the cover of *Time* magazine.

Of course, besides his brother, he had no family to speak of—no wife or children, at least not yet. But by way of compensation he had a family of another sort, the Inklings, his writing and conversation group which included his closest friends. Among them was his colleague J. R. R. Tolkien, who had just finished a long fictional epic about a ring and a race called hobbits and was now working on getting it published.

And so in the summer of 1948, as Professor Lewis looked back over his fifty years, he must have found much to be proud of. But with the greater part of his life behind him, his thoughts must also have turned to all he still hoped to accomplish.

One project kept forcing its way back into his reflections: a story he had started nine years ago during the war . . . a story he had written the opening paragraph for, and then put away . . . a story about four children who went to stay with an old professor . . . a story based on a picture which had been in his head since he was sixteen, the image of a faun from Greek mythology, carrying an umbrella and parcels as he walked home through a snowy wood. . . .

In the summer of 1948, as he approached his fiftieth birthday, C. S. Lewis picked up pen and paper and resumed the story he had started nine years earlier, shortly after a group of schoolgirls evacuated from London had come to stay with him.

What he could not have known was that he was beginning what many would later consider to be one of his greatest accomplishments.

༼ ༽

On October 16, 1950, six weeks before Lewis's fifty-second birthday, *The Lion, the Witch and the Wardrobe* was released in England by Geoffrey Bles Publishers. Three weeks later, Macmillan issued the U.S. version of the novel. Although he had supported Lewis's other works, fellow writer J. R. R. Tolkien did not like the book, responding, "It really won't do, you know!" (Green and Hooper 241). Tolkien's biggest complaint was Lewis's "jumble of unrelated mythologies"—the Roman fauns and nymphs, the Germanic dwarfs, Father Christmas, and the new characters of Lewis's own invention—all in the same work (Sayer 312).

Despite Tolkien's misgivings, *The Lion, the Witch and the Wardrobe* was an instant success and has remained widely popular over the years, with copies of the individual volumes and the boxed set of the Chronicles of Narnia selling into the tens of millions. After the initial volume, Lewis published one Chronicle each year until the seven-book set was complete. When *The Last Battle* came out in 1956, it won the Carnegie Medal, an award given by children's librarians to the year's most outstanding book for young people, though in Lewis's case perhaps given as much in recognition for the whole series as for the final book.

The Lion, the Witch and the Wardrobe was the first of the seven Chronicles of Narnia that Lewis wrote. While he was alive it was always listed as the first volume in the series. In 1980, seventeen years after Lewis's death, Collins, part of what would later become

HarperCollins, first published the stories with a somewhat different numbering; *The Magician's Nephew*—originally listed sixth—was moved to first, and *The Lion, the Witch and the Wardrobe* was numbered second. This revised order appears on all editions published today along with this statement on the copyright page: "The HarperCollins editions of The Chronicles of Narnia have been renumbered in compliance with the original wishes of the author, C. S. Lewis."

The change was in part based upon a letter Lewis wrote in 1957 to a young boy named Laurence Krieg. In response to a question about which order the Narnia books should be read in—the way they were originally numbered, which corresponded with their order of publication, or their chronological order—Lewis came down in a qualified way slightly on the side of chronology, which was the way Laurence Krieg had proposed. Maybe Lewis really felt renumbering the Chronicles would be an improvement, but quite possibly he was simply trying to be supportive of a young fan's suggestion, as he went on to add, "perhaps it does not matter very much in which order anyone reads them" (1995, 68).

In his book *Imagination and the Arts in C. S. Lewis*, Hope College professor Peter Schakel includes an essay which questions the meaning of the phrase from the copyright page "the original wishes of the author." He writes, "Does original mean from the time at which *The Magician's Nephew* was completed? If so, why did Lewis not request the Bodley Head to include this renumbering in the new book, or in *The Last Battle* the following year, or have Geoffrey Bles change the order in later reprints of the other books?" (Schakel 2002, 43). Schakel takes a firm stand regarding Lewis's statement to Laurence Krieg, arguing that the reading order in fact "matters a great deal" (44) and that if readers are going to share the wonder and suspense of the children in the story, they need to read the Chronicles in the order they were published. This means reading *The Lion, the Witch and the Wardrobe* first.

Lewis's letter to Laurence Krieg is famous among Narnia enthusiasts for another reason. From it we learn about Lewis's plans, or rather his lack of plans, for further Chronicles. Lewis told Krieg,

"When I wrote *The Lion, the Witch, and the Wardrobe* I did not know I was going to write any more. Then I wrote *Prince Caspian* as a sequel and still didn't think there would be any more, and when I had done *The Voyage of the* Dawn Treader I felt quite sure it would be the last" (1995, 68).

Questions, controversy, and mixed opinions about the Chronicles of Narnia still abound today. An article headlined "Narnia books attacked as racist and sexist" appeared in the June 3, 2002, issue of the British newspaper *The Guardian*. In it John Ezard quotes Philip Pullman, the Whitbread Book Award–winning author of the His Dark Materials trilogy, who calls Lewis's work "propaganda" and accuses it of being "monumentally disparaging of girls and women" and "blatantly racist." Laura Miller, senior editor for the online magazine *Salon*, has also been critical of the Narnia books in certain ways. In an article titled "Personal Best" which appeared in the September 30, 1996 issue, Miller described an experience shared by a number of readers as they grew older. She states, "Lewis's books are very, very English and very Christian, in a particular way. The latter I didn't realize until I was a good deal older, and this discovery filled me with anger and bitterness. I had been tricked into giving my heart to the very noxious, twisted religion I had tried so hard to elude."

Children's literature scholar Peter Hunt has also cast a less-than-favorable eye on Lewis's series for young people, claiming that "not far beneath the genial surface of the books lie some very sexist, racist, and violent attitudes" (2001, 200). About the widely varying responses which the books have generated, Hunt claims, "If there is a single, central example of the divergence of popular and critical taste, then the seven books concerning the mythical land of Narnia . . . must qualify" (199).

Another anti-Narnia voice comes from a very different source—the radical right of fundamental Christianity, a somewhat strange bedfellow of other critics. A website titled Balaam's Ass Speaks includes a section called "C. S. Lewis: The Devil's Wisest Fool." In it Mary Van Nattan claims, "The Chronicles of Narnia are one of the most powerful tools of Satan that Lewis ever produced. Worst of all, these books are geared toward children." The leading criticism raised in the essay, one which given its source may not be completely unexpected, is that the series is an "indoctrinating tool of witchcraft."

While opponents often raise strong, even vehement, objections, fans' support for *The Lion, the Witch and the Wardrobe* has remained unwavering. In British bookseller Waterstone's voting for "Best Books of the Century," *The Lion, the Witch and the Wardrobe* finished twenty-first, ahead of works by such acclaimed authors as Franz Kafka, Virginia Woolf, John Steinbeck, and Toni Morrison. In The Big Read series sponsored by the BBC in fall 2003, voters ranked *The Lion, the Witch and the Wardrobe* as their number nine choice.

To coincide with the fiftieth anniversary of the publication of *The Lion, the Witch and the Wardrobe*, HarperCollins released a special deluxe hardcover edition with nineteen full-color plates by the original illustrator Pauline Baynes. In the United States, the Focus on the Family Radio Theatre has produced audio adaptations of all seven of the Narnia stories, with Douglas Gresham, Lewis's stepson, serving as host. Some of the famous voices include Paul Scofield as the narrator and David Suchet as Aslan.

The first film adaptations of the stories were made by the BBC in the late 1980s. Rather low-budget projects, they still have their share of devoted fans, though many viewers see them now as somewhat dated. The major motion picture version of *The Lion, the Witch and the Wardrobe*, directed by Andrew Adamson and scheduled for release in December 2005, builds on the positive reception given to the *Harry Potter* films and Peter Jackson's *Lord of the Rings*.

Anyone looking at the fairy tale Lewis put to paper around his fiftieth birthday must wonder at its enduring popularity and wide acceptance. How is it that its appeal has not waned over the years but has remained steady and even grown?

For one answer, we can turn to a distinction used by Lewis himself. In an essay titled "On Three Ways of Writing for Children," Lewis described what he called a Boy's Book or a Girl's Book. In it, he says, we find "the immensely popular and successful schoolboy or schoolgirl," the one who "discovers the spy's plot or rides the horse that none of the cowboys can manage" (Lewis 1982e, 38). The problem with this book, he claims, is that while we find pleasure in reading it, we always return to our own world feeling as though our own life can never measure up. We will never catch the spy; we will never ride the unrideable pony; we will not be friends with magicians. We run to this book, Lewis states, to escape from "the disappointments and humiliations of the real world" but then afterwards return "undivinely discontented" to reality, to a world and to a life in that world which have been made a little less wonderful than before.

A second type of book, Lewis suggests, wipes away the film of the ordinary from our world and makes the events of our daily lives and the people we encounter more special, not less. After reading this type of book, we do not despise our friends, our robins, or our wardrobes for being unmagical. These stories cast a spell over our world and make all robins and wardrobes a little marvelous, a little more wonderful than before. We see with a new perspective that indeed our friends in a sense *are* magicians. As Lewis states, the reader of this second kind of book "does not despise real woods because he has read of enchanted woods: the reading makes all real woods a little enchanted" (1982e, 38).

While Lewis intended this distinction to refer to young people's books in general, *The Lion, the Witch and the Wardrobe* certainly fits his description of this second type of book rather than the first, and one of its chief functions is to re-enchant a disenchanted world.

Lewis biographer A. N. Wilson has observed that since the publication of *The Lion, the Witch and the Wardrobe* in 1950, "a whole generation has grown up of people who read the Narnia stories in childhood" (1991, 220) and then passed them on to their own children and even to their grandchildren, making the stories a part of the cultural heritage for three generations of readers on both sides of the Atlantic. Another explanation for the enduring popularity of *The Lion, the Witch and the Wardrobe* is that the Narnia stories represent, as Green and Hooper note, "a new mythology" (1994, 251) and as such can play an integral role in the personal growth and development of those who read them. Roland Hein, author of *Christian Mythmakers*, has argued, "With Lewis, myth was a vehicle by which supernatural reality communicates to man" (1998, 206).

The difficulty in achieving worldwide recognition in even a single genre makes Lewis's ability to switch from the expository writing in his early works to the mythic-style fiction seen in the Chronicles of Narnia all the more remarkable. Clearly Lewis understood the need for a creative format rather than a discursive one in order to address life's most fundamental questions. Speaking of himself as well as of others writing in a similar vein, he said that "there may be an author who at a particular moment finds not only fantasy but fantasy-for-children the exactly right form for what he wants to say" (Lewis 1982e, 36). Lewis believed that by conveying vital insights through an imaginary mode, one could make them "for the first time appear in their real potency" (1982f, 47).

Lewis saw myth not as "misunderstood history, . . . nor diabolical illusion, . . . nor priestly lying, . . . but, at its best, a real though unfocused gleam of divine truth falling on human imagination" (Lewis 1996d, 134) and as a form which "enables man to express the inexpressible" (Kilby 1964, 81). In the preface to the anthology of George MacDonald that Lewis compiled, he wrote that myth "gets under our skin" and "hits us at a level deeper than our thoughts" (MacDonald 1996, xxviii).

Lewis further clarifies what he saw as the function of myth for its readers by saying, "In the enjoyment of a great myth we come nearest to experiencing as a concrete what can otherwise be understood only as an abstraction" (1996e, 66). In another context Lewis wrote that the experience of myth "is not only grave but awe inspiring. . . . It is as if something of great moment had been communicated to us" (1996a, 44).

Clyde Kilby, one of the first scholars to write about Lewis, has noted Lewis's recognition of the importance of myth-making as "one of man's deepest needs and highest accomplishments" (Kilby 1964, 80). Kilby argues that Lewis wrote "hardly a single book in which he does not, in one way or another, discuss and illustrate this subject." What, according to Lewis, was behind myth-making? Kilby explains that Lewis envisioned a "great sovereign, uncreated, unconditioned Reality at the core of things" (81) and viewed myth as "a kind of picture-making which helps man to understand this Reality" as well as a response to "a deep call from that Reality."

In describing Lewis's decision to write in a fictional rather than expository mode, Donald Glover states that Lewis did so because he believed that this "indirect" approach could "bring the reader closer to the truth" (1981, 3). In his book *C. S. Lewis: The Art of Enchantment*, Glover suggests that Lewis was well aware of the power of myth "to present in understandable form concepts which could be approached in no other direct fashion" (51).

"Let us suppose that this everyday world were, at some point, invaded by the marvelous" (Lewis 1982b, 21). C. S. Lewis penned these words to describe the feeling evoked by the novels of his friend Charles Williams. However, Lewis's description could equally be used to describe the effect produced by his own stories. More than fifty years after it was first published, readers from all over the world, young and old, continue to share the perception that as they read *The Lion, the Witch and the Wardrobe*, their everyday world truly *is* invaded by the marvelous.

ONE

Lucy Looks into a Wardrobe

Depending on the edition they have, as readers first open the book, they may find a map of Narnia included before chapter one. Because the events in *The Lion, the Witch and the Wardrobe* (which I will typically refer to from here on as *TLWW*) occur within a relatively small section of Narnia, the map will have more relevance for later books in the series. Before jumping into the story itself, it may be helpful to say a few words about Lewis's dedication here and about the illustrations which will appear throughout the work.

The Dedication

Lewis's dedication of *TLWW* appears just before the contents page. Lucy Barfield, addressed as "My dear Lucy," was Lewis's goddaughter and the adopted daughter of Owen Barfield, one of Lewis's best friends and an occasional member of Lewis and Tolkien's writing group, the Inklings. Barfield met Lewis when they were students together at Oxford and later served as the solicitor for the charitable trust into which Lewis put most of the royalties from his books. Lewis described Barfield as the kind of friend who "disagrees with you about everything" (1955, 199) and dedicated *The Allegory of Love* to him, referring to Barfield as "the wisest and best of my unofficial teachers" (1992, v).

In the dedication Lewis tells Lucy, "I wrote this story for you." Lewis did not intend these words to mean he wrote in the same way that, for example, Lewis Carroll wrote *Alice in Wonderland* particularly for Alice Liddell. In his essay "On Three Ways of Writing for Children," Lewis described one kind of writing which seeks to give "what the modern child wants" (1982e, 31). A second kind, he noted, "grows out of a story told to a particular child" and was the source for stories written by "Lewis Carroll, Kenneth Grahame, and Tolkien" (32). Lewis continued, "The third way, which is the only one I could ever use myself, consists in writing a children's story because a children's story is the best art-form for something you have to say: just as a composer might write a Dead March not because there was a public funeral in view but because certain musical ideas that had occurred to him went best into that form."

Lewis's practice was to dedicate nearly all of his books to someone close to him, and the Narnia dedications were always to children. Later Narnia books were dedicated as follows: *Prince Caspian* (1951), to Mary Clare Harvard, daughter of fellow Inkling Dr. R. E. "Humphrey" Harvard; *The Voyage of the* Dawn Treader (1952), to Lucy's foster brother Geoffrey Barfield; *The Silver Chair* (1953), to Nicholas Hardie, son of Inkling Colin Hardie; *The Horse and His Boy* (1954), to Lewis's future stepsons David and Douglas Gresham; and *The Magician's Nephew* (1955), to the Kilmer family, an American family whose children Lewis corresponded with in his *Letters to Children*. *The Last Battle* (1956) is the only Narnia book which has no dedication.

In his dedication to *TLWW*, Lewis goes on to write that he fears in the time it has taken to complete the book Lucy has already become "too old for fairy tales." Lucy Barfield was born in November 1935 and so would have been twelve when Lewis began writing the story and nearly fifteen when it was finally released. Whether she indeed felt herself too old for the book when it appeared in 1950 has not been recorded. Lucy Barfield died on May 3, 2003.

The suggestion that young people may at some point think they have outgrown Narnia reappears again at the end of the Chronicles in *The Last Battle*. There Susan is reported as telling her siblings that their adventures in Narnia were just "funny games we used to play when we were children" (1994b, 154). In the dedication to *TLWW*, Lewis concludes with the hope that someday Lucy "will be old enough to start reading fairy tales again," and in this statement readers may find a parallel, and thus hope, for Susan also.

Despite the disclaimer in his dedication, Lewis was in fact adamant that good fairy stories would be enjoyed by all ages. In fact, he insisted "a book worth reading only in childhood is not worth reading even then" (1982f, 48), an assertion which children's literary scholar Peter Hunt has called "one of the worst critical dicta" (2001, 200). Though all the Chronicles' dedications are to young people, Lewis stated that in his stories about Narnia he was not intending to write something "below adult attention" (1982f, 47), and in fact the stories have very loyal fans among both younger and older readers.

In the final chapter of *That Hideous Strength*, the third volume of his space trilogy which had been published five years earlier, Lewis included a passage which his dedication to Lucy here reprises. At that point in the story, Mark Stoddard has recently come to his senses and has stopped at a little country hotel on his way to rejoin his wife and the forces of good. After tea and a hard-boiled egg, he picks up an old volume of *The Strand*. There Mark finds a serial children's story "which he had begun to read as a child but abandoned because his tenth birthday came when he was half way through it and he was ashamed to read it after that" (2003, 358). We are told, "Now, he chased it from volume to volume till he had finished it. It was good." In both this passage and in the dedication to *TLWW*, Lewis was actually echoing his own experience, which he described this way: "When I was ten, I read fairy tales in secret and would have been ashamed if I had been found doing so. Now that I am fifty I read them openly" (1982e, 34).

This idea of never being too grown-up for fairy tales is so important that Lewis will focus on it again in the second Narnia book. When Caspian expresses delight in the tales of naiads, dryads, dwarfs, and "lovely little fauns," his Uncle Miraz reprimands him, saying, "That's all nonsense, for babies. . . . Only fit for babies, do you hear? You're getting too old for that sort of stuff. At your age you ought to be thinking of battles and adventures, not fairy tales" (1994e, 42). Miraz banishes the nurse who has been telling Caspian these stories, but Lewis's point is made clear when Miraz is defeated in the end and Caspian and his old nurse are reunited (204).

The Illustrations

Most readers see the illustrations as an integral part of *TLWW* and can hardly imagine the book without them. Because Lewis approved of each of the drawings and since from the start they have been included in every edition, we should explore both what they contribute and how they contribute to our experience of the book. While not every illustration warrants comment, as we go through the text many will be discussed because of something special they add to our understanding of the story or because of a particular issue they raise.

Pauline Baynes, who did the illustrations for all seven Narnia books, was born in England in 1922. In advance of the Lewis Centenary and the fiftieth anniversary of *TLWW*, she was asked by HarperCollins to go back and add color to her original black-and-white drawings. As with many issues related to Narnia, readers have strong feelings about both versions—some insist the original black-and-white drawings are superior; others accept or even prefer the colored ones since they were done by the original artist herself.

Lewis became associated with Baynes as a result of the pictures she had drawn for J. R. R. Tolkien's *Farmer Giles of Ham*, published in

1949. Besides the illustrations which appear in the seven Chronicles, Baynes also created two maps of Narnia. One was part of the original hardback edition, and one was made into a poster which on some editions can be found printed inside the book's back cover.

Lewis personally met with Baynes several times to discuss her drawings. In a letter written in 1967, she described in part what it was like to work with him:

> When he *did* criticize, it was put over so charmingly, that it wasn't a criticism, i.e., I did the drawings as best as I could—(I can't have been much more than 21 and quite untrained) and didn't realize how hideous I had made the children—they were as nice as I could get them—and Dr. Lewis said, when we were starting on the second book, 'I know you made the children rather plain—*in the interests of realism*—but do you think you could possibly pretty them up a little now?'—was that not charmingly put? (Hooper 1996, 406–7)

George Sayer, Lewis's student and later his good friend, has recorded that Lewis considered illustrating the stories himself but decided that "even if he had the skill, he would not have the time" (1994, 314). Readers who would like to see what these pictures might have looked like can see examples of Lewis's early attempts at drawing in *Boxen*, a book named after the world Lewis created when he was a boy and published in 1985, many years after his death. Sayer notes that Lewis once said about Baynes, "She can't draw lions, but she is so good and beautiful and sensitive that I can't tell her this" (315).

Except for the one rather anthropomorphic drawing of Aslan talking with the White Witch which appears in chapter thirteen (Lewis 1994c, 143; note that future references to the book will indicate page number only unless further clarification is needed), Lewis's opinion of Baynes's lions does not seem to be one generally shared by readers. Colin Duriez has written that in joining up with Baynes, Lewis was paired with an illustrator "whose imagination complemented his own" (2000, 30).

Baynes went on to illustrate works by many other authors—books by Alison Uttley, Rumer Godden, and Mary Norton as well as editions of the stories by Hans Christian Andersen and Beatrix Potter—but when she began the Narnia project, she was young and inexperienced. Because of this, the drawings were "modestly paid work for hire," and years later Baynes would note that "even minimal royalties would have 'supported' her for life" (Lindskoog 1998c, 93).

After Baynes had drawn the illustrations for the fifth book, *The Horse and His Boy*, Lewis sent her a letter expressing his pleasure with her work, although in a somewhat backhanded way. Lewis wrote:

> I lunched with Bles [the publisher] yesterday to see the drawings for *The Horse and His Boy* and feel I must write to tell you how very much we both enjoyed them. It is delightful to find (and not only for selfish reasons) that you do each book a little bit better than the last—it is nice to see an artist growing. (If only you could take six months off and devote them to anatomy, there's no limit to your possibilities.) . . . The result is exactly right. Thanks enormously for all the intense work you have put into them all. (1993, 436)

When the final book in the Narnia series, *The Last Battle*, was awarded the Carnegie Medal, a prize similar to America's Newbery Medal, Baynes wrote Lewis to congratulate him. He graciously responded, "Is it not rather 'our' Medal? I'm sure the illustrations were taken into consideration as well as the text" (Hooper 1996, 408). After finishing the drawings for the Narnia books, Baynes went on to illustrate Tolkien's *The Adventures of Tom Bombadil* (1962) and *Smith of Wootton Major* (1967). She won Britain's Kate Greenaway Medal in 1968 for her illustrations in Grant Uden's *Dictionary of Chivalry*.

Chapter One: Lucy Looks into a Wardrobe

The first sentence of *TLWW* introduces four children who have come to stay at the house of an old professor because London, where their home is located, is under attack during the air raids of World War II. Not until two books later, in *The Voyage of the Dawn Treader*, do we find out that their last name is Pevensie (Lewis 1994g, 3). In an interview which appeared in the June 28, 2004, *New Zealand Herald*, film director Andrew Adamson said this about his forthcoming adaptation of Lewis's book: "I've really tried to make the story about a family which is disenfranchised and disempowered in World War II." Lewis will say almost nothing about the rest of the family in *TLWW*. After this brief mention of the air raids on the opening page, no concern or anxiety is ever expressed about the mother and father who, presumably, have remained in London. In fact, the only mention of Mr. and Mrs. Pevensie in *TLWW* comes about because Peter and Susan are worried about Lucy's safety, not their parents' (46–7).

A girl named Lucy (perhaps a nod to Lucy Barfield from the dedication) appears as the last named, the youngest, and the most sympathetically portrayed of the four children. Paul Ford, a leading Narnia scholar, has suggested that Lucy is the character "through whom the reader sees and experiences most of Narnia" and that through her Lewis expresses his own "religious and personal sensibilities" (1994, 275). Colin Manlove notes that Lucy is the most spiritually perceptive and suggests that "not for nothing is her name Lucy," a name which comes from lucidity or *lux*, meaning *light* (1987, 135). Don King argues that Lucy is one of Lewis's most endearing characters. King observes, "We follow her from her initial entry into Narnia and share her wonder and excitement as she encounters the Narnian world. Later, when she meets abuse from Edmund and skepticism from Peter and Susan, we sympathize with her" (1986, 20).

When Owen Barfield was asked about the connection between his own daughter and the character Lucy in the novel, he responded, "The question whether Lucy Pevensie was 'named after' Lucy Barfield is one I never put to Lewis. I should have thought the opening words of the dedication were a sufficiently appropriate answer" (Hooper 1996, 758). As to whether Lewis had Lucy Barfield directly in mind in portraying Lucy Pevensie, Barfield replied, "I think the answer must be no; because, although he had very willingly consented to be her Godfather, they saw very little of each other in the latter years of his life."

During the war, a group of children—all girls—did in fact come to stay at Lewis's home, the Kilns. On September 5, 1939, Lewis wrote to his older brother Warren, or Warnie, who had been recalled up for active service: "Our schoolgirls have arrived and all seem to me . . . to be very nice, unaffected creatures and all most flatteringly *delighted with their new surroundings*" (1993, 323; emphasis added). In this last detail, the real children particularly matched their fictional *TLWW* counterparts. As soon as the Pevensie children are alone, Peter exclaims, "We've fallen on our feet and no mistake. . . . This is going to be perfectly splendid" (4).

Two weeks after his first letter about his houseguests, Lewis wrote to Warnie about them again, stating, "I have said that the children are 'nice,' and so they are. But modern children are poor creatures. They keep on coming to Maureen and asking 'What shall we do now?'" (1993, 326). Years later as he was creating the fictionalized account of four children staying with an old professor in *TLWW*, Lewis would depict them quite differently—as wonderfully, perhaps miraculously, self-reliant.

Lewis biographers Roger Lancelyn Green and Walter Hooper note that Lewis's "knowledge of actual children was slight, and his own two stepsons did not arrive on the scene until after the Narnian stories were completed" (1994, 241). What would the effect have been on *TLWW* if Lewis had not been host to these schoolgirls during the Second World War? Would the novel have even been written? While no one will ever be able to answer these questions with certainty, John Bremer claims that the presence of these young people in his home "taught Jack something" (1998, 47). As Bremer explains, Lewis, who used Jack as a first name rather than Clive, "had always been shy around children and did not understand them. He now learned how to relate to them and to have affection for them. Without this experience, the Chronicles of Narnia might never have been written or not written so well."

One of the schoolgirls who stayed at the Kilns was Jill Flewett, and so it is perhaps no accident that a girl named Jill appears as a main character in *The Silver Chair* and *The Last Battle*. Jill Flewett was sixteen when she arrived at the Lewis household in 1943, and she lived there until 1945 when she entered the Royal Academy of Dramatic Arts. Like the children in *TLWW*, Flewett remained close with the real-life professor with whom she had become friends, and in later years she returned to visit several times (Lindskoog 1998a, 175). In an interesting turn of events, Jill Flewett later married Clement Freud, the grandson of Sigmund Freud, the Austrian father of psychoanalysis and the figure who is often named as Lewis's intellectual opposite.

In 1984, slightly more than a decade after Warnie's death, the Kilns was purchased by the C. S. Lewis Foundation of Redlands, California, and visitors may by prior arrangement tour the home. How much resemblance is seen between the house Lewis owned and the Professor's? The Kilns is nearer to five than "ten miles" from the railway station (3) and is located in the city of Headington Quarry, a suburb of Oxford. So, unlike the house described in the novel, it is not in "the heart of the country," though during Lewis's time the area was certainly less built up than it now is. The Kilns also lacks the "long passages" and the "rows of doors leading to empty rooms" which the Professor's house has (5). The Professor's house and the nearby woods and mountains can be seen in Baynes's second illustration in chapter five (52).

The Professor's house, the neighboring mountains, and even the rain which the children encounter on their first morning may have come more from Lewis's memories of Little Lea—his boyhood home on the outskirts of Belfast, Northern Ireland—than from anything around Oxford. Evidence for this can be seen in the following passage written by Warnie about their childhood: "We would gaze out of our nursery window at the slanting rain and the grey skies, and there, beyond a mile or so of sodden meadow, we would see the dim high line of the Castlereagh Hills—our world's limit, a distant land, strange and unattainable" (1993, 21).

In *TLWW* we find this parallel: "But when the next morning came there was a steady rain falling, so thick that when you looked out of the window you could see neither the mountains nor the woods nor even the stream in the garden" (5).

In 1969, the pond and the woods next to the Kilns were made into the Henry Stephen/C. S. Lewis Nature Reserve and opened to the public. Readers might be interested to learn that the house used for filming *Shadowlands*, the 1993 movie about Lewis's marriage to Joy Gresham, was not the real property. In *The Magician's Nephew* we find out that the Professor's house had originally belonged to his old great-uncle Kirke, and there we find the following description which makes it seem even more grand: "the great big house in the country, which Digory had heard of all his life and never seen, would now be their home: the big house with the suits of armor, the stables, the kennels, the river, the park, the hot-houses, the vineries, the woods, and the mountains behind it" (Lewis 1994d, 200).

After first seeing the Kilns and the large parcel of land surrounding it, Warnie recorded the following depiction in his diary and expressed the same excitement used to describe the setting of the Professor's house:

> We did not go inside the house, but the eight-acre garden is such stuff as dreams are made of. I never imagined that for us any such garden would ever come within the sphere of discussion. . . . To the left of the house are the two brick kilns from which it takes its name—in front, a lawn and a hard tennis court—then a large bathing pool, beautifully wooded, and with a delightful circular brick seat overlooking it: after that a steep wilderness broken with ravines and nooks of all kinds runs up to a little cliff topped by a thistly meadow; and then the property ends in a thick belt of fir trees, almost a wood: the view from the cliff over the dim blue distance of the plain is simply glorious. (W. Lewis 1988, 68)

Lewis lived at the Kilns from October 1931 until his death in November 1963. During this time, like many of his colleagues, he also would often spend the night in his rooms at Oxford and then later at Cambridge where he taught. After his brother's death, Warnie continued to live at the Kilns off and on for ten more years and died there in 1973.

Immediately after meeting the four children, we meet the old Professor himself. As Walter Hooper has observed, the Narnian character closest to Lewis himself is "the old Professor" (1996, 427). Lewis also was a professor, though he was in his early forties during the war and thus perhaps not quite as old as the "very old" character described in the novel, who seems to be retired (3). In later notes that Lewis made about the events in Narnia, he indicated that the Professor was born in 1888 and that the Pevensie children came to stay with him in 1940, which means he would have been fifty-two (Hooper 1996, 421). Lewis was forty-two in 1940, but it is perhaps not coincidence that he had just turned fifty-two, the exact age of the Professor, when *TLWW* was published in 1950.

Like the Professor, Lewis was unmarried at the time that the schoolgirls from London stayed at the Kilns. However, the clean-shaven and balding Lewis looked nothing like the bearded and tousled-headed Professor who is described as having "shaggy white hair, which grew over most of his face as well as on his head" (3). In the first illustration in chapter five (50), readers can see Pauline Baynes's rendering of Lewis's description.

As a teenager Lewis hated Malvern College, the boarding school he attended. Because of this, in 1914 when he was sixteen, he convinced his father Albert to allow him to be privately tutored by William Kirkpatrick, or Kirk, who had been the headmaster at Albert's alma mater, Lurgen College in Northern Ireland. In *The Magician's Nephew*, we go back to a time before *TLWW* to meet the Professor when he was a young boy, and we learn there that his name is Digory Kirke—and similar names will not be the only aspect the two share.

Lewis's tutor, who did have white hair and shaggy white mutton chops, was noted for his rigorous logic, a trait which Lewis came to love. The Professor's famous appeal to logic will appear in chapter five of *TLWW* (48). Later, in *The Voyage of the* Dawn Treader, Peter does not appear in the story because he is away at the Professor's being coached for his exams (Lewis 1994g, 4), just as Lewis himself went to William Kirkpatrick's to be prepared. Given all these details, one could argue that a great deal of the old Professor was drawn from Lewis's memories of his former tutor.

In his autobiography, *Surprised by Joy*, Lewis records his first impressions after meeting Kirkpatrick, writing, "His wrinkled face seemed to consist entirely of muscles, so far as it was visible; for he wore mustache and side whiskers with a clean-shaven chin like the Emperor Franz Joseph" (1955, 133). Readers who are interested can find a photograph of Lewis's tutor in Green and Hooper's biography, which is listed in the Reference List section of this book.

Two of the servants named on the first page of *TLWW*, Ivy and Margaret, may be echoes of a single character, Ivy Mags, from *That Hideous Strength*, published in 1938. Mrs. Macready, the Professor's housekeeper, may be a variation of Mrs. McCreedy, the housekeeper Lewis and his brother knew in their Belfast childhood (Lindskoog 1998b, 110). Her name might also be a pun on the words "make ready" (Ford 1994, 285). Edmund's rudeness on meeting the old Professor—he wants to laugh at the Professor's odd looks—is not only characteristic of his youth, as the narrator suggests here (4), but also part of Lewis's characterization of Edmund, a portrayal which will be seen to be consistent from the start.

Walter Hooper, who was Lewis's personal secretary near the end of his life and later his biographer, has put forth what he believes may have been Lewis's first words about Narnia. According to Hooper, Lewis wrote the following paragraph, partly in response to his young houseguests, in 1939 on the backside of a manuscript he was working on:

> This book is about four children whose names were Ann, Martin, Rose and Peter. But it is mostly about Peter who was the youngest. They all had to go away from London suddenly because of the Air Raids, and because Father, who was in the army, had gone off to the war and Mother was doing some kind of war work. They were sent to stay with a relation of Mother's who was a very old Professor who lived by himself in the country. (Hooper 1996, 402)

Peter is the only character from this earliest start of the novel to make it into the later version of the story, where his age is reversed from youngest to oldest. Lewis kept the original number and gender for his protagonists—two girls and two boys. Unlike the passage above, in *TLWW* there is no indication that the Professor and the children are relatives, although Colin Manlove has suggested that the Professor is their uncle (1993, 32). Finally, one might note that if Lewis's original intention was to make the story "mostly about Peter who was the youngest" (Hooper 1996, 402), to some extent he kept this focus in the book's final form, where more attention is placed on the youngest of the four children, although this character is now Lucy.

After the children say goodnight to the Professor and go up to their rooms, they have their first real conversation, one which raises several issues.

First, in this short exchange we see Lewis early on establishing each of the four children's basic personality traits: Peter as the upbeat leader; Susan as sympathetic but also motherly and pretentious; Edmund as negative, rebellious, and argumentative; and Lucy as good-natured and seeking to please. Second, we also begin to see some of the motivation that will be a part of Edmund's character. He is described as "tired and pretending not to be tired" (4), and the narrator tells us that this always "made him bad-tempered." The characters which are brought to life throughout the Narnia books, both the human and the imaginary, will be quite believable. One of the ways Lewis achieves this is by always giving his readers reasons for the ways the characters behave, and thus we can say they are motivated and not simply one-dimensional like characters in some children's stories are.

While most readers will probably just skim over Peter's use of "old chap" in his opening words (4), some may find it a bit archaic or even artificial. In chapter six, one of the first things Peter will say upon arriving in Narnia is "by jove" (55), and a few pages later he will exclaim, "Great Scott!" (62). Peter is not the only character to sometimes speak in ways that may seem stiff to modern readers. When Edmund gets into Narnia he will try to apologize to Lucy by stating, "Make it Pax" (30).

Contemporary readers may wonder if any young boys in Lewis's time really talked the way Peter does here. And readers may further wonder whether some of their expressions sounded as affected then as they do now. A. N. Wilson has complained that the children "jaw" rather than talk (1991, 221) and "seem no more to belong to the mid or late twentieth century than Lewis did himself." According to Green and Hooper, before the book was published Lewis was aware that some of his dialogue was outdated and was persuaded to delete all the instances of the word *crikey* used by the children (1994, 242).

Having briefly commented on Peter's occasionally stilted language, it should be noted that young people typically have no trouble identifying with the Pevensie children. As Wilson has observed, "generations of children can now testify to the irresistible *readability* of the Narnia stories" (1991, 221). However, one may be interested to see how Lewis's schoolboys—with their shorts, knee socks, caps, and school blazers and their use of phrases like "old chap" and "by jove"—will resonate with readers in the coming decades, readers from times and places which will grow more and more removed from the quaint Oxford countryside of the early 1940s. This is not to suggest that the Narnia stories are likely to become less popular or that readers will not enjoy these aspects but simply to point out that Lewis's ratio of familiar and marvelous elements will continue to change over time as many of what he viewed as ordinary elements become part of an increasingly distant past. To future generations the boys' exclamations, the wardrobe, and even World War II may to some extent seem as alien as Narnia's fauns, centaurs, and unicorns.

We are given our first really good view of both the boys in their school outfits in the illustration showing them in the Beavers' house in chapter seven (75). Although throughout *TLWW* Pauline Baynes will always depict the boys in shirts, ties and sweaters, with Edmund in shorts and knee socks and Peter in long pants, Lewis gives virtually no indication in the text what any of the four children look like or what they wear. Perhaps because Lewis gets to the action so quickly in *TLWW* and uses the children's own words and actions rather than descriptive passages to reveal what kind of young people they are—strategies which are typically thought of positively—he misses the chance here at the beginning to tell us anything about how the children look. Once the opportunity is missed, for Lewis to stop halfway through the novel and tell us about their appearances seems impossible; so, for example, not until the final chapter will we discover that Susan has black hair while Lucy's is golden (183–84).

Up in their rooms, the four children are immediately excited by the possibility of seeing animals in the woods near the Professor's house. Some scholars have seen significance in the animal that each child names in the passage about exploring (Lindskoog 1998b, 111; Ford 1994, 309). For example, Peter's animals—eagles, stags, and hawks—could be said to be associated with chivalry; and one could claim that the girls soon find themselves hunted and having to hide like the badgers and rabbits they name.

Exactly what, if anything, is indicated by matching each child with an animal here is a question open to speculation. However, some evidence hints that Lewis may have been more intentional than may first appear: he went to the trouble of changing the animals for an early American edition of the novel (Ford 1994, 164). In that version Lewis has Edmund keyed up about the possibility of seeing snakes, and Susan is the one overjoyed about foxes. In any case, as Colin Manlove has pointed out, from the very beginning the children are "quite strongly individuated" (1987, 135). All editions published after 1994 use Lewis's original animals in this passage.

The next morning the children have plans to explore outside, but they wake to find a rain "so thick that when you looked out of the window you could see neither the mountains nor the woods nor even the stream in the garden" (5). The rain by preventing outdoor activities leads to Lucy entering the wardrobe and then Narnia itself, and in this sense it may be seen to be providential.

A number of interesting parallels exist between Lewis's fiction and that of his friend J. R. R. Tolkien. The seemingly insignificant fact of weather leading to the start of a great adventure was an aspect also used by Tolkien in *The Fellowship of the Ring*, the first book in his epic *The Lord of the Rings*. In that work we read that Sam "had a good deal to think about. For one thing, there was a lot to do up in the Bag End garden, and he would have a busy day tomorrow, if the weather cleared" (Tolkien 1994a, 44). As David Mills has noted, "Because the weather is good, Sam can work in the garden, and because he can work in the garden, he can sneak under the window and listen to Gandalf and Frodo's discussion of the Ring. Because he listens to it, he gets caught doing so, and because he gets caught doing so, he is ordered to go with Frodo" (Mills 2002, 24). According to Mills, because of the providential weather that morning, Sam goes on the quest and helps Frodo "in ways that no one else could have," and the Ring "is destroyed against all odds."

In the same way, Edmund's statement, "Of course it *would* be raining!" will resonate a page later when readers realize that precisely because of this rain the children explore the house (5). Because they are exploring, Lucy enters the wardrobe, and because she enters the wardrobe, she is able to enter Narnia. This same hand of providence will be seen again in chapter five when a group touring the house seems to follow the children everywhere, making them run from room to room. There we are told that it was as though "some magic in the house had come to life and was chasing them," so that they are almost forced into the wardrobe (53).

Later, in writing *The Magician's Nephew*, Lewis will again turn to this device of providential rain showers leading to the start of an adventure. There readers learn that Polly and Digory's adventures "began chiefly because it was one of the wettest and coldest summers there had been for years. That drove them to do indoor things: you might say, indoor exploration" (1994d, 7).

In Susan's very first words, she called the Professor "an old dear" (4). Here in her comments about the weather, she again takes a somewhat affected, motherly tone, again one not quite in harmony with her age. "Do stop grumbling, Ed," she says. "Ten to one it'll clear up in an hour or so" (5). And then, like any mother would, she offers suggestions of things to do, adding, "And in the meantime we're pretty well off. There's a wireless and lots of books."

Peter, assuming the role that he will hold throughout the series, takes the lead, saying, "Not for me. I'm going to explore in the house" (6). Everyone agrees, and the adventure begins.

Lewis's description of the Professor's house comes next, and we find that it has several rooms that might be expected as well as a couple which may leave readers, along with the children, somewhat mystified. It has lots of spare bedrooms, a long room full of pictures, and a suit of armor—all familiar staples of the British country manor. It has a library full of old books, some of them, because of their large size, likely to have been old handwritten or hand-printed manuscripts. Readers learn later that visitors come to see the "rare books in the library" (51). Exactly what the room "all hung with green, with a harp in one corner" is used for (6), we are never told. Perhaps it is simply a harp room for music, and to complement the harp comes the green of Celtic Ireland.

Finally the children come to a room that is "quite empty except for one big wardrobe" and "a dead blue-bottle on the window-sill" (6). Modern readers who have closets in their bedrooms and are curious what the wardrobe might look like can see Pauline Baynes's first rendition of it here in chapter one (7). In this illustration we can also see the shadows of the four children extending, almost pointing, toward the wardrobe doors, Baynes's literal way of foreshadowing their later entrance. Some readers may not know that a blue-bottle is a type of fly. The dead fly here suggests the room is seldom used and seldom cleaned. It also may give readers a feeling of stagnation, a feeling that nothing happens in the room and that the wardrobe has not been used for a long period of time. The two mothballs which drop out when Lucy opens the door further reinforce these impressions. Perhaps, as we find later, it has been waiting to come alive.

On the last two pages of *The Magician's Nephew*, readers will find Lewis's explanation of the wardrobe's origins and the source of its magic (1994d, 201–2). But at this point anyone who is reading the novels in their original order will find the wardrobe as mysterious as the children do and will uncover its secrets along with them. As mentioned earlier, this sharing of the children's curiosity and wonder, here and throughout the story, is the strongest argument for retaining the original reading order.

The Professor's wardrobe is described as "the sort that has a looking-glass in the door" (6), which may suggest that it has one door, not the two that Pauline Baynes includes in her drawings of the wardrobe here in chapter one (7) and again in chapter seventeen (188). Later, when Lucy enters it, Lewis will take note about her not shutting "the door," again in the singular (7). When the four children enter, we are told that Peter "held the door closed but did not shut it" (53), further evidence that Lewis may have had in mind a wardrobe with a single door, making this one of the few times when Lewis's text and Baynes's drawings perhaps do not match up.

As the other three children troop out, Lucy lags behind to try the door of the wardrobe and ends up going inside it because, as we are told, she liked nothing so much "as the smell and feel of fur" (7). Imagining scores of his young readers becoming locked inside wardrobes all over Britain and America, Lewis immediately adds that Lucy kept the door open "of course" and notes that "it is very foolish to shut oneself into any wardrobe." Lewis was so concerned about this problem of children playing Narnia and getting trapped inside wardrobes that he repeats this warning two pages later and then again in chapter five (53). A reverse warning appears when Edmund enters the wardrobe, as we are told that he "jumped in and shut the door, forgetting what a very foolish thing this is to do" (28).

In his second caution about the wardrobe, Lewis puts his warning in parentheses: "(She had, of course, left the door open, for she knew that it is a very silly thing to shut oneself into a wardrobe.)" (8–9). By using this parenthetical structure, Lewis inserts his narrator more directly into the story. Here the punctuation of the narrator's comments gives the feeling of an aside, further emphasizing the relationship with the reader. Technically, one might say that the narrator is always the one telling the story. However, sometimes the narration is interrupted in a special way—with the use of the pronouns *I* or *you*, or with parenthetical comments like the one here. While other ways to describe these two different styles of narration could be proposed, a useful distinction may be referring to the speaker who intrudes in this special way as the narrator and to the person who tells us things in the ordinary way as Lewis.

Much has been written about the various narrators who break into Lewis's fiction (Schakel 2002, 74; Gibson 1980, 134), which except for these interruptions is typically told from the third person point of view. In *TLWW* readers will encounter this narrator again from time to time. When Lucy meets Mr. Tumnus, Lewis writes, "One of his hands, *as I have said*, held the umbrella: in the other arm he carried several brown-paper parcels" (10; emphasis added). The narrator intrudes again in his description of the Professor's house: "All manner of stories were told about it, some of them even stranger than the one I am telling you now" (51). The narrator will also interrupt the description of the meal with the Beavers, pointing out: "And all the children thought—and I agree with them—that there's nothing to beat good freshwater fish if you eat it when it has been alive half an hour ago and has come out of the pan half a minute ago" (74).

A different kind of intrusion occurs near the start of chapter five—this time using the first person plural, rather than first person singular: "And now we come to one of the nastiest things in this story" (44). The narrator will open chapter six, "And now of course you want to know what had happened to Edmund" (88). Readers find a similar comment at the start of the following chapter, serving as a transition to the next episode: "Now we must go back to Mr. and Mrs. Beaver and the three other children" (100).

Evan Gibson argues that Lewis's narrator has a special position in the Chronicles, one "different from that in any of his other stories," and that this difference can be found in the narrator's "relationship with the reader" (1980, 134). Gibson continues:

Perhaps the word *raconteur*, a skilled spinner of tales, describes Lewis's relationship to the story. He is not so much a narrator as a storyteller, if I can make that distinction. It is as if he is here in the room with us, his feet spread out to the fire, his hands gesturing. . . . Notice how often in *The Lion, the Witch and the Wardrobe* he reminds us of his presence. . . . The *I*'s and *you*'s scattered throughout the book referring to the storyteller and his friend, the reader, establish a common ground which is almost a one-to-one relationship. (134)

Peter Schakel also describes how Lewis's use of this occasionally intrusive narrator adds to our experience as readers. As Schakel explains, "The use of 'we' gives substance and identity to the story-teller. The narrative is no longer impersonal and objective: a person is telling this story and commenting on the events. The statement, with its evaluative comment, is the kind an adult is more likely to make than a young person. The 'we,' at the same time, draws the reader into the tale at a new level" (2002, 75).

In his use of occasional interruptions from this unnamed narrator, Lewis was following a pattern also used by Tolkien in his novel for young people *The Hobbit*, published in 1937. By placing one of the passages from *TLWW* mentioned earlier alongside a parallel passage from Tolkien, their similar tone is revealed. First Lewis:

It was the sort of house that is mentioned in guide books and even in histories; and well it might be, for all manner of stories were told about it, some of them even stranger than the one I am telling you now. (51)

By some curious chance one morning long ago in the quiet of the world. . . . Gandalf came by. Gandalf! If you had heard only a quarter of what I have heard about him, and I have only heard very little of all there is to hear, you would be prepared for any sort of remarkable tale. (Tolkien 1994b, 13)

Perhaps the greatest effect of this unnamed narrator found in *TLWW* and throughout the rest of the Chronicles is to give a distinctly personal impression to the narration. As we read, the narrator jumps in just often enough and just long enough to give readers the feeling that they are being *told* a story rather than just reading it on their own.

Lucy finds a second row of coats behind the first and the wintry land of Narnia behind that. In making a wardrobe the entranceway to another world, Lewis unconsciously used a device from "The Aunt and Amabel," a story by Edith Nesbit published in 1908 that he would certainly have come across as a child. In the summer of 1948, Lewis is recorded as making a remark to Chad Walsh about completing a children's book which he had begun writing "in the tradition of E. Nesbit" (Walsh 1979, 129). Green and Hooper argue that it is likely that Lewis had come across "The Aunt and Amabel" when it appeared in *Blackie's Christmas Annual* for 1909, when Lewis was ten, but they also point out that he "had forgotten the Nesbit story entirely until reminded of it" (1994, 250–1).

Amabel, like the Pevensie children, has been sent away from home. In Amabel's case, she has been sent to stay with a great aunt, not because of air raids but because of "measles or a new baby or the painter in the house" (Nesbit 1994, 192), and in her room she finds a "large wardrobe with a looking glass in it that you could see yourself in" (194).

On the dressing table in the spare room where she is staying, Amabel finds a strange timetable for trains, and in it she sees a station named "*Bigwardrobeinspareroom*" (Nesbit 1994, 196), a name which will perhaps be echoed in Mr. Tumnus's references to the land of "Spare Oom" and the city of "War Drobe" (*TLWW*, 13, 21). We are told that Amabel, thinking that she will find only hats inside, "went straight to the Big Wardrobe and turned its glass handle" (Nesbit 1994, 197). Nesbit then writes: "Of course it wasn't hats. It was, most amazingly, a crystal-cave, very oddly shaped like a railway station. It seemed to be lighted by stars, which is, of course, unusual in a booking office, and over the station clock was a full moon."

While Lewis may have had a faint recollection of Nesbit's story in the back of his mind as he began *TLWW*, travel through Lewis's wardrobe is much more like a birth than Nesbit's train ride. Lucy begins in the dark, cozy womblike enclosure and moves through the fur coats and a narrow tangle of branches to emerge into a whole new world. While a Freudian reading of this passage is possible—and in fact, is even joked about by the fictional Inkling named John in the pub scene in the film *Shadowlands*—it is not required. The birth that Lucy and that later her brothers and sisters will undergo is more of a rebirth, a passage from one condition in England to a more vital one in Narnia or, as Colin Manlove describes it, the development "out of an old awareness into a new" (1993, 35).

At this point in the story, the question might be raised, how is Lewis going to make the imaginary world of Narnia seem real? One of the primary techniques he will use, both now in Lucy's first passage to the make-believe country and also later throughout the story, is to provide readers with vivid, concrete descriptions of specific, familiar objects which they can see, hear, touch, and smell. Here Lucy pushes aside "soft folds of coats" and hears a crunching under her feet (8). She stoops down to feel what is making the sound, and instead of feeling "the hard, smooth wood of the floor," she feels something "soft and powdery and extremely cold." Next she comes up against something "hard and rough and even prickly" which rubs against her face and hands. Finally, with the help of a dim light off in the distance, she recognizes "snowflakes falling through the air." As Walter Hooper has pointed out, "Lewis's close observations of nature and his ability to describe what he saw, heard, and smelled, are nowhere so evident as in the Narnian stories" (1980, 80).

The late Joseph Campbell was one of the world's foremost scholars of mythology. While his assumptions about the origins of myth were fundamentally different from those Lewis held, his observations about the aspects which all myths share have proven to be insightful and can shed light upon ways that the Narnia stories may serve as myths for our time. Campbell presents several stages which each mythic hero will go through. The first is what he labels the call to adventure. Campbell points out that this call often comes unexpectedly and may sometimes seem to invade the hero's safe, secure world by "merest chance" (1968, 51). However, according to Campbell it is not chance which has produced the call but rather the hero's own subconscious readiness, his or her need to progress to the next psychological level. Campbell explains: "A blunder—apparently the merest chance—reveals an unsuspected world, and the individual is drawn into a relationship with forces that are not rightly understood." Certainly Lucy's entrance into Narnia has almost seemed to come about by chance, by the simple fact of her lagging behind to try the wardrobe door.

The exploration of the Professor's house and Lucy's subsequent entrance into the wardrobe occurred after "they had just finished their breakfast" (5). Now the fact that Lucy finds herself standing in the middle of a wood "at night-time" (8) is the first hint to readers that time in Narnia is different than time in England.

The first image that Lucy sees, and Pauline Baynes's first illustration of Narnia, captures the essence of the imaginary world. After walking "about ten minutes" toward the light she has noticed, Lucy comes upon "a lamp-post in the middle of a wood" (9). Narnia is characterized as being a mystical blend of worlds, a place where the very real and the very imaginary come together. In creating this mingling of robins and fauns, of hot tea and miraculous cordials, of enchanted woods and London lamp-posts, Lewis delighted his readers but put off his friend J. R. R. Tolkien, who insisted on a more rigid separation between what he called the primary world and the secondary or fictional—a separation that appears more completely in Tolkien's imaginary realm of Middle-earth. Later in *TLWW*, Father Christmas will be introduced (107), and Lewis defended this inclusion alongside figures with very different origins such as Aslan or Mr. Tumnus by saying that they all exist happily together in our minds in real life. To this Tolkien responded, "Not in mine, or at least not at the same time" (Sayer 1994, 313).

Colin Manlove has described this magical blending of different ingredients which occurs in Narnia. He observes:

The very title of the book, *The Lion, the Witch and the Wardrobe*, suggests that it is a kind of amalgam of different things: and that is indeed the case. . . . It is as if Lewis delights in the juxtaposition of as many different things as he can, and in refusing us any settled view or position. The book is almost a cornucopia, or in other terms, rather like a Christmas stocking, full of various and mysterious objects all held together in one container. (1987, 126–7)

Peter Schakel sums up the point saying, "The distinctive atmosphere of Narnia is shaped by the blending of familiar things with unfamiliar, and by placing of familiar things in an unfamiliar context" and also on its blending of "the ordinary and the impossible" (2002, 59–60).

Paul Kocher makes a similar point about Tolkien's Middle-earth, which combines "the ordinary with the extraordinary," making the fantasy world "familiar but not too familiar, strange but not too strange" (1972, 2). Kocher argues, "No audience can long feel sympathy or interest for persons or things in which they cannot recognize a good deal of themselves and the world of their everyday experience" (1). In this respect, both Lewis and Tolkien are following Tolkien's dictum from his essay "On Fairy-Stories." In that essay Tolkien maintained, "*Faerie* contains many things besides elves and fays, and besides dwarfs, witches, trolls, giants, or dragons: it holds the seas, the sun, the moon, the sky; and the earth and all things that are in it: tree and bird, water and stone, wine and bread" (1966, 38). Walter Hooper has claimed that in the Chronicles of Narnia Lewis provides readers with "descriptions which somehow familiarize, without making dull, the strangeness of another world, and which quietly convince us that we are in a *real* world that we should enjoy living in if we could get there" (1980, 82).

Narnia is intentionally a hodgepodge collection of widely diverging elements, often with no relation to each other, giving it a dreamlike quality. At the same time Narnia is also a blend of more specific, intentionally chosen pairs of opposites: "the ordinary and the fabulous, the contemporary and the medieval, the childlike and the 'adult,' and the secular and the religious" (Manlove 1993, 10).

In *The Magician's Nephew* we will learn the origin of the mysterious lamp-post out in the middle of the deepest woods (Lewis 1994d, 119), but as with the wardrobe, at this point in the story readers are as amazed by it as Lucy is.

The second image we have of Narnia is as famous and as distinctive as the lamp-post. Lucy hears a pitter-patter of feet, and then out steps a faun carrying an umbrella and "several brown-paper parcels" (10). Lewis claimed that this picture, which first came to him when he was a teenager, was the beginning of Narnia. In a short essay titled "It All Began with a Picture," Lewis wrote:

> All my seven Narnian books, and my three science-fiction books, began with seeing pictures in my head. At first they were not a story, just pictures. *The Lion, the Witch and the Wardrobe* all began with a picture of a Faun carrying an umbrella and parcels in a snowy wood. This picture had been in my mind since I was about sixteen. Then one day, when I was about forty, I said to myself: "Let's try to make a story about it." (1982a, 53)

In this first image of Mr. Tumnus walking in Narnia, often the picture used for the book's cover, we have the same blending of worlds first seen with the lamp-post in the middle of the woods. In the homey extras which Lewis adds—Mr. Tumnus's umbrella, his red woolen muffler, and the brown wrapped packages—familiar, domestic England is united with the mythology of ancient Greece. In the faun itself we have, of course, a further blending: the mixture of human and animal.

The very first words in the novel uttered by a Narnian are "Goodness gracious me!" (10). Some readers may see this utterance as merely an expression someone might make after being startled. At the least, Lewis's choice of this particular expression adds to the characterization of Mr. Tumnus. As readers get to know the creature with "a strange, but pleasant little face," they will see that this is exactly the kind of thing he would say. But since these are the first words spoken by a Narnian, perhaps they hold more significance than just developing Mr. Tumnus's character. Perhaps in these opening words readers are meant to hear intimations of the goodness and the grace which will play fundamental roles all throughout the story.

These first words are also remarkable in that they happen to be in English. Certainly Lewis could have used a different language in Narnia as he did in his earlier space trilogy. In *The Magician's Nephew*, Lewis will explain how the animals in Narnia came to speak (1994d, 125–7), and from this account one may argue that Mr. Tumnus and the rest of the talking animals in Narnia speak English because Frank and Helen, the first king and queen of Narnia, came from England. However, unless readers have read *The Magician's Nephew*, when they encounter Mr. Tumnus's exclamation here, they have no explanation for the English, and neither did Lewis at this point. Like the wide variety of foods that Mr. Tumnus will serve for tea (in spite of the fact that the Narnian winter has lasted for years and years), his use of English here in the final sentence of chapter one is something that is simply accepted.

TWO

What Lucy Found There

Chapter one opened with the children's arrival at the Professor's and closed with Lucy's arrival in Narnia. Chapter two will have a similar symmetry. It opens with Lucy's meeting with Mr. Tumnus and will conclude with her saying good-bye to him and returning through the wardrobe.

After Mr. Tumnus picks up the parcels which he has dropped, his first concern is to know if, in fact, Lucy is "a Daughter of Eve" (11). At the end of this chapter, Lewis will return to this point when we are told that the White Witch has been on the lookout for Sons of Adam and Daughters of Eve (20). At that time we also learn that four thrones wait at Cair Paravel and when they are filled, something will happen with the creatures the Witch has turned into statues, but it is not until chapter eight that readers learn precisely what the prophecy is (82).

Mr. Tumnus tells Lucy that he has never met a Son of Adam or a Daughter of Eve before and that he is "delighted" (11). He stutters over what to say next, and Lewis tells us that the faun "stopped as if it had been going to say something it had not intended but had remembered in time" (12). What is Mr. Tumnus faltering about here? Readers have no clue and may even miss Lewis's hint of what is to come. We will learn at the end of the chapter that Mr. Tumnus is in the employ of the White Witch and is supposed to hand over any humans he happens to encounter. One rule of writing is that if you are going to fire a cannon in act five, you must put it on the wall in act one. (The converse is also true: if you put a cannon on the wall in act one, you must fire it in act five.) Following this rule, if Mr. Tumnus is going to turn out to be an agent of the Witch at the end of this chapter, we need to have this suggestion early on that all is not quite as it seems.

Next the faun introduces himself as Tumnus. While he will be the only faun readers meet in *TLWW*, in *Prince Caspian* Lewis will briefly mention nine others by name. By giving them Latin-sounding names such as Tumnus here, and later Mentius, Obentinus, Dumnus, and so on (1994e, 82–3), Lewis clearly intended to evoke the fauns' connection to Roman mythology. Paul Ford notes that the origin of Mr. Tumnus's name "is not clear, although it is a Latin diminutive of some sort" and may be "from *tumulus*, meaning 'hill,' as Tumnus lives in hilly country" (1994, 428).

In a letter Lewis wrote in 1957 to Jane Gaskell, whose first novel *Strange Evil* had just been published, he offered several tips so that her next book might be "twice as good" (1993, 468–9). One of Gaskell's characters had been named Enaj, and among Lewis's corrections was that the names in a book "ought to be beautiful and suggestive as well as strange: not merely odd." Lewis certainly followed his own advice. Throughout the Chronicles, Lewis takes pains to ensure that the names he creates for characters in Narnia are not "merely odd" like Enaj but also "beautiful and suggestive" and memorable as well—not just the name he here gives to Mr. Tumnus, Narnia's first character, but also later the names Aslan, Reepicheep, Tirian, Shasta, Bree, Hwin, and all the others.

Mr. Tumnus asks how Lucy came into Narnia, and this is the very first time readers hear the name of the imaginary land (12).

How did Lewis come up with the name *Narnia?* While scholars have found several references to a historical city called Narnia, whether Lewis took the name from one of these references or made it up independently remains unclear. Paul Ford suggests that Lewis named his make-believe country Narnia simply "because he liked the sound of the word" (1994, 297). He adds "there is no indication that he was alluding to the ancient Umbrian city Nequinium, renamed Narnia (after Nar, a tributary of the Tiber) by the conquering Romans in 299 B.C." At the same time Ford acknowledges that since Lewis had majored in the classics and ancient history at Oxford before getting a second degree in English, he quite possibly came across at least seven references to the Roman Narnia in Latin literature (298).

Several critics have suggested a comparison between Mr. Tumnus and the White Rabbit from *Alice's Adventures in Wonderland* (Glover 1981, 138; Manlove 1987, 127; Kilby 1964, 141). Like Mr. Tumnus, the White Rabbit—who wears a waistcoat and has a pocket watch—is a wild creature who has been transformed into a civilized one and thus also demonstrates a blending of two worlds. When Alice speaks to him, the rabbit is startled and, like Mr. Tumnus, drops what he has been carrying, white gloves and a fan. Like Narnia, Alice's Wonderland is bigger on the inside than it seemed from the outside and is entered through a tunnellike or holelike opening. After Lucy and Alice enter their imaginary lands, both encounter hostile queens.

Mr. Tumnus offers Lucy "a roaring fire—and toast—and sardines—and cake" if she is willing to come for tea (13). Narnia, an imaginary land, is again brought to life through Lewis's use of vivid and familiar specifics that the reader can see, smell, touch, and in this instance also taste. Celebrations, hospitality, and feasting will be an essential element of proper living there. Wesley Kort has pointed out that in the Narnia stories, "the children often encounter the talking animals in their homes," and that the "warmth, hospitality, and relative safety" which the homes provide influences the relationship that the children and animals have (2001, 56). As with Lewis's decision to make English the language spoken in

Narnia, again one might note that Lewis has chosen for the food in Narnia to be the same as it is in England. Certainly if he had wanted to, Lewis could have invented alien foods, as he did in the first two books of his space trilogy.

When Lucy and Mr. Tumnus arrive at the faun's cave, he lights a "lamp" with "a flaming piece of wood" from the fireplace (14), possibly the kerosene-type lamp that Pauline Baynes puts on his mantel (15). Except for its being a cave, Mr. Tumnus's home could have come straight from England sometime in the nineteenth century, before electricity. Earlier Mr. Tumnus referred to "the" lamp-post (12), suggesting that it is the only one in Narnia. There is no explanation in *TLWW* of how the lamp-post is powered or how it came to be in the middle of the woods. Later, Mrs. Beaver will have a sewing machine, but one which appears to be nonelectric, possibly a hand- or foot-operated type (72). Throughout the Chronicles, the battles will be fought with swords, clubs, bows, and arrows, evidence that in addition to being pre-electricity, Narnia is also pre-gunpowder. Later in *TLWW*, the White Witch and Father Christmas will travel by sleighs, not by train or automobile.

Having said all this, terms like *pre-electricity* and *pre-gunpowder* may be somewhat inaccurate. After the seven Chronicles were published, Lewis went back and created for himself what he titled "An Outline of Narnian History so far as it is known." In this record, Lewis indicates that the country comes to an end in the Narnian year of 2555 (Hooper 1980, 53). Over the course of these twenty-six centuries, certain technological advances are made, such as the ability to build sailing ships like the *Dawn Treader*. However, perhaps Narnia would not have necessarily followed England in terms of advancing technology. Electricity and gunpowder may never have been developed even if Narnia had lasted millions of years.

The warmth and snugness of Mr. Tumnus's cave stand in stark contrast to the cold outside. Here and in the similarly cozy and comfortable home of the Beavers found in chapter seven, Lewis is inserting his own tastes into the story. Several years after finishing *TLWW*, Lewis would write in a letter, "I like to feel in-doors when I'm in" (1967, 46).

Among the books Lucy looks at on Mr. Tumnus's shelves are two that refer to humans: *Men, Monks, and Gamekeepers; a Study in Popular Legend* and *Is Man a Myth?* (15), titles which suggest that humans have already had an encounter with Narnia prior to the events in *TLWW*—but possibly one which was either very fleeting or in the distant past. In *The Magician's Nephew*, set in a time long before Lucy's visit, Lewis will have a human couple—a London cabdriver named Frank and his wife Helen—serve as the first king and queen of Narnia. King Frank and Queen Helen later have human children who will then marry with Narnians. In that story readers will be told, "The boys married nymphs and the girls married wood-gods and river-gods" (1994d, 200). We are left to assume that the children's offspring also married with Narnians, so that by the time of *TLWW* their human genes and any memory of humans have long since dissipated. Presumably the myths and legends of man that Lucy finds in Mr. Tumnus's cave have their origins in this earlier time.

The Horse and His Boy, one of the later books in the Narnia series, is set during the time when Peter, Susan, Edmund, and Lucy are reigning as adult kings and queens in Narnia. In that story we find that human beings are living in Archenland, a country to the south of Narnia, and in *The Magician's Nephew* we are told that the second son of Frank and Helen would go on to become king there. At this point in writing *TLWW*, Lewis had not yet conceived of Archenland and the humans who would be there or why the author of Mr. Tumnus's book would think of man as a myth or legend. Perhaps the Witch's imposed winter has prohibited any contact with the outside world for a long time.

Lewis's inclusion of these books on Mr. Tumnus's shelves leads to the question raised by Colin Manlove, "Whether our own world is more or less real or fictional than Narnia, a question answered in *The Last Battle*, when both are shown to be of equal (un)reality" (1987, 128). The use of monks and gamekeepers in the title of Mr. Tumnus's book is Lewis's humorous attempt to reverse the situation from our world, where we might expect to find a title like *Fauns, Centaurs, and Unicorns: A Study in Popular Legend*.

If readers look closely at Baynes's illustration of Mr. Tumnus's cave, across the room from the bookshelf they can find the portrait of Mr. Tumnus's father over the mantelpiece (15). The picture will play a role in this chapter (19) and again later in chapter six (57).

Lewis himself wrote little in the way of explanation about his fiction, which may be seen as both a good and a bad thing: bad because it might have been very interesting to see what his reasons were for writing as he did; good because, as he certainly knew, the best way for us to understand his works is to be rooted primarily in the texts themselves. However, in an essay about ways of writing for children, we find one of the few moments where Lewis happened to describe his intentions. About creating this scene in *TLWW*, he wrote:

> In my own first story I had described at length what I thought a rather fine high tea given by a hospitable faun to the little girl who was my heroine. A man, who has children of his own, said, "Ah, I see how you got to that. If you want to please grown-up readers you give them sex, so you thought to yourself, 'That won't do for children, what shall I give them instead? I know! The little blighters like plenty of good eating.'" In reality, however, I myself like eating and drinking. I put in what I would have liked to read when I was a child and what I still like reading now that I am in my fifties. (1982e, 31)

Besides the obvious points that Lewis raises here about putting in elements that he personally would have liked as a child and still likes as an adult, we also learn that he thought of Lucy as his heroine and that Mr. Tumnus's prime motive here was to be hospitable rather than to entrap Lucy.

Mr. Tumnus serves Lucy "a wonderful tea" (15), one which is more homey than fancy. Readers are told, "There was a nice brown egg, lightly boiled, for each of them, and then sardines on toast, and then buttered toast, and then toast with honey, and then a sugar-topped cake." Hooper has observed that while throughout the Chronicles, "sumptuous feasts very properly follow corona-tions and victories" (1980, 82), the majority of readers "are more vulnerable to the descriptions of the more ordinary Narnian fare." Readers can see the sugar-topped cake and the other marvelous, ordinary elements of Mr. Tumnus's tea arrayed on the table in Baynes's drawing (15).

After the tea, Mr. Tumnus has "wonderful tales to tell of life in the forest" (15), stories of midnight dances, of hunting the milk-white stag, of treasure seeking with Red Dwarfs, and of summer visits from old Silenus—scenes depicted in the illustrations (16–17). Later Lewis will revisit several of these images. Fauns and dryads frolic in a midnight dance in *The Silver Chair* (1994f, 217), the milk-white stag will appear near the end of *TLWW* (184), and Silenus will appear in *Prince Caspian* (1994e, 158–60). Silenus, another character from Greek mythology, was the teacher and faithful companion of the wine-god Bacchus. The first book that Lucy sees on Mr. Tumnus's shelf is *The Life and Letters of Silenus*. In the next story in the series, *Prince Caspian*, when Lucy and Susan encounter Silenus and Bacchus, Lucy will comment, "Don't you remember Mr. Tumnus telling us about them long ago?" (1994e, 160), a reference to a discussion that must have occurred during the time of *TLWW* but which is not depicted.

Finally, one should note that when Lewis wrote *TLWW* and had Mr. Tumnus tell stories about "summer when the woods were green," he had not fully conceived the timeline of Narnian history. In later books this time period will be referred to as the "Hundred Years of Winter" (Lewis 1994e, 169; 1994f, 61; 1994b, 49), leaving three ways to interpret Mr. Tumnus's remarks about summer. Perhaps Mr. Tumnus is over a hundred years old and is remembering the actual summers of his youth from a time before the Witch's arrival. How-ever, the fact that he will become "stout" and "middle-aged" over the relatively short course of the novel may undercut this possibility (184). Alternatively, he may simply be recounting tales he has heard of events which took place before he was born. Finally, readers could choose to read this passage as one of the handful of inconsistencies which resulted from the fact that when Lewis wrote *TLWW* he did not foresee that it would lead to a series and so had not yet decided that the Witch's winter would last a hundred years.

Next we are told that Mr. Tumnus picks up "a strange little flute that looked as if it were made of straw" to lull Lucy to sleep (16). In the drawing by Baynes on the next page, this instrument is pictured more as a set of Pan pipes than what most readers might think of as a flute (18). Although in mythological tradition fauns have the power to cast their listeners under spells by playing music, Mr. Tumnus is unable to put Lucy into the trance he intends, presumably due to a lack of real commitment to betraying her. Lewis will include a scene much like this one in *The Silver Chair*, where the Queen of Underland attempts to cast a spell with the help of "a musical instrument rather like a mandolin" which she strums (1994f, 173).

Mr. Tumnus begins to cry and ends up using Lucy's handkerchief, which he must wring out again and again. Soon Lucy finds herself standing in "a damp patch" (18), and in this last detail Lewis lapses momentarily into a clichéd triteness which is untypical in his otherwise fresh portraits of characters and events in Narnia. A similar image can be found in an early scene in *Alice's Adventures in Wonderland*, where Alice is described as "shedding gallons of tears, until there was a large pool around her" (Carroll 1998, 17). Perhaps another echo from Lewis Carroll can be heard in Mr. Tumnus's first words, "Goodness gracious me" (10), an expression which could be said to parallel the first words of the White Rabbit, "Oh dear! Oh dear!" (Carroll 1998, 9).

Mr. Tumnus confesses that he has "taken service under the White Witch" (19). What exactly this service involves besides keeping watch for humans is not clear, nor is it evident that his service was entirely voluntary. Here at the first mention of the Witch, readers may be momentarily confused by the use of the color white, a designation that often signals a good character rather than a bad one. In Narnia, readers will find two types of magic, good and evil, and two types of practitioners. In *The Silver Chair* Jill and Eustace encounter the Queen of the Underland, who is said to be "of the same crew" as the White Witch (Lewis 1994f, 61) and has a similar desire to dominate Narnia. In *Prince Caspian* Doctor Cornelius, a good character, will claim to be "a very minor magician" (Lewis 1994e, 58), and later Caspian will accuse Nikabrik of attempting to use the "black" sorcery of a hag (170). Other examples of good and bad magicians include Coriakin in *The Voyage of the* Dawn Treader and Uncle Andrew in *The Magician's Nephew*.

Next Mr. Tumnus utters what has become a famous line, that in Narnia it is "always winter and never Christmas" (19). Lewis was a lover of weather of all kinds, and so for Narnia to be always in winter would not necessarily be a bad condition for him. One December a few years after completing *TLWW*, he wrote to Mary Willis Shelburne, who was living in America, "One part of me almost envies you that deep snow: *real snow*" (Lewis 1967, 25). But by having the Witch remove Christmas from winter, Lewis may be suggesting that she has stolen the magic and mystery of the season, the incarnation of life into a season where nothing seems alive, leaving winter as simply a time of cold barrenness which is under her control.

Colin Manlove points out that the Witch "simply spreads herself over all Narnia in the form of a dead white frost, allowing nothing else independent life: the unchanging monotony of winter is her symbol" (1987, 130–1). He further suggests that in doing so, the White Witch has converted Narnia to "a mirror image of herself" (1993, 38). Evan Gibson notes that "a winter without spring is without hope, and a winter without Christmas is without love" (1980, 141), and surely the White Witch has been nearly though not quite successful in her attempt to eliminate these two virtues from the imaginary country.

Mr. Tumnus finds that he cannot carry through with his plans of kidnapping Lucy and decides instead to risk the consequences should the Witch find out he has disobeyed her orders. He mentions the possibility of being turned into stone (20), preparing readers for the statues that Edmund will later find at the Witch's castle (96). Then Mr. Tumnus makes a vague allusion to what seems to be a prophecy about the statues remaining stone until "the four thrones at Cair Paravel are filled," but then questions "whether it will ever happen at all" (20). Readers may wonder exactly what Mr. Tumnus is talking about, and of course Lewis intended this first allusion to the prophecy to be cryptic, as a way to raise our curiosity and create suspense. It will not be until chapter eight that he will have Mr. Beaver explain the saying in full (81).

As Mr. Tumnus prepares to escort Lucy back to the lamp-post, he warns her that the wood is full of spies, noting that "even some of the trees are on her side" (21), a statement which suggests that at one time all of the trees were good. Mr. Beaver will reiterate Mr. Tumnus's observation about the good and bad trees when he meets the children in chapter seven (66–7).

If Narnia is like England in a number of ways, such as its language and food, it is also unlike England in some aspects. One of the most significant ways it differs is that like most traditional fairy lands, Narnia will have three distinct types of sentient beings—those who by their very nature are evil (or at least have become totally evil), those who by their very nature are good, and finally those who have potential for both good and evil. Besides the Witch, some of the other creatures in this first category can be found in the list of evil forces that the Witch summons in chapter thirteen: the werewolves, Ghouls, Boggles, Ogres, Cruels, Hags, Spectres, and so on (136). Any creature with an animal head on a human body is part of this group, creatures like the minotaurs found in the list, later referred to as bull-headed men (151). Since there seems to be no possibility of redemption for beings in this category, no sorrow is expressed when they are killed.

Later in chapter eight, Mrs. Beaver will make it clear that the Witch is completely evil, claiming, "She's bad all through" (81), a claim Mr. Beaver concurs with. As Paul Ford has observed, the Beavers' comments suggest that the Witch is "totally depraved" (1994, 133), that she is "so aligned with evil that she is incapable of being won over to the good." Mr. Beaver will go on to point out that "there may be two views about humans," meaning that there will be some good humans and some bad, since humans have the potential for both good and evil. He will conclude, "But there's no two views about things that look like humans and aren't"—his way of saying that the Witch and the other creatures like her are fully evil.

The second category of beings in Narnia are those who by their very nature are good. Aslan and his father the Emperor are the only characters who fit this description. As Lewis will have Mr. Beaver state, Aslan "isn't safe, but he's good" (80). Paul Ford has referred to this aspect as Aslan's "essential goodness" (1994, 43). In *The Last Battle* many of the Narnians will be tricked into believing that Aslan is behind the evil commands which the ape issues. Jewel will ask Tirian how Aslan could be commanding such wicked things, how could it be that "Aslan is not Aslan" (Lewis 1994b, 31). The end of the story makes clear that Aslan has not been evil and by his very nature could not have been.

The final category of beings are those who have the potential for both good and evil. This group is the largest and most interesting, and it is the one Lewis focuses most of his narrative on. It includes the humans, half-humans, animals, dwarfs, giants, and the trees mentioned by Mr. Tumnus. Exactly how trees rooted in the ground are able to commit evil (or good) is not made entirely clear in TLWW. In chapter fourteen readers are told that "spirits of evil trees" are present at Aslan's slaying (151). In *The Magician's Nephew* Aslan creates "walking trees" at the same time he creates talking beasts (Lewis 1994d, 126). One of these walking oak trees is part of Aslan's first council and is pictured in Baynes's illustration looking much like one of Tolkien's Ents (Lewis 1994d, 130).

Mr. Tumnus stealthily escorts Lucy through the woods back to the lamp-post, where she leaves him after granting his request for forgiveness and allowing him to keep her handkerchief as a remembrance, as a knight might keep the scarf of the lady he serves. Like a cannon put on the wall here, Lucy's handkerchief will appear again later as Mr. Beaver's "token" of honesty (67). Apologies and forgiveness, first seen here, will play an important role throughout the story. After shaking hands, Lucy says, "I do hope you won't get into dreadful trouble on my account" (22), Lewis's way of hinting at what is to come for Mr. Tumnus.

The first clue that time is different in Narnia is the fact that Lucy left England in morning but arrived in Narnia in nighttime. As Lucy returns back through the wardrobe to the Professor's house after being away for so long, the fact that it is still raining in England and the other children have barely moved on are Lewis's next clues that time in the two countries is different, a fact which Colin Manlove has noted gives Narnia a dreamlike feel (1993, 33).

As Susan will report to the Professor later, to them Lucy seemed to have been gone for "less than a minute," but she will claim to have been away "for hours" (49). Had someone else been missing this long, Lucy would have been worried sick, and so chapter two ends with Lucy, who is always thinking of others, immediately crying out in reassurance, "I'm here. I've come back. I'm all right" (23).

THREE

Edmund and the Wardrobe

While *The Lion, the Witch and the Wardrobe* was not written to be published serially, like for example many of Charles Dickens's novels, each of the early chapters in *TLWW* will end with one foot in whatever action comes next, a device which keeps readers reading. The final pages of the first chapter ended with Lucy's initial arrival in Narnia and the first moments of her encounter with Mr. Tumnus. Chapter two ended with Lucy stepping out of the wardrobe and back into the Professor's house. Chapter three picks up there and will conclude with the first moments of Edmund's exchange with the White Witch. By finishing one step into the action that follows, Lewis provides incentive for readers to go on to the next chapter, but as many parents know, also makes it hard for anyone reading the story aloud to young people to find a satisfying stopping point.

As chapter three opens, Lucy emerges from the wardrobe and runs out of the room to find the other three children just ahead of her in the passageway. Peter's response to Lucy's report that she is "back" is to gently tell her that if she wants them to notice she has been hiding, she will need to hide longer (24). When Lucy declares that she has been away for hours, Edmund bluntly concludes she is "batty." Susan's somewhat milder but still negative verdict is that Lucy is being silly, but Peter again kindly tries to ease his youngest sister's embarrassment by suggesting that Lucy is not being silly but simply "making up a story for fun" (25). The idea that Narnia is a reality that is storylike will return again in the novel (56, 61). Lucy insists that she has really visited Narnia, but when she tries to show her siblings how she was able to reach the magic land, they find "no wood and no snow, only the back of the wardrobe, with hooks on it" (25). Peter, always the good brother, goes so far as to rap his knuckles on the back to ensure it is solid.

Paul Karkainen has written about the wardrobe's on-again, off-again properties. "True to its nature," he notes, "mystery cannot be invoked at one's discretion. The wardrobe is not an automatic door to Narnia. It can provide transit between the two worlds only at the destined times" (1979, 17). The wardrobe will be seen to have a will of its own, although to whom or what this will is subject is left somewhat unclear. At the end of the novel, the Professor will tell the children, "Don't *try* to get there at all. It'll happen when you're not looking for it" (188), instructions which make it clear that the forces at work in Narnia are not subject to human wishes. In the final chapter a similar statement will be made concerning Aslan when Mr. Beaver tells the children, "He's wild, you know. Not like a *tame* lion" (182).

One could say that the wardrobe also is wild in the sense that it cannot be forced to allow entrance into Narnia. That Peter understands this concept is made clear later when the children are in Narnia debating what to do about Mr. Tumnus. Worried about their lack of food, Peter is in favor of returning to the Professor's for supplies, except that as he observes, "there doesn't seem to be any certainty of getting in this country again when once you've got out of it" (60). The fact that the wardrobe does not always allow passage forms the basis for Peter's initial belief that Lucy has made it all up, as he tells the Professor, "If it was real why doesn't everyone find this country every time they go to the wardrobe? I mean, there was nothing there when we looked; even Lucy didn't pretend there was" (49). The idea that entrance to Narnia is not subject to human wishes is an element which Lewis will continue throughout the stories. As Eustace will tell Tirian in *The Last Battle*, "You can't go just by wanting to" (Lewis 1994b, 58).

If you cannot be certain that you *can* get in through the wardrobe, you might also assume that neither can you be sure that you can *not* get in. However, the Professor's words at the end of the novel suggest he has some additional knowledge, because he will declare, "I don't think it will be any good trying to go back through the wardrobe to get the coats. You won't get into Narnia again by *that* route" (188). We are never told how the Professor happens to know this fact, but as is seen through the rest of the series, he is correct. After the trips depicted in *TLWW*, the children are never able to travel through the wardrobe again.

While the wardrobe has a will of its own, or is subject to another will, in allowing or not allowing entrance into Narnia, it should be pointed out that the wardrobe passage does seem to always be available from the other direction, from Narnia back to the Professor's—at least it is on the three occasions when the children try to use it in *TLWW* (22, 43, 187). Lewis authority Don King has made some interesting suggestions which may help explain why the passageway is not at the children's bidding from our side but is always open from the Narnia side. King first notes:

> The fact that the entries [from our world] tend to be unplanned suggests two things. On the one hand, the unexpected entries parallel Lewis's own realization about his life long quest for joy. As he records in *Surprised by Joy* it became a kind of obsession. The one characteristic thing about his experiences of joy was that its occurrence was always unexpected. If he tried to seek it or find it or produce it, he never had success; it had to occur spontaneously. . . . In a similar vein, I believe he arranges the unexpected entries into

Narnia so that the children will experience the awe and wonder of Narnia not at their own bidding, which could become cheap and worn out, but at the bidding of Another. (1987, 27)

But why then should travel in the reverse direction, the opening back to our world, be at the children's "bidding"? King points out that all who enter into Narnia are called, but "none are compelled to stay" (1987, 25). In *TLWW* the four children are allowed entrance into the imaginary world only at specific moments; once there, however, the implication is that they may leave at any time they choose by simply returning to the wardrobe opening just past the lamp-post.

Just as readers may wonder about whether any real-life antecedents existed for the children, the Professor, or his house, a similar question may be raised concerning the wardrobe. Did Lewis know an actual wardrobe that might have served as the basis for the one depicted in *TLWW*?

In fact, two wardrobes may lay claim to having been the model for the one in the Professor's house. One was the wardrobe Lewis knew as a boy in Belfast, a piece made by his grandfather which is now housed at the Wade Center at Wheaton College in Wheaton, Illinois. The other wardrobe was the one Lewis knew as an adult at the Kilns, a piece now on display at Reynolds Hall at Westmont College in Santa Barbara. The Wade Center website mentions that "C. S. Lewis's family wardrobe" is among the pieces the Center has on display. The Westmont website goes further, claiming that Westmont has the wardrobe "that belonged to C. S. Lewis and served as a model for the magical one he described in his famous children's book, 'The Lion, the Witch, and the Wardrobe.'"

Should anyone be confused by the presence of a second wardrobe at Wheaton, the Westmont website specifically explains: "In *The Lion, the Witch, and the Wardrobe*, Lewis refers to the wardrobe through which the Pevensie children reach Narnia as 'a perfectly ordinary wardrobe, the kind with a looking-glass in the door.' The Wheaton wardrobe is ornate and has two doors—neither of which has a looking-glass."

Readers continue to make pilgrimages, both real and virtual, to both wardrobes and must decide for themselves what role, if any, they may have played in Lewis's depiction of the Professor's wardrobe in *TLWW*.

Lewis's stepson Douglas Gresham, who served as the host for the Focus on the Family Radio Theatre series adaptation of the Chronicles of Narnia, grew up with the Kilns' wardrobe and had this to say about it at the start of production of *The Horse and His Boy*: "I remember going to the house for the first time and seeing a large, oak wardrobe in the hall. Wide-eyed, I asked Jack if it was *the* wardrobe from the famous story. Jack smiled and said, 'It might be.' It was years before I dared to hang a coat in that wardrobe." Lewis's statement, "It might be," keeps open the question about whether there was a particular real wardrobe that inspired the fictional one. The film *Shadowlands* includes a moving scene where the young Douglas Gresham investigates a wardrobe in the attic of the Kilns.

Over the next few days Susan and Peter continue to disbelieve Lucy, though with compassion. Edmund, on the other hand, is characteristically "spiteful" and jeers at his sister with questions about whether she has found "other new countries in other cupboards all over the house" (26). Paul Karkainen has characterized Edmund's behavior here as a "slide" into evil where gradually he becomes "more and more confused, wrongheaded, bitter, and unhappy" (1979, 22). In his earlier work *The Screwtape Letters*, Lewis had the devil Screwtape observe, "The safest road to Hell is the gradual one—the gentle slope, soft underfoot, without sudden turnings, without milestones, without signposts" (1996i, 54).

One of Lewis's greatest strengths, though one that is not always noted, is his stunning ability to realistically portray wrongdoing. His characters are not completely good one moment and then wickedly bad the next. Rather, Lewis will make it clear that the descent into transgression occurs step by step. Lewis will later tell readers that Edmund was "becoming a nastier person every minute" (45). As Chad Walsh has pointed out, at this point Edmund is "not a complete scoundrel" although he is "weak" and "unable to resist temptation" (1979, 140). Here Edmund cannot, or will not, resist the temptation to torment Lucy, who is younger than he is. At each step his behavior will become more and more egregious and, much like Macbeth's, will grow harder and harder to turn back from.

One wet afternoon a few days later, during a game of hide-and-seek, Lucy and Edmund both enter the wardrobe—Lucy because it is the only last-minute hiding place she can think of and Edmund because he has seen Lucy go in and wants "to go on teasing her" (27). Both children are able to enter Narnia this time, although when Edmund arrives, Lucy is so far ahead of him that he is unable to see her. This fact is in keeping with the concept that time in Narnia goes much faster than in our own world. Lucy would presumably have been a few of our seconds ahead of Edmund, but this seems to translate into perhaps an hour or more in Narnia, enough time for her to have lunch with Mr. Tumnus and then to return just after Edmund has had his conversation with the White Witch.

Since Edmund had foolishly shut the door (28), the inside of the wardrobe is dark. After not being able to find Lucy, Edmund decides he would like some light and tries unsuccessfully to find the door to reopen it. Seeing a light, he moves toward it, mistakenly assuming that it is coming from the door, which he assumes has "swung open of its own accord" (29). Stepping out from under the shadow of a fir tree, Edmund finds himself alone under a blue sky in the snow-covered woods.

Lucy, even though she is younger than Edmund, was delighted when she first discovered Narnia. Here Lewis notes that Edmund "did not much like being alone in this strange, cold, quiet place" (30). Lewis's point here speaks to the general trust which the trustworthy may display in new situations, in contrast to their less moral counterparts. Edmund's characteristic distrust will be seen again on his second visit to Narnia.

Next in a continuation of Lewis's layered characterization, Edmund issues what may seem to be an honest apology for his actions, although there is the suggestion he is uttering it more out of fear or loneliness than true contrition. The narrator notes that Edmund "did not like to admit he had been wrong" but nevertheless shouts out, "I say, Lu! I'm sorry I didn't believe you. I see now you were right all along. Do come out. Make it Pax" (30). As the story progresses, readers will learn that Edmund is actually not all that different from his mostly kind and compassionate siblings, that he is not truly as mean as he seems to be at the start of the story. Later we are told that something at his "horrid" school has brought on the cruelty Edmund demonstrates toward Lucy and to a lesser extent toward Peter and Susan (180).

Edmund's moment of apology here, while containing some aspects of legitimacy, is short-lived. When Lucy does not respond, he wrongly imagines her doing what he would do in her stead and declares, "Just like a girl . . . sulking somewhere, and won't accept an apology" (30). As Evan Gibson points out, Edmund is best thought of here as "a small boy whose tendency to selfishness and bullying needs to be checked before it colors his whole life" (1980, 136). At the end of the next chapter Edmund will have another chance to apologize to Lucy for not believing her, and his second attempt will be seen to be even less authentic (41).

Paul Ford explains what he believes is driving the choices Edmund makes at this point in the story:

> He is struggling with his older brother Peter, who is always considered better than he, and his older sister Susan, who has appropriated to herself the role of his mother. The only person he ranks above is his younger sister Lucy. Out of this tangle of sibling relationships comes his will to power, his desire to have life his own way. Lewis doesn't try to make the reader feel too sympathetic toward Edmund—he has designed him to be the temporary villain—but Edmund's insecurity, fostered by his war-time dislocation, could make any child a difficult case until he knows he is loved. (1994, 160–1)

Almost immediately after his halfhearted apology, Edmund hears the sound of bells, signaling the arrival of the sledge bearing the White Witch. In chapter ten Lewis will return to this sound of bells as a false warning of the Witch's arrival (105). The British term *sledge* is unfamiliar and so perhaps distracting to first-time

American readers, and its use here raises the question of whether there was ever any discussion about replacing it with *sleigh* in versions sold in the United States. Chad Walsh recalls that when he met with Lewis in 1948, the author mentioned he was "beginning to see more pictures," including one picture of "a queen on a sledge" (1979, 129), as Edmund encounters here.

Though the Witch is described here as "a great lady, taller than any woman that Edmund had ever seen" (31), readers will later learn that "there isn't a drop of real human blood" in her (81), that she is not "a daughter of Eve." Besides her size, the other notable aspect about the Witch is, of course, her coloring. We are told, "Her face was white—not merely pale, but white like snow or paper or icing-sugar, except for her very red mouth" (31).

Colin Manlove has suggested that Lewis's White Witch comes "straight out of the pages of Hans Andersen" (1987, 127–8), a reference to Andersen's story "The Snow Queen." Kay, the main character in that fable, is, like Edmund, a good boy gone bad. Similarities between Andersen's character and the White Witch can be seen in the following passage where Kay first meets the Snow Queen:

> All at once . . . the great sledge stopped, and the person who had driven it rose up. The fur and the cap, which were made entirely of snow, fell off, and he saw a lady, tall and white, it was the Snow Queen.
>
> "We have driven well," said she, "but why do you tremble? here, creep into my warm fur." Then she seated him beside her in the sledge, and as she wrapped the fur round him he felt as if he were sinking into a snow drift.
>
> "Are you still cold," she asked, as she kissed him on the forehead. The kiss was colder than ice; it went quite through to his heart, which was already almost a lump of ice; he felt as if he were going to die, but only for a moment; he soon seemed quite well again, and did not notice the cold around him. (Andersen 1984, 58)

Like the Snow Queen, the White Witch in *TLWW* will make similar offers of warmth. In the next chapter she will invite Edmund into her sledge and wrap her mantel around him (35). She will warm him with a magical drink rather than a kiss (36).

Manlove sees in the White Witch's whiteness a vampirelike quality that "drains the vitality from Narnia" and literally "bleeds it white" (1987, 131). In *The Magician's Nephew* readers will learn how the Witch originally came to be in Narnia, but as with the other magical elements already encountered—the wardrobe, the lamp-post, and Narnia itself—if readers are reading *TLWW* first, they share in the children's surprise, and here will be as startled as Edmund. In *The Magician's Nephew* Lewis will explain that the Witch was not always white. This quality appears only after she has stolen and eaten a magic apple. When Digory comes upon her, she is described as looking "stronger and prouder than ever" (Lewis 1994d, 174), but her face has changed and become "deadly white, white as salt."

Thomas Howard has suggested that the sledge the Witch uses here and later in the story, with its bells and reindeer, is an imitation of the one belonging to Father Christmas, a character encountered later. Howard explains that the difference is that the sledge belonging to the White Witch is "a counterfeit, exactly like the real thing but a cheat" (1980, 42). This is because "evil can only parody goodness, it cannot invent new forms of real beauty and joy. That is why in fairy tales you have to beware of attractive disguises—nice old crones selling apples in the forest, say, or angels of light." We might add another "attractive disguise" to Howard's list: tall, beautiful queens with hot drinks and candy. Tolkien followed the same pattern, making his villain Sauron beautiful to behold in his earlier form, and Paul Kocher notes how it was through this "seductive charm of body and mind" that Sauron was able to deceive the king of Numenor (1972, 56).

Joe Christopher has noted a series of parallels between Lewis's world of Narnia and Tolkien's world of Middle-earth and suggests that Lewis produced "a work that, in its overall pattern, is close to Tolkien's" (1987, 111). As Christopher points out, Lewis and the other Inklings would have listened to *The Lord of the Rings* in installments as it was being written in the twelve years between

1937 and 1949. (The three-book series was not published until 1954 and 1955, a number of years after *TLWW*.) Later Tolkien would write about "the unpayable debt" that he owed to Lewis for his encouragement, suggestions, and support, stating: "He was for long my only audience. Only from him did I ever get the idea that my 'stuff' could be more than a private hobby. But for his interest and unceasing eagerness for more I should never have brought *The Lord of the Rings* to a conclusion" (Tolkien 2000, 362). Given Lewis's long and deep involvement with the shaping of *The Lord of the Rings*, we should not be surprised to find similarities occurred when Lewis set out to write *TLWW* in 1948.

While a sizable number of parallels can be discovered between the two writers' fiction, determining who—Lewis or Tolkien—was first with a particular feature may be impossible. For example, even if one could determine that some incident or aspect was present in an early manuscript of *The Lord of the Rings*, long before Lewis would have begun writing *TLWW*, probably no way can be found to determine whether Lewis might have originally given Tolkien the suggestion for it. Additionally, when a parallel is found, the possibility exists that both authors borrowed the same element from an earlier tradition, as they do with their dwarfs, for example.

Leaving the question of origin aside, a key benefit of examining a few of the most significant Lewis-Tolkien similarities is that doing so can help to bring out key aspects in a way that allows us to see them more clearly. For example, one parallel between Lewis and Tolkien which Christopher does not mention is the Witch's lack of ability to create; she can only imitate, a quality which is found in Tolkien's villain Sauron also. In *The Two Towers*, Tolkien has Treebeard tell Pippin and Merry, "Trolls are only counterfeits, made by the Enemy in the Great Darkness, in mockery of Ents, as Orcs were of Elves" (1994d, 474). At another point, Frodo is talking to Sam about orcs and says, "The Shadow that bred them can only mock, it cannot make: not real new things of its own" (Tolkien 1994c, 893). Later in *TLWW* readers will be told that part of the Witch's magic is to "make things look like what they aren't" (138), a motif which occurs again and again. Even the winter imposed over Narnia is not a real one she has created but a perversion or a distortion of a real winter. The Turkish Delight the Witch gives to Edmund in the next chapter will be her less-than-satisfying imitation of "good ordinary food" (88).

Evidence that Lewis intended for readers to draw a comparison between Father Christmas and the Witch can be found in the way that Father Christmas's sledge is introduced later. Readers will be told, "It *was* a sledge, and it *was* reindeer with bells on their harness. But they were far bigger than the Witch's reindeer, and they were not white but brown" (106). In addition, when Father Christmas arrives in his sledge, the three children and the beavers are expecting it to be the Witch who is arriving, making the connection even stronger.

In the portrait of the Witch's sledge, readers may notice that Lewis uses a color scheme which emphasizes three colors in a way that suggests intention. The three colors we find are white for the reindeer, the dwarf's polar bear fur, and the Witch's fur and skin; gold for the reindeer's horns, the dwarf's tassel, and the Witch's wand and crown; and red for the harness, the dwarf's hat, and the Witch's mouth (31). While the colors can be interpreted in a number of ways, the white may be said to reflect the Witch's never-ending winter, the gold her royalty, and the red her imitation of Father Christmas.

The Witch's golden wand, which plays such a major role in *TLWW*, is not mentioned as belonging to the Witch when she enters Narnia from her world in *The Magician's Nephew*, suggesting that it is perhaps something she acquired during the long years she was far away from Narnia in "the North of the world," a time when she was "growing stronger in the dark Magic" (189). Here in *TLWW* the wand is described as "long" and "straight" (31), aspects which will contribute to the theme of narrowness that the Witch displays, seen later when Edmund arrives at her castle with its "long pointed spires" that are "sharp as needles" (92). In Baynes's first illustration of the Witch (32), her wand is perhaps even longer and more pointed than readers may have imagined.

The Witch spies Edmund and orders an abrupt stop which is brought to life by the concrete details Lewis provides. The reindeer are pulled up so sharply that they "almost sat down." After they recover, they stand "champing their bits and blowing" in the frosty air, the breath "coming out of their nostrils like smoke" (31–2).

The "lady" asks Edmund twice, "What are you?" He first tells her his name, failing to address her as Queen, something which readers will notice is supremely important to the Witch. In his second answer, Edmund tries to indicate that he is a student, or was a student before the holidays started. Lewis ends chapter three with this second answer, one which also serves to explain why the children have not been required to attend school during their stay at the Professor's.

FOUR

Turkish Delight

In the fourth chapter, Lewis continues his pattern of beginning each new chapter already one step in the following action and then concluding it with one foot in what comes next. Chapter four starts with Edmund still working on the Witch's first question. It will end with Edmund and Lucy having arrived back at the Professor's and heading out to find their siblings.

The White Witch has to ask Edmund "What are you?" yet a third time before she gets an answer. She wonders if he might be "a great overgrown dwarf that has cut off his beard" (34). If the Witch had never seen a human boy before, this conjecture would seem appropriate. However, as we learn in *The Magician's Nephew*, the Witch saw quite a bit of the Professor when he was a boy. Thus we have another small inconsistency caused by Lewis not knowing when writing *TLWW* what was going to happen in *The Magician's Nephew*, or, alternatively, one could argue that the Witch has not seen a human in Narnia in hundreds and hundreds of years and so she is justified in first thinking that Edmund might be an oversized dwarf.

Edmund finally understands the Witch's question and admits he is a boy. This news causes the Witch to worry: "This may wreck all" (35). But she then reasons that Edmund is "only one" and easily dealt with, a comment which should lead readers to recall Mr. Tumnus's earlier remark about four empty thrones at Cair Paravel to be filled one day (20).

The Witch raises her golden wand and is about to turn Edmund into one of the stone statues we have already heard about (20), but at the last moment she changes her mind and decides to get information from him about the possibility of more humans coming to Narnia. To obtain this information she takes on the semblance of kindness. Like Andersen's Snow Queen in the passage previously discussed, she invites Edmund into her sledge to warm up and then offers him a magical hot drink.

In the drink which the Witch creates to warm Edmund, readers can find another parallel with Tolkien, as both authors depict unwholesome drinks that warm the drinker in an unhealthy way. Lewis writes, "Edmund felt much better as he began to sip the hot drink. It was something he had never tasted before, very sweet and foamy and creamy, and it warmed him right down to his toes" (36). In *The Two Towers* Pippin and Merry receive a similar drink, not from an evil dwarf but from one of the orcs which have captured them. Tolkien describes Pippin's experience: "Ugluk thrust a flask between his teeth and poured some burning liquid down his throat: he felt a hot fierce glow flow through him" (1994d, 438).

Just as the Witch's sledge may be seen to imitate the one belonging to Father Christmas, both Lewis's and Tolkien's evil hot drinks mirror or parody wholesome ones found elsewhere in the stories. The White Witch's magic brew can be seen as a counterfeit of the hot tea which Lucy is given by Mr. Tumnus, the first character that she encounters, as well as imitating the steaming tea which the other children are given first by the Beavers and then later by Father Christmas (74, 109).

The drink from Tolkien's orcs may be viewed as an imitation of the warming drink of *miruvor* which is given to the hobbits first by Glorfindel and then again by Gandalf during the snowstorm on Caradhras (Tolkien 1994a, 206, 283). Additionally, the orc drink may be seen as an imitation of the *lembas* bread which the elves give to the hobbits. In fact, Tolkien has Merry himself make the comparison, saying, "*Lembas* does put heart into you! A more wholesome sort of feeling, too, than the heat of that orc-draught" (1994d, 448). In his *Preface to Paradise Lost*, Lewis discussed evil as a sickly form of the good, observing, "What we call bad things are good things perverted" (1961b, 66), and he traces this perspective back to Milton and before him to St. Augustine.

Lewis provides readers a foreshadowing of what is to come by having the dwarf bow and smile as he hands the drink to Edmund—but "not a very nice smile" (36)—another time when appearances in Narnia are deceiving.

Next the White Witch creates a round box filled with "several pounds" of Turkish Delight, and Edmund greedily devours it all (37). Donald Glover has called Lewis's specific choice of Turkish Delight here a "master stroke" (1981, 138), one made with clear intention. What would have been lost if the Witch had tempted Edmund with oatmeal cookies, for example, or a chocolate bar? What in particular does the use of Turkish Delight contribute? Glover argues that Turkish Delight is "a highly overrated sweet," and Narnia fans who have gone in search of the candy after reading about it in *TLWW* may agree, wondering how Edmund could have fallen prey to this overly sugary confection. Surely the name promises more than the candy delivers, and this, perhaps, is Lewis's point. Furthermore, it is not just "Delight" but "Turkish Delight," a title containing, as Glover has observed, "Oriental and romantic overtones," further promises which are never fulfilled.

Gilbert Meilaender, in a chapter appropriately titled "The Sweet Poison of the False Infinite" (1998, 8), provides an analysis of the spell that the Witch's magic candy casts upon Edmund. As Meilaender explains, the phrase "the sweet poison of the false infinite" comes from Lewis's novel *Perelandra* (1996g, 70) and refers to any love of secondary things which has become inordinate. Meilaender points out that this theme—that human beings are to take delight in material objects and in physical pleasures but are not to worship them—is one to which Lewis "often returns" (8).

Later, at the Beavers' house, the children will be served wholesome food of which the Witch's candy is a sickly imitation. They will eat boiled potatoes, bread and butter, and "good freshwater fish" (74). Edmund will be unable to enjoy the Beavers' meal, for as Lewis explains, "He had eaten his share of the dinner, but he hadn't really enjoyed it because he was thinking all the time about Turkish Delight—and there's nothing that spoils the taste of good ordinary food half so much as the memory of bad magic food" (88).

Lewis's point here with the Turkish Delight is not that enjoying sweets is bad; in fact, his position is quite the contrary. Enjoyment of life's pleasures in all their variety and plentitude will be an essential quality of proper Narnian life, as has been seen already in the tea that Mr. Tumnus provided for Lucy which included "a nice brown egg, lightly boiled, for each of them, and then sardines on toast, and then buttered toast, and then toast with honey, and then a sugar-topped cake" (15). In both his fiction and nonfiction, Lewis suggests over and over that "to be fully human involves a certain stance toward the things of creation" (Meilaender 1998, 8), one of enjoyment but not slavish adoration.

In an essay which he titled "First and Second Things," Lewis made a point similar to the one here in *TLWW*, writing:

> By valuing too highly a real but subordinate good, we . . . come near to losing that good itself. The woman who makes a dog the center of her life loses, in the end, not only her human usefulness and dignity but even the proper pleasure of dog-keeping. The man who makes alcohol his chief good loses not only his job but his palate and all power of enjoying the earlier (and only pleasurable) levels of intoxication. . . . Every preference of a small good to a great, or a partial good to a total good, involves the loss of the small or partial good. . . . You can't get second things by putting them first. (1996b, 280)

Twelve years earlier in *Out of the Silent Planet* (1938), Lewis addressed this subject of the sweet poison of the false infinite in a conversation which Ransom, the philologist who has been kidnapped to Mars, has with one of its inhabitants named Hyoi. Ransom states that if something is a pleasure, a man "wants it again" (1996f, 74). For Hyoi repeating a pleasure over and over again is inconceivable, and he asks, "But why? Would he want his dinner all day or want to sleep after he had slept?"

In *Perelandra*, the next book in the space trilogy, Ransom travels to the planet Venus, and while eating the delicious native fruit there, he is able to avoid the endless repetition and enslavement which Edmund succumbs to here. We read:

> He let the empty gourd fall from his hand and was about to pluck a second one, it came into his head that he was now neither hungry nor thirsty. And yet to repeat a pleasure so intense and almost so spiritual seemed an obvious thing to do. . . . It appeared to him better not to taste again. Perhaps the experience had been so complete that repetition would be a vulgarity—like asking to hear the same symphony twice a day. (Lewis 1996g, 37–8)

Part of the reason that Edmund devours one piece after another of the Witch's Turkish Delight, one reason why he "wants it again," is because it is not *real* candy but only an imitation. While tasty, it is not satisfying. In fact, it is the opposite of satisfying, creating a craving which can never be fulfilled no matter how much is eaten. Readers are told that anyone who eats enchanted Turkish Delight "would want more and more of it, and would even, if they were allowed, go on eating it till they killed themselves" (38).

Don King has pointed out an interesting antecedent for this scene, one which Lewis certainly would have been familiar with and so may have had in the back of his mind. King observes that Edmund's excess here with the Turkish Delight "recalls Eve's gluttonous indulgence in Milton's *Paradise Lost* where she first eats the apple" (1984, 15). The parallel becomes apparent when passages from the two scenes are put side by side. In *TLWW* we read: "At first Edmund tried to remember that it is rude to speak with one's mouth full, but soon he forgot about this and thought only of trying to shovel down as much Turkish Delight as he could, and the more he ate the more he wanted to eat, and he never asked himself why the Queen should be so inquisitive" (37). In book nine of *Paradise Lost* we find this corresponding depiction:

> . . . for Eve
> Intent now wholly on her taste, naught else
> Regarded, such delight till then, as seemed,
> In fruit she never tasted, whether true
> Or fancied so, through expectation high
> Of knowledge, nor was God-head from her thought,
> Greedily she ingorged without restraint . . .
>   (Milton 1969, 785–91)

Besides exploiting his greed for the magic candy, the other means the White Witch uses to draw information out of Edmund and turn him into a traitor is the promise of dominance over his siblings. Significantly, she never refers to herself as a witch but from the very start as "the Queen of Narnia" (33), because her desire to dominate all else is the trait which most clearly defines her. As Colin Manlove states, "The Witch is a tyrant. Her evil is one of selfishness. What she does with it is never clear" (1987, 130).

Here again readers can see a parallel to Tolkien's character Sauron, whose central desire is also dominance, seen in his "One Ring to rule them all" (Tolkien 1994a, 49). Paul Kocher's description of Sauron sheds light on this aspect of the White Witch, for as he states, Sauron "is an obsessed being, driven by his fever to dominate everything and everybody. He cannot rest. He is always on the offensive, always reaching out to draw all life to himself in order to subdue it" (1972, 58). As Gandalf explains to Frodo, "Hobbits as miserable slaves would please him far more than hobbits happy and free" (Tolkien 1994a, 48). Similarly, in *The Magician's Nephew* readers will be told the Witch "had taken no notice of Polly" because "Digory was the one she wanted to make use of" (Lewis 1994d, 79). The narrator will offer this explanation: "I expect most witches are like that. They are not interested in things or people unless they can use them." The Witch will justify her destruction of all the residents of her kingdom by stating, "I was the Queen. They were all *my* people. What else were they there for but to do my will?" (67).

W. H. Auden has noted that this kind of evil "is not satisfied if another does what it wants; he must be made to do it against his will" (1976, 57). Manlove, in summing up the Witch's love of power for its own sake, states: "She is concerned only with maintaining her power over Narnia. She does nothing with it" (1993, 36). Manlove points out that the Witch's dominance "exists for no other reason than to keep it."

Finally, one might argue that in her desire for domination, the White Witch also parallels one of Lewis's own villains: the devil Screwtape found in *The Screwtape Letters*, published eight years before *TLWW*, in 1942. In Screwtape's final letter we learn that his nephew Wormwood has lost the young man he was trying to bring to hell, and so as punishment Wormwood is going to be given to Screwtape. Writing with irony, Screwtape tells Wormwood of his plans to dominate him: "I have always desired you, as you (pitiful fool) desired me. The difference is that I am the stronger" (1996i, 109).

In *The Magician's Nephew*, readers learn that the White Witch has come to Narnia from another world which was destroyed because the Witch wanted to overthrow her sister and rule the world herself. In that story, the White Witch, there known as Jadis, offers this explanation for the conflict, one which is characteristically lacking any trace of self-criticism: "It was my sister's fault. She drove me to it. . . . At any moment I was ready to spare her life too, if only she would yield to me the throne. But she would not. Her pride has destroyed the whole world" (Lewis 1994d, 66). Of course it was the Witch's pride that was to blame, but like Sauron, who is portrayed as a single eye, the White Witch sees every event from only one perspective—her own.

As mentioned, the self-styled Queen insists on being addressed as "your Majesty" (33), and she tempts Edmund with this same lust for domination, promising to make him a prince and later a king, with the other children serving as his "courtiers and nobles" (39), for what is the use of being a ruler if there is no one to rule over? Edmund falls into her trap, responding, "There's nothing special about *them*" (39). Readers will learn that Edmund's desire to dominate, the trait that the Queen now snares him with, was present in him before their encounter. In the next chapter Peter will tell his younger brother, "You've always liked being beastly to anyone smaller than yourself; we've seen that at school before now" (46).

Long before he created the White Witch or the devil Screwtape, Lewis described another character whose sole desire was to dominate. In *A Preface to Paradise Lost*, Lewis described Milton's Satan, and in his description we can find a prefiguring of Lewis's own portrait of evil in *TLWW*. According to Lewis, when a creature becomes "more interested in itself than in God" and wishes to exist "on its own" (1961b, 66), it is guilty of "the sin of Pride." Lewis notes that the first creature to commit this sin was Satan, "the proud angel who turned from God to himself, not wishing to be a subject, but to rejoice like a tyrant in having subjects of his own."

In the Witch's promise to make Edmund "King of Narnia" after she is "gone" (39), we can find two points worth taking notice of. First, as readers will learn in *The Magician's Nephew*, the Witch is immortal unless killed in battle (Lewis 1994d, 190). Her promise to Edward is all a lie, for she has no plans to ever be "gone." In *The Magician's Nephew*, Lewis will have the Witch make a similar promise—one that is a similar lie—to Digory. She urges him to eat the apple that will grant endless days with the assurance, "You and I will both live forever and be king and queen of the whole world—or of your world, if we decide to go back there" (1994d, 175). Digory will reject the temptation offered by the Witch in a way that Edmund does not.

Secondly, her plan as stated here is actually a false imitation of Aslan's plan for Edmund. In fact Edmund is to rule as a king after Aslan is gone. However, Aslan's conception of being a king or queen is radically different from the Witch's. Rather than being a position of endless privilege, Aslan will tell King Frank, Narnia's first ruler, that to be king means being "the first in the charge and the last in the retreat" (Lewis 1994d, 152).

In Edmund's conversation with the Queen, he reveals not only that his sister Lucy has been to Narnia already but also that she "had met a Faun there" (37), information which will have dire consequences for Mr. Tumnus, who up until now has been able to keep his meeting with Lucy and disobedience of the Queen's command a secret. The Queen keeps returning to the fact that there are four children, making clear the connection with Mr. Tumnus's earlier prophecy about the four thrones. The Witch finally insists that Edmund must return to his own country so that he can bring his brother and sisters to her. Presumably what she fears most is their uncontrolled entrance to Narnia, the kind of entrance which Lucy has made twice now.

Edmund claims not to know the way back to the wardrobe, and here the Witch appears to contradict her prior lack of information. Earlier it had seemed that the entrance to Narnia was something she had no direct knowledge of, as she stated, "A door from the world of men! I have heard of such things" (35). Now she tells him, "Do you see that lamp? Straight on, beyond that, is the way to the World of Men" (40). In *The Magician's Nephew* Lewis tells the story of how the Witch came through a door of sorts from her original world of Charn to London and then to Narnia, which may explain how she has "heard of such things" but not how or why she knows the location of the wardrobe passageway here.

One possible explanation for how the Witch knows that beyond the lamp-post is a doorway to the World of Men, although one which can never be any more than speculation, is that Lewis may have envisioned a story telling how the Professor had traveled through the wardrobe himself. At least three clues in *TLWW* support this possibility: (1) as noted, the Witch has already heard of the wardrobe doorway, meaning that someone has used it before; (2) at the end of the story, the Professor will somehow know that the wardrobe will not allow the children further passage, as though perhaps he himself was denied entrance to Narnia after a certain number of trips; and (3) also at the end of the story, the Professor will somehow know the maxim which Aslan tells the children, "Once a King in Narnia, always a King in Narnia" (188).

One explanation for these three otherwise inexplicable facts is inadvertent oversight by Lewis, and these might have been items that Lewis had planned to tidy up in a later revision which he never got to. Another explanation might be that Lewis was planning to write a story set in the past where the much younger Professor traveled to Narnia through the wardrobe and was a king himself. This would also account for the books about man seen earlier on Mr. Tumnus's shelf. Of course, a third explanation is that Lewis merely wanted to suggest this possibility but leave it unstated, a bit of a mystery. In a letter written to his friend Arthur Greeves, Lewis noted how ancient myths were "suggestive of meanings beyond my grasp" (1993, 288), and certainly in other places throughout the Chronicles Lewis's goal is to suggest rather than fully explain.

Having said all this, it could also be noted that at the end of *The Magician's Nephew* readers will be told that the Professor "did not discover the magic properties of that wardrobe, someone else did" (Lewis 1994d, 202). Most readers will probably just assume that this "someone else" is Lucy Pevensie, but in the first chapter of *The Voyage of the* Dawn Treader, Lewis provides one further clue that the Professor or someone else not named made an unrecorded visit to Narnia. At the start of the story, Lucy and Edmund are staying with their aunt and uncle while their parents are in America, and as the first chapter opens we find them up in Lucy's room looking at a picture of a Narnian sailing ship. Readers are told Aunt Alberta did not like the picture but had not gotten rid of it "because it had been a wedding present from someone she did not want to offend" (1994g, 6).

Who is this person Aunt Alberta does not want to offend? Who could have had a picture of a Narnian sailing ship to give as a present? At this point in time, only six people in England had been to Narnia—Polly, Digory, and the four children. Given Eustace's age, we must believe that the wedding took place well before the events in *TLWW*. This leaves Polly or Digory, characters who are never mentioned as knowing Eustace's parents but are older figures and thus perhaps the kind of people that Aunt Alberta would not wish to offend. However, in *The Magician's Nephew* Digory and Polly travel to Narnia at the time of its creation, a time long before it would have had sailing ships. In his inclusion of this painting, Lewis implies that someone besides the four children must have traveled to Narnia on a trip which is not recorded in the Chronicles. One last detail supports this claim. Lewis would later make what he called an "Outline of Narnian History," which has been published in several books (Ford 1994, 454–5; Hooper 1980, 50–1; Hooper 1996, 420–3). The full title of this list of dates and events is "Outline of Narnian History so far as it is known," and the latter part of the title suggests that there have been more visits to Narnia than Lewis recorded.

The Witch drives off in her sledge just as Lucy arrives, and Edmund is very ready to lie, saying nothing about his meeting with the Witch and even going so far as to falsely claim, "I have been looking for you everywhere" (41). He makes what could be taken as an apology—or not—telling her, "I'll say I'm sorry *if you like*" (emphasis added). Lucy characteristically does not take him up on his offer, and so Edmund again fails to genuinely apologize. He will have a third and last chance to ask for forgiveness later in the story, one which he will finally take advantage of (139). In spite of Edmund's weak attempt at making up, Lucy responds with her typical goodness, saying, "If I'd known you had got in I'd have waited for you" (41). When she mentions that the White Witch has not yet done anything to Mr. Tumnus, Edmund's response is to say, "The White Witch? Who's she?" (42), a reaction which, since she was introduced to him not under that name but as the Queen of Narnia, may be somewhat genuine, although it is perhaps more plausible to assume he suspects that this name must refer to the uniquely white person he has just met and so is just covering up the fact that he has met her.

As Lucy then tells Edmund, the White Witch "calls herself the Queen of Narnia" (42). Except for a few evil Narnians in her service, no one else will ever call her this. Lewis as narrator uses all three terms somewhat interchangeably—the Witch, the White Witch, and the Queen—but will use "the Queen" the least. Later, in chapter six of *TLWW*, readers will learn that the Witch has a personal name, Jadis (58), the same name she was known by in *The Magician's Nephew*'s land of Charn, but this is a designation which is never used except that one time, perhaps suggesting that her identity is based solely on her evil (hence the term *Witch*) or her desire for power over others (hence the title *Queen*).

Edmund tries to convince himself that the Queen is not as evil as Lucy has suggested. To justify his position, he declares to Lucy, "You can't always believe what Fauns say," and claims this is something that "everyone" knows. Lewis points out that Edmund particularly wants to sound "as if he knew far more about them than Lucy" (42). Rather than going on with this argument which he knows has no basis, Edmund quickly shifts the conversation to complaining about the snow, and together he and Lucy return back through the wardrobe to the Professor's house.

At this point in the story readers may be interested to take a closer look at exactly how Lewis describes the children's return from Narnia, because it is a process that he intentionally leaves somewhat vague. Both when Lucy came back in chapter two and now at the end of chapter four, we find no indication that they actually climb into the back of the wardrobe. Instead, they simply keep going in the direction where they can see the wardrobe door, and "presently instead of branches" and snow they find coats, the wooden boards of the wardrobe, and finally the empty room (43). In both cases Lewis's description makes it seem as though another world is actually inside the wardrobe.

In later Narnia stories, Lewis will purposely not have travel occur in the same way again, and the children will travel through devices that seem more like doorways that connect the worlds. Though this image of a world inside a wardrobe will not be used in later books, in *TLWW* Lewis will have both Susan and Peter picture Narnia in this way. As they are debating whether they should take the fur coats, Susan argues, "It isn't as if we wanted to take them out of the house; we shan't take them even out of the wardrobe" (55).

Peter will agree, stating, "No one could say you had bagged a coat as long as you leave it in the wardrobe where you found it. And I suppose this whole country is in the wardrobe."

Finally, we might also note that when Lucy came back after her first visit, she ran toward a "far-off patch of daylight" coming from the open doorway of the wardrobe (22). Since Edmund had shut the door when he entered (28), no mention is made of any daylight coming from the wardrobe on their next return (43). They simply walk "a good way" and suddenly feel the fur coats.

Chapter five ends with Lucy's optimistic declaration that "wonderful adventures" are going to immediately follow because, as she states, "we're all in it together" (43). Part of Lewis's success in keeping readers' interest high comes through his use of the elements of surprise, unpredictability, and reversal. In fact, the next chapter will be anything but "wonderful" for Lucy, as she will find that instead of all of them being "in it together," the other three children are all aligned against her.

Back on This Side of the Door

As Edmund and Lucy emerge from the wardrobe, once again little or no time has passed, and so as chapter five opens, they have to go hunting for Peter and Susan, who are still playing hide-and-seek.

When Lucy announces that Edmund has been to Narnia with her, Lewis provides Edmund with a complex response. He first provides time for Edmund to come up with his disavowal of being in Narnia. If Peter and Susan had been standing right outside the wardrobe the moment that Edmund and Lucy came popping out, perhaps Edmund would have found it more difficult to deny where he and Lucy had been moments before. Instead we are told that because the game of hide-and-seek was still in progress, "it took Edmund and Lucy some time to find the others" (44).

Secondly, Lewis provides motivation—not an excuse but at least a way to understand the spiteful disavowal that Edmund makes. Readers are told that Edmund had been feeling "sick, and sulky, and annoyed with Lucy for being right" (44). As has been noted, Edmund does not like to admit he has been wrong (30). While these reasons might spur Edmund's dishonesty, Lewis makes it clear that they do not excuse it. In spite of the way Edmund feels, he has a conscious choice to make here, a fact that Lewis takes pains to point out several times in a short space. We read: "Up to that moment Edmund . . . hadn't *made up his mind* what to do. When Peter suddenly asked him he *decided* all at once to do the meanest and most spiteful thing he could think of. He *decided* to let Lucy down" (44, emphasis added).

While acknowledging that his characters may be influenced by external events, thus making their behavior believable, Lewis will never allow externals to serve as a justification for wrong actions. Instead he will always preserve and even highlight their free will, their personal choice and their responsibility for those choices. Tolkien takes a similar stance in *The Lord of the Rings*, as Paul Kocher points out, "For Tolkien every intelligent being is born with a will capable of free choice, and the exercise of it is the distinguishing mark of his individuality. Nothing can be more precious" (1972, 60). If the Witch's reign is characterized by her domination of free will, the reign of the four Pevensies will be marked by the opposite attitude. One of the few specific tasks they will be noted as accomplishing as adult kings and queens will be to stop "busybodies and interferers" and to encourage ordinary people who want "to live and let live" (183), a position which the Professor will emphasize during his conversation with Peter and Susan (51).

Worth noting is that Lewis's narrator calls Edmund's cruelty to Lucy here "one of the nastiest things in this story" (44). Certainly some nasty moments are yet to come—the moment when Edmund actually betrays his siblings to the Witch, Peter's brutal moment fighting the wolf, and of course Aslan's execution. When Lewis rates Edmund's decision to hurt Lucy here as being as nasty as any of the things that follow, he wants his readers to see that misdeeds which may seem small can carry as great a weight as those which may seem larger.

Peter acknowledges that their younger sister was "perfectly all right" when they left home (45) but now seems to be "going queer in the head" or is becoming "a most frightful liar." In spite of this evaluation, he harshly criticizes Edmund for "jeering and nagging at her one day and encouraging her the next." Peter then comments on Edmund's general pattern of behavior and in doing so, raises a possible contradiction. Peter tells his younger brother, "You've always liked being beastly to anyone smaller than yourself" (46). However, at the end of the story, when Edmund is healed, the narrator will comment that he looks better than he had for ages, better than "ever since his first term at that horrid school which was where he had begun to go wrong" (180). Did Edmund always have a beastly side, one which only comes out when he starts school? Or was he a good boy who only began to go wrong at a bad school? Perhaps Lewis wants readers to see that Edmund, like all humans, always had the potential for wrongdoing and that Edmund's potential for bad behavior began to be realized at school.

In spite of Edmund's denial that they had been to Narnia, Lucy sticks by her story, so much so that Peter and Susan become worried that their younger sister is losing her mind. As a result, the next morning they go to see the Professor. Here in the first extended scene with the Professor, readers discover that he is really quite an extraordinary person to go to for advice. He pulls up chairs for Peter and Susan and becomes "quite at their disposal" (47), listening attentively with his fingertips pressed together and "never interrupting" until they have completely finished. He says nothing "for a long while" as he thinks carefully about what he has been told. Then his response is largely to ask Peter and Susan questions, leading them in a Socratic way to come to the truth themselves.

In the short span of three pages, the Professor asks eight questions. The first is: "How do you know that your sister's story is not true?" (47). Not until readers get to *The Magician's Nephew*—where the boy who will later become Professor Kirke has his own journey to Narnia—do they find out that his asking this question is not quite as extraordinary as it seems here. At this point in *TLWW*, the Professor simply seems remarkably open to strange ideas, and as has been mentioned previously, if readers are to share Peter and Susan's astonishment, they would need to be reading *TLWW* first.

Through his questioning, the Professor makes it clear Lucy is not mad and in fact is by far the more trustworthy of the two younger children. Susan responds, "But this couldn't be true—all this about the wood and the Faun" (48), to which the Professor somewhat cryptically replies, "That is more than I know." Paul Ford sees in the Professor's responses here a Platonic undercurrent that runs throughout the Chronicles. Ford notes:

> In admirable Socratic fashion he replies not with answers but with questions that invite the children to step beyond their typical un-examined opinions about what is and what is not possible. The net effect of the conversation is to steer the children into a searching and thoughtful openness, which is precisely the method Socrates employs throughout the dialogues of Plato. (1994, 316)

Near the end of *The Last Battle*, Lewis will reassert his Platonic theme by having the old Narnia be a shadow of the new and by having the Professor exclaim, "It's all in Plato, all in Plato" (1994b, 195).

The Professor continues by telling Susan, "A charge of lying against someone whom you have always found truthful is a very serious thing; a very serious thing indeed" (48). These are words that Susan will appear to forget when in *Prince Caspian* Lucy will again be the first to experience something—in this case she will be the first to see Aslan. While Peter and Edmund also find it hard to believe Lucy, Susan goes further and implicitly again accuses her of lying (Lewis 1994e, 147), an action which she ultimately will apologize for (152).

In his conversation with Peter and Susan, we also find the Professor making what will become a famous pronouncement: "Logic! Why don't they teach logic at these schools?" (48). The Professor points out, "There are only three possibilities. Either your sister is telling lies, or she is mad, or she is telling the truth. You know she doesn't tell lies and it is obvious that she is not mad. For the moment then and unless any further evidence turns up, we must assume that she is telling the truth." The Professor's thought process here would have been characteristic of Lewis's tutor, William Kirkpatrick. Lewis set down this description of him in his autobiography: "If ever a man came near to being a purely logical entity, that man was Kirk. . . . The idea that human beings should exercise their vocal organs for any purpose except that of communicating or discovering truth was to him preposterous" (1995, 135–6).

In the Professor's question "Why don't they teach logic at these schools?" and later when he mutters, "I wonder what they *do* teach them in these schools" (50), we can find traces of Lewis's own personal encounters with the British educational system. As Paul Ford has noted, Lewis thought of schools as at best merely "a necessary evil" because his own experiences with them "were not happy" (1994, 363–4). As a young man Lewis attended a series of different institutions and there found serious learning to be quite difficult, and consequently he disliked them all. So it is perhaps no wonder that bad schools and a dislike for school will appear throughout the Chronicles. As mentioned, in *TLWW* Edmund's wrong-turning is connected with a negative school experience (180), and one of the specific accomplishments of the children later during their reign as kings and queens will be to liberate "young dwarfs and young satyrs from being sent to school" (183). Lewis will add emphasis to his critique of modern education by having the Professor repeat his question about school curriculum at the close of the novel (189) as well as at the close of *The Last Battle* (1994b, 195).

Lewis's most scathing indictment of modern trends in British education can be found in his portrait of Experiment House, the school Eustace and Jill attend in *The Silver Chair*. There Lewis will revisit the Professor's concern about teaching as the narrator suggests that learning is out of fashion and bullying is in, stating, "Owing to the curious methods of teaching at Experiment House, one did not learn much French or Math or Latin or things of that sort; but one did learn a lot about getting away quickly and quietly when They were looking for one" (1994f, 10–11). One can safely assume that the students at Experiment House did not learn much logic either.

When Susan points out the apparent time problem, that Lucy was gone "for less than a minute" but claimed to have been in Narnia "for hours," the Professor responds that this "is the very thing that makes her story so likely to be true" (49). In his reasoning he notes that if Lucy had gone to another world, he "should not be at all surprised to find that the other world had a separate time of its own; so that however long you stayed there it would never take up any of *our* time," and that this is not something that a girl Lucy's age would be likely to make up. What the Professor does *not* say here is that he has experienced this same time shift himself, as Lewis will have him exclaim at the end of *The Magician's Nephew*, "I believe the whole adventure's taken no time at all" (1994d, 195).

If readers later do go on to the story of young Digory Kirke, they may wonder why the Professor chooses not to say any more than he does here in this conversation with Peter and Susan—since, as they will discover, he already knew about and had visited Narnia, had already met the Witch, and had been told by Aslan she would cause problems one day (154). Perhaps the Professor's reticence at this point in *TLWW* is because whether Peter and Susan are also going to enter Narnia is not yet clear. At the end of *TLWW*, the Professor will advise the children, "Don't mention it to anyone else unless you find that they've had adventures of the same sort themselves" (188–9). Here, early in the novel, the Professor may be simply following his own admonition.

In *The Magician's Nephew*, readers will learn that the Professor was directly responsible for the Witch's presence in Narnia, as Aslan tells the newly created talking animals that the evil was "waked and brought hither by this son of Adam" (Lewis 1994d, 148). The Professor's lack of surprise in learning that Lucy has traveled to Narnia through the wardrobe can be attributed to the fact he was present when Aslan prophesied that "as Adam's race has done the harm, Adam's race shall help to heal it," a prophecy which can be seen as applying both to Digory and to the Pevensie children. While he cannot be certain, the Professor must hope, and perhaps believe, that Lucy's initial visit here signals the start to fully undoing the wrong that he had done as a young boy.

What may be the most unique aspect of the children's conversation with the Professor is his resort to logic to support Lucy's claim about the existence of an imaginary world. In Susan's view of reason, such claims must be discarded before looking at the evidence. The conversation ends with the Professor suggesting, "We might all try minding our own business" (51), a comment full of good sense and one which runs exactly counter to the Witch's main goal, which is to mind and even to control everyone's business.

Early in *The Fellowship of the Ring*, Frodo has an encounter similar to Peter and Susan's, a meeting where like them he turns to an older, wiser character for advice. Frodo meets with Gildor the elf and, like Peter and Susan, receives little in the way of real answers or little real advice (Tolkien 1994a, 81–3). In the initial stage of their adventures, both Lewis and Tolkien have their young protagonists receive vague assurances—but no more than this. Basically all they are told is that they should continue to act as they have been doing. What is the point of keeping these assurances vague? In these scenes both authors imply that the doubts and questions their inexperienced protagonists encounter are a part of the adventure and are something which they for the most part need to face on their own.

Next Lewis, as narrator, returns to the discussion of the Professor's house, which we are told is "so old and famous that people from all over England used to come and ask permission to see it" (51). Readers are told that "all manner of stories were told about it," some "even stranger" than the tale told in *TLWW*. Unfortunately, as far as we know, Lewis never put any of these strange stories about the Professor's house on paper.

In *The Magician's Nephew*, Lewis records the details of how the young Digory Kirke first came to live in the house with his parents. Lewis writes, "There came a long letter from Father in India, which had wonderful news in it. Old Great-Uncle Kirke had died and this meant, apparently, that Father was now very rich. He was going to retire and come home from India forever and ever. And the great big house in the country, which Digory had heard of all his life and never seen, would now be their home" (1994d, 200). Pauline

Baynes's illustration of the house shows it to be big, surrounded by woods, and backed by mountains in the distance (52). The three figures she pictures there, two with walking sticks, presumably are visitors coming to tour the house, some of the "strange grown-ups" that Edmund refers to (52), not any of the main characters we meet in the story.

Earlier the catalyst to Lucy's adventure in the wardrobe was the rain that led to their exploring the house rather than playing outside. Back in chapter one, readers learned "that was how the adventures began" (6). Here at the end of chapter five the children have been told to keep out of the way of the visitors, and now they find themselves running from one room to the next and finally being forced to take shelter in the wardrobe. As mentioned earlier, these visitors take on the same providential aspect that the rain had earlier, and to underscore the similarity, Lewis includes the phrase, "That was how the adventures began for the second time" (52). Lewis makes it clear that this has not happened by chance, but rather that "some magic in the house had come to life and was chasing them into Narnia" (53). As Peter claims as he guides the others into the wardrobe, "There's nowhere else."

In the chapter's final sentence, Lewis revisits his admonishment about how "you should never shut yourself up in a wardrobe" and has Peter modeling the proper behavior for all the young readers who will play Narnia. Lewis notes that he "held the door closed but did not shut it" (53). As Paul Ford has observed, in all of his actions including this one, Peter represents "the figure of the fine older brother" to his siblings and later will become "the paradigmatic king" in Narnia (1994, 309).

SIX

Into the Forest

For the first time since the start of *TLWW*, Lewis does not move into the next scene before the chapter break. Chapter five ends with the children still at the Professor's sitting in the wardrobe. As chapter six begins, we find them still sitting there. Through varying his pattern of ending chapters with one foot in the following action by now keeping the children in the same scene over the chapter break, Lewis signals that something special is about to happen. This will be the turning point for the first part of the book.

The children gradually come to be no longer in the wardrobe but in the woods of Narnia. This quality of gradual change, seen also in chapter one in Lucy's gradual transition into Narnia, is something which Lewis will continue to revisit. Colin Manlove has described this "gradualness" which Lewis uses over and over again in *TLWW*:

> First the children are withdrawn from society by being
> sent away from the London air raids in wartime to

their uncle's house in the remote country. . . . There is a hint here of likeness to the landscape of the world the children are to enter. The discovery of Narnia, too, is gradual . . . a marvelous tapering of everyday world into fantastic realm. . . . First one, then two, then four children have entered Narnia. Once there, there are further gradations. (1993, 32–3)

During this time of gradual transition, Susan complains about being cramped and cold. Edmund grumbles about the "filthy smell of camphor" (54) and then is the first to suggest, "Let's get out, they've gone." Perhaps in Edmund's words we are meant to hear a reluctance to enter Narnia again. Significantly, Lucy is the only one of the children to say nothing, a continuation of her attitude of withdrawal taken when no one believed her.

The moment they realize they are in a different land, Peter turns "at once" to Lucy and makes a sincere apology for not having believed her (55). He first says, "I apologize," then he adds, "I'm sorry," and finally asks if she will shake hands. With the exception of Aslan, the good characters in the Narnia stories will not be all good; they will not be idealized figures. Instead they will all make mistakes from time to time, and when they do, genuine apologies and forgiveness will be required. Note, though, that unlike Peter, Susan decides not to apologize to Lucy here, perhaps because in her eyes technically she has not wronged her younger sister.

Back in chapter two when Lucy learned that Mr. Tumnus had been trying to lull her to sleep so he could betray her, Lucy's reaction was carefully described. There readers were told that Lucy "wanted to be truthful and yet not be too hard on him" (19), a statement which embodies Lewis's own approach toward his protagonists. Lewis will be careful to tell the truth about the flaws in his central figures, and at the same time he will be understanding of the weaknesses which make these characters susceptible to mistakes. So while being honest, Lewis is also sympathetic—in Lucy's terms, he is truthful but yet "not too hard" on them.

Peter then proposes that they explore the new country. Susan immediately responds to the coldness with a characteristic "ugh!"

and suggests they should each put on one of the fur coats from the wardrobe (55). On her earlier two trips, Lucy seemed not to notice the cold or feel the need for a coat, although Edmund did. In this difference, perhaps Lewis is simply noting that young children left to themselves will often go outside without a coat, and if they stay active will not always be aware of the cold—and Lucy did stay active in her walk to Mr. Tumnus's, while Edmund did not as he stood in conversation with the Witch. Taking an alternate approach, Donald Glover sees the different ways that Lucy and Edmund react to the cold as "a barometer of their spiritual condition" (1981, 138), and if this observation is accurate, Susan's negative reaction could also be seen as indicative of her state. Whether Lewis included these varying reactions to indicate an inner condition or not, a big difference is certainly seen in the ways Lucy and Edmund each responded earlier to Narnia's winter. The contrast is clearly seen in comparing Baynes's drawing of Lucy in her light dress being led by Mr. Tumnus through the snowy woods in chapter two (13) with the drawing of the children all bundled up in the coats seen in chapter seven (71).

Donning the fur coats here serves several purposes. First, Susan's complaints about the cold help to establish her as a somewhat reluctant adventurer, and her suggestion that everyone bundle up before going out continues her attempt to seem more adultlike than she really is, an attempt that Kath Filmer has labeled as "a tendency to pseudo-sophistication" (1993, 106). Second, the coats will allow the children to stay for an extended time in Narnia—they will be there a couple days before the winter weather is driven out by Aslan's arrival, a significantly longer stay than either of Lucy's two earlier visits. Third, and most significantly, wearing fur coats will further erase the division between the children and the talking animals, creating a unity that provides much of Narnia's enchantment. When they encounter the Beavers, the animals will be humanlike on the inside, and the children will appear animallike on the outside. This resemblance is seen most clearly in Baynes's illustration, already referred to, of the four children in their overly long fur coats following Mr. Beaver into his house (71).

In the pub scene early in the film *Shadowlands*, one of Lewis's colleagues questions the presence of fur coats, wondering who they belong to since the Professor is a bachelor. In the film, Lewis explains that they could have once belonged to the Professor's mother. In *The Magician's Nephew* readers will meet the Professor's mother, Mabel Kirke, and her sister, Digory's Aunt Letty, both possible prior owners of the garments. In *TLWW*, no direct explanation is ever given for the Professor's rather large collection of fur coats, nor is there any indication whether they are men's or women's.

Peter, as we would expect, is uncomfortable with Susan's suggestion to take the coats, stating, "They're not ours" (55). In Susan's response that technically they are not taking them out of the wardrobe, Lewis makes it clear that the wardrobe is not a passage or doorway to Narnia but that, as Peter concludes, "This whole country is in the wardrobe."

They all agree to Susan's "very sensible" suggestion (55), and Peter leads them "forward into the forest" with the coats like "royal robes" (56), a foreshadowing of their coronations to come. Readers are told that "each thought the others looked better in their new get-ups." A man who was well-known as somewhat of a shabby dresser, Lewis made a rather large deal of fancy clothing in his imaginative works. At the end of *Prince Caspian*, Lewis will note that it was "odd, and not very nice" when the four children have "to take off their royal clothes and come back in their school things" (1994e, 222). In *The Last Battle* Tirian will find Eustace and Jill's British clothing not only "queer" but "dingy" (Lewis 1994b, 53). As Peter Schakel has noted, "such an emphasis on clothing is intriguing" (2002, 155) because, as Warren Lewis had observed about his brother, "His own clothes were a matter of complete indifference to him" (1993, 36).

As Peter begins leading the way forward into the forest, Lewis takes a moment to point out that heavy clouds hang overhead and that it looks "as if there might be more snow before night" (56). At this point in the story, this detail may seem merely descriptive. Later it will be seen to be craftsmanship, since this is a factor which is needed further along in the story. In chapter nine Edmund will

As noted earlier, the Witch's lack of a positive identity is also sig-
naled by the names she is called. Readers learn that her name is
Jadis, yet except for the one mention in Maugrim's letter (58), no
one calls her this. She is referred to as the Witch, the White Witch,
or in a few cases as the Queen—names which, as mentioned earlier,
reflect her evil or, in the latter case, her domination.

Lewis takes special care at this point in the story to emphasize
the wholesome, everyday goodness of the food, giving it almost
a sacramental quality in its ordinariness. Readers are told by the
narrator, "You can think how good the new-caught fish smelled
while they were frying" (73–4). He tells us about "a jug of creamy
milk for the children," a "great big lump of deep yellow butter in
the middle of the table," and finally the "great and gloriously sticky
marmalade roll, steaming hot" and cups of tea (74). As Paul Ford
notes, the Chronicles "are filled with the delights of domesticity"
(1994, 145), and in the meal here and the tea from Mr. Tumnus
earlier, Lewis served up the simple fare that he himself enjoyed.
Warren Lewis, in writing of his brother's preferences, stated, "Plain
domestic cookery was what he wanted, with the proviso that if the
food was hot the plates should be hot as well. What he really disliked
was 'messed-up food,' by which he meant any sort of elaborately
dressed dish" (1988, 36). The familiar dishes in *TLWW* will always
be accompanied by hot tea, another Lewis necessity. Warren notes
"the immense importance" he attached to afternoon tea, stating,
"When we were off on a walking tour together, or out on my motor-
cycle with Jack in the sidecar, the whole day had to be planned
around the necessity of finding ourselves at four o'clock in some
place where afternoon tea would be available."

In contrast to Edmund, who is plagued by cravings for Turkish
Delight, after the others finish eating, they shove their stools back
and lean against the wall as each gives "a long sigh of contentment"
(75). Readers will probably enjoy the meal at the Beavers' house, as
the children do, without questioning where, in this land of eternal
winter, the potatoes might have come from, or how they had the
cream or the butter without having grass or hay for cows, and so on.
Peter Schakel describes how the poet Ruth Pitter, who was Lewis's

trudge to the Witch's castle with "snowflakes swirling all round him" (90), making his journey even more unpleasant. The snow will be falling again in chapter ten as the children and the Beavers flee (103), a weather condition which will be essential when the Witch's wolves arrive and find that "even the footprints were covered up" (113).

Forgetting that he is not supposed to know anything about Narnia, Edmund suggests that they need to bear left if they hope to reach the lamp-post. Realizing his brother's deceit, Peter refers to him as a "poisonous little beast" (56), while the girls say nothing. As they continue walking, Edmund thinks to himself, "I'll pay you all out for this." But what exactly is it that Edmund's brother and two sisters have done? They have simply recognized the wrong that Edmund has committed and, in Peter's case, labeled him correctly. While Edmund is the one who has wronged his siblings, in his mind somehow the reverse is true, and in this lack of capacity for self-condemnation he will resemble the Queen.

Tom Shippey in his chapter on concepts of evil in *The Lord of the Rings* describes a similar condition for Tolkien's orcs, who "have no self-awareness or capacity for self-criticism" (2000, 133). In *TLWW* both the Queen and Edmund illustrate the old saying "no one does evil in his own eyes." Later in the story, Edmund will continue in his belief, or in his attempt to convince himself, that all the difficulties which befall him "had been Peter's fault" (92).

In a final gesture to make up for his earlier disbelief, Peter, the natural leader, asks Lucy if she will lead them, allowing her to decide where they should go. In this story of four children—two boys and two girls—Lewis will not always give identical roles to the females, an aspect which becomes more prominent later when the issue of the girls' role in battle is raised (109). Paul Ford has written a good deal on the topic of attitudes toward gender in Narnia (1994, 368–75), noting that "the issue of sexism in the Chronicles is more complex than might at first be supposed" (368). Here Lewis makes a point of telling readers that Lucy proves to be "a good leader" (57).

Readers will come across a similar scene in *The Last Battle*. There King Tirian, Eustace, and Jill are crossing through a thicket at night, and the dense branches make it "hard to pick up their bearings" (Lewis 1994b, 68). Lewis describes what happens next:

> It was Jill who set them right again: she had been an excellent Guide in England. And of course she knew her Narnian stars perfectly, having traveled so much in the wild Northern Lands, and could work out the direction from other stars even when the Spear-Head was hidden. As soon as Tirian saw that she was the best pathfinder of the three of them he put her in front. (1994b, 68–9)

Ford argues that the last three Narnia books Lewis wrote "reflect a writer more in touch with the reality of women and therefore more willing to see them as free individuals, capable of exploding cultural strictures and stereotypes" (1994, 374–5). However, it should be noted that even at this point early in *TLWW*, the first book of the series, Lewis is willing to have a female lead two males, and also to have the youngest child lead three who are older. Here Lucy keeps her head, recognizing "an odd-looking tree in one place" and "a stump in another" (57), and competently brings her siblings to their destination. Of course it is also true that Peter defers to Lucy because she has been to Narnia before and therefore knows her way better than the rest. Still the point can be made that Peter lets Lucy make the decision about where they should go and has confidence in her ability to guide them.

When they arrive at Mr. Tumnus's cave, the children find that it has been ransacked by the Witch or her forces. In contrast to its warm and inviting condition when Lucy had visited earlier, the interior is now described as "dark and cold" (57), a state similar to the Witch's castle, seen later with its "gloomy" hall where the only light comes from a single lamp (98–9). Edmund, rather than expressing any remorse when faced with what has been the direct result of his own personal actions—his statement to the Witch that Lucy had already been in Narnia and "had met a Faun there" (37)—callously replies, "This is a pretty good washout. Not much good coming here" (57). As Thomas Howard comments, "Edmund's disinclination to bother about Mr. Tumnus, small enough at the moment, is, alas, a deadly accurate index to what Edmund *is:* a selfish and egoistic cad" (1980, 46). Besides the indifference in Edmund's comment, readers may also hear a criticism of Peter's decision to allow Lucy to lead them.

Peter finds a notice which states that Mr. Tumnus has been arrested and is awaiting trial for high treason. From the notice readers learn the Queen's name, Jadis, and also that she is not content with ruling only Narnia but envisions herself the "Chatelaine of Cair Paravel, Empress of the Lone Islands, etc." (58). Mr. Beaver will later dispute her claim to the title of queen (140).

The announcement is signed by Maugrim, the captain of the Queen's secret police. His name seems to have no direct antecedent but in sounding like *grim maw* may suggest "savage jaws" or, alternatively, may allude to the French *maugre*, meaning "ill will" (Ford 1994, 189). The first interpretation seems particularly likely since Lewis's first description of him is as having "a great, red mouth" (98).

Because of labor union rules, the text of the Chronicles of Narnia had to be reset for the American editions. As Lewis prepared the new proofs, he took the opportunity to make a number of minor revisions. In the original American versions of the novel, Lewis changed the wolf's name to Fenris Ulf, a name which Paul Ford traces to the great wolf of Scandinavian mythology (1994, 189). While readers with older American copies may find this name, all current versions return to the use of Maugrim from the original British edition.

Two further details which Lewis includes in his description of the ravaged cave are worth commenting on. First, the snow which has drifted in through the open door has been mixed with "something black" (57). Lewis heightens our suspense before explaining that the black comes from the remains of a fire which someone has flung about the room and then stamped out. What has caused this inordinate reaction to what might have been expected in any fireplace during the Witch's long winter? Perhaps the Witch or her minions are enraged to find that the Narnians are able to be quite cozy and comfortable in spite of the imposed cold outside.

Lewis also describes how the picture of the Faun's father has been "slashed into shreds with a knife" and thrown onto the floor (57). This, of course, is the same picture which Mr. Tumnus pointed out to Lucy when he was unable to go through with his attempt to put her to sleep so he could hand her over to the Witch. The picture seems to have been a factor in his decision not to betray Lucy, as Mr. Tumnus's words at the time were "My old father, now, that's his picture over the mantelpiece. He would never have done a thing like this" (19).

Readers never learn anything more about the faun's father, but the destructiveness seen here suggests either that the Witch and her henchmen personally knew of Mr. Tumnus's father and his stance as a resister or that they destroyed the picture simply because it was something Mr. Tumnus treasured. Lewis takes the time here to point out that the picture has been slashed with "a knife." Later in the story, readers will see the Witch's stone knife with its "strange and evil shape" (155) and, looking back, may imagine her using it to shred the picture.

Susan's response to the devastation is to claim, "I don't know that I'm going to like this place after all" (59). She then complains, "I—I wonder if there's any point in going on. . . . I mean, it doesn't seem particularly safe here and it looks as if it won't be much fun either. And it's getting colder every minute, and we've brought nothing to eat. What about just going home?" In his portrait of Susan's weaknesses, Lewis was drawing upon his own exaggerated concerns for safety. In the introduction to *The Problem of Pain* (published in 1940), Lewis confessed, "I have never for one moment been in a state of mind to which even the imagination of serious pain was less than tolerable" (1996h, 9–10). Later in *The Four Loves* (1960) he would admit, "I am a safety-first creature. Of all arguments against love none makes so strong an appeal to my nature as 'Careful! This might lead you to suffering'" (1988, 120).

Joseph Campbell has noted how in many of the myths from around the world, the call to adventure is at first refused, for "it is always possible to turn the ear to other interests" (1968, 59), specifically the interests of safety, comfort, and security which staying in the same condition promises. Although readers may not realize it at this point, the answer to Susan's question, "What about just going home?" bears more weight than first might appear, for both Narnia and the children. Should Peter, Susan, Edmund, and Lucy decide to refuse the call, possibly Narnia would have remained under the spell of the Witch and Mr. Tumnus's doom would have been sealed. Additionally, we must ask, what would have become of the children if at this point they had decided to turn their backs on the situation, retraced their steps back to the lamp-post, and returned through the wardrobe to the comforts and protection of the Professor's home?

Campbell offers this description of the refusal of the call: "Often in actual life, and not infrequently in the myths and popular tales, we encounter the dull case of the call unanswered. . . . Refusal of the summons converts the adventure into its negative. Walled in boredom, hard work, or 'culture,' the subject loses the power of significant affirmative action and becomes a victim to be saved. His flowering world becomes a wasteland of dry stones and his life feels meaningless" (1968, 59). Although Susan will repeat her suggestion to go home once more (64), in *TLWW* she ultimately decides to heed the call. This will not always be the case. Always a somewhat reluctant adventurer, Susan will later in the Chronicles choose to reverse her decision here and refuse a further call (Lewis 1994b, 154).

Lucy is quick to counter her sister's concern about their own safety, saying, "Oh, but we can't, we can't" (59). Later in the story, when Father Christmas gives Lucy a dagger which is to be used only for defense because he does not want her to enter the battle, she will respond, "I think—I don't know—but I think I could be brave enough" (109). Father Christmas does not question Lucy's courage. For all her sweetness and light, in the face of difficulty and danger Lucy is also very brave. When she is a Queen of Narnia, the name by which she will be known is not "Lucy the Sweet" or "Lucy the Compassionate" but "Lucy the Valiant" (184).

Colin Manlove points out that Susan changes in a positive way "during the narrative" (1987, 135). At this point in the story, he notes that she is "rather inclined to give up at difficulties" and is "less perceptive than Lucy." However, after they have been in Narnia for a while, "it is she who sees before Lucy how Edmund must be spared the knowledge of how Aslan gave his life for him." When Peter asks what Susan thinks of Lucy's claim here that they must attempt to help Mr. Tumnus, Susan, in spite of her fear, immediately asserts that they "must try to do something" (60). Here, as Evan Gibson suggests, Susan's "sense of duty is stronger than her timidity" (1980, 136).

The children (at least three of them) decide that they will go on rather than going back to the wardrobe. The problem of where to go on to is solved when a robin appears and seems to be wanting them to follow him. Later Mr. Beaver will mention that a bird gave him firsthand information about Mr. Tumnus's arrest, a reference to a bird which, unlike the robin here, can talk. Lucy notes that the robin "almost looks as if it wanted to say something to us" (60). Though unable to speak, it does seem to be able to understand.

Paul Ford has suggested that the robin who appears here can be viewed as "the first bird of spring" (1994, 82), a small but perceptible evidence that the Witch's power has begun to crack. Twelve years before writing *TLWW* Lewis had published a poem titled "What the Bird Said Early in the Year." It was based upon an experience he had while walking along Addison's Walk, which runs next to Magdalen College. There Lewis "heard a bird's song promising that this particular summer would not fade, that autumn would never come" (King 1998, 112). In the poem, the bird finishes his prophecy with the words, "This year, this year, as all these flower foretell, / We shall escape the circle and undo the spell" (Lewis 1964, 71). Ten years later when writing *TLWW*, Lewis would again use a bird and blossoming flowers to proclaim escape and the undoing of a spell.

In Narnia there will be two types of animals: talking animals and dumb beasts. Animals which can speak will be larger and somewhat more upright than their nonspeaking counterparts. They are not typically worked or ridden as if they were regular animals and are never eaten for food. Except for the robin in this chapter and the nontalking mice which gnaw through the ropes in chapter fifteen, nonspeaking animals in Narnia will have the same mental abilities and the same status as they do in England. For example, in the next chapter Mr. Beaver will catch fresh trout, apparently nontalking, which will then be fried for dinner. In later Narnia books, Lewis will not use hybrids like the robin. The animals who cannot speak will not be able to understand human speech either.

In an essay where Lewis considers the reason that readers young and old like fairy tales, he makes reference to the theories of Tolkien and then adds a theory of his own. Tolkien, Lewis points out, argued that "the appeal of the fairy story lies in the fact that man there most fully exercises his function as a 'subcreator,'" making not just a "comment upon life" but also "a subordinate world of his own" (1982e, 35–6). Lewis goes on to explain that in Tolkien's view, this act of subcreation "is one of man's proper functions" and because of this, "delight naturally arises whenever it is successfully performed."

Lewis then continues, "I would venture to add to this my own theory" about one feature of the fairy tale, "the presence of beings other than human which yet behave, in varying degrees, humanly" (1982e, 36). Lewis argues that these nonhuman humans function as "an admirable hieroglyphic" which can in some ways convey human nature more powerfully than human forms could. Certainly Lewis's nonhuman characters—figures such as Mr. Tumnus and Mr. Beaver in *TLWW* as well as characters from the later books, such as Reepicheep and Bree—are in fact more human than animal and as such provide great insight into human temperament and character.

Lucy, as the most intuitive of the children, is the first to discern that the robin wants them to follow. Susan also shares this intuition, "an idea" it wants to take them somewhere (61), and so the four children trail the bird from tree to tree with, it should be noted, the two girls leading.

We might ask how Lewis is able to bring readers to suspend their disbelief and accept that a robin which seems to understand English is leading four children through an imaginary land. Here as in other places, Lewis again makes use of concrete images, descriptions firmly rooted in the ordinary senses. Lewis tells the readers that the robin "kept going from tree to tree, always a few yards ahead of them, but always so near that they could easily follow. In this way it led them on, slightly downhill" (61). Lewis takes the time to add even more concrete details, noting: "Wherever the Robin alighted a little shower of snow would fall off the branch. Presently the clouds parted overhead and the winter sun came out and the snow all around them grew dazzlingly bright."

As the boys lag behind a bit, Edmund, who has been untrustworthy himself, raises the question of whether they should be trusting the robin, and here he matches an observation Tolkien has Gandalf make about Saruman: that "the treacherous are ever distrustful" (Tolkien 1994d, 568). Edmund begins by declaring to Peter, "If you're not still too high and mighty to talk to me, I've something to say which you'd better listen to" (61). Readers may recall that the last words Peter said to his brother were, "Shut up—you!" (59). Later when Aslan arrives, Peter will confess about Edmund's betrayal, "That was partly my fault, I was angry with him and I think that helped him to go wrong" (128), an admission with which Aslan will neither agree nor disagree.

In answer to Edmund's questioning of their guide, Peter replies, "Still—a robin, you know. They're good birds in all the stories I've ever read" (61). Peter's response implicitly casts the four children as characters in their own story. Earlier when Lucy had suggested, "We can pretend we are Artic explorers," Peter reminded her, "This is going to be exciting enough without pretending" (56). As Colin Manlove points out, "One of the recurrent motifs of the story is the relation of fiction to reality" (1987, 127). Having once questioned whether Lucy's world of Narnia was real or imaginary, the children have been swept up into the kind of story that previously they had encountered only in books. In fact, Peter, Susan, Edmund, and Lucy are characters in an additional story—not just the story of *TLWW* but the internal story or prophecy about how the four thrones at Cair Paravel will someday be filled.

When Edmund raises the question of whether they should follow the robin, his action may remind readers of yet another Tolkien parallel: the scene in *The Fellowship of the Ring* when Sam has doubts about whether they should trust Strider to lead them. Sam states, "He knows something, that's plain, and more than I like; but it's no reason why we should let him go leading us out into some dark place far from help" (Tolkien 1994a, 162–3). Both Narnia and Middle-earth are places where things are not always as they seem. Edmund may already have a suspicion, though he will not admit it, that he has been misled by the White Witch, and this may lead him to mistrust further creatures they encounter. In the end, both the robin and Strider are trusted as leaders, and both prove reliable.

Lewis ends chapter six with Edmund's observation that they have now gone so far that they have lost the way back to the wardrobe. Edmund has the final words, noting that there is "no chance of dinner either" (62), perhaps an indication that memories of Turkish Delight are still playing on his mind.

SEVEN

A Day with the Beavers

As chapter seven opens, the readers are still with Peter and Edmund, who have been lagging behind discussing the trustworthiness of the robin who is guiding them. Suddenly the girls cry ahead of them, "Oh!" (63), and Lewis uses this to move our attention along with the boys' focus to Lucy and Susan. We learn that the robin has flown away, and Edmund gives Peter a look which says, "What did I tell you?" (63), his attempt to point out he was right and Peter was wrong. Among the trees something is moving, something "that doesn't want to be seen" (64).

Always a safety-first person, Susan responds to the unknown by saying, "Let's go home" (64), another temporary refusal of the call which causes everyone to realize they do not know which way home is. Joseph Campbell sees the hero's adventure as "a passage beyond the veil of the known into the unknown" (1968, 82) and describes how in all of the world's hero myths, at some time early in the adventure comes a point of no return where a threshold is crossed, a moment in the story after which there is no turning back. *TLWW* takes its place alongside the great myths by sharing this pattern and others which Campbell has observed. This moment just after the robin leaves, when in response to Susan's suggestion everyone realizes they cannot go home because they are "lost," becomes the children's crossing of the threshold.

For more than a page, Lewis keeps his readers in the same suspense as the children about what awaits them, and here once more we find the aspect of gradualness injected again into the novel, Lewis's technique of unveiling mysteries slowly in a way that rivets the attention of his readers on what is to come. The children see "a whiskered furry face" that looks out at them from behind a tree, but still they cannot recognize what it is (64). The creature puts its paw to its mouth in an intriguing signal to remain quiet. Finally out steps "the stranger" and motions for the children to make no noise and to come closer. Peter recognizes it as a beaver and then once again turns to Lucy for her opinion. Lucy shares her feeling that it is a "nice" beaver (65), a belief which is met with Edmund's characteristic skepticism. Susan, without reversing her earlier inclination toward safety, sees no alternative and so urges, "Shan't we have to risk it?" Part of her motivation, she admits, is that she is getting hungry.

Lewis has used a gradual introduction to the first of the important good animals in the story. He will use a parallel technique in chapter twelve when the children (minus Edmund) have their first encounter with a bad animal. His descriptive method there will function in the same way to arouse our curiosity and build suspense. First Peter will see Susan fleeing something that is described only as a "huge gray beast" (131). Next it will be portrayed as something that Peter thinks is a bear. Then he will observe that it looks "like an Alsatian" but is "too big to be a dog." After these other steps comes the final realization that it is a wolf.

Lewis, in an essay titled "On Stories," briefly discusses the specific choices surrounding the type of animals who appear in *The Wind in the Willows*. He asks, "Does anyone believe that Kenneth Graham made an arbitrary choice when he gave his principal character the form of a toad, or that a stag, a pigeon, a lion, would have done as well?" (1982d, 13). From this remark we might conclude that similar intention stood behind Lewis's own choices of the animals for Narnia—from beavers to robins to lions. As Walter Hooper notes, Lewis "had an uncanny eye" for the specific traits of animals and was aware of "those physical similarities that men and beasts have in common" (1980, 26). Perhaps a beaver's qualities of ordinariness or industriousness were the reasons for this choice. Readers are never told what kind of fur the coats from the wardrobe are made from, but based on the Professor's somewhat upper-middle-class status, perhaps they are beaver rather than a more expensive fur such as mink or ermine. If so, when the children don the coats, they could be said to become beaverlike on the outside themselves and in this way akin to the first talking animal they meet in Narnia.

At this point in the story, we discover one of the most significant aspects of Narnia—that some of its animals can talk. Earlier when Lucy met Mr. Tumnus, the fact that he could talk was perhaps not a surprise since he is half-human. Given that the beaver has been making signs that he wants the children to stay quiet, readers are somewhat prepared for the fact that he too can speak. His first words—the first words spoken to the children by a talking beast in Narnia—are, "Further in, come further in" (65). Very similar words will be prominent at the end of *The Last Battle*, where the penultimate chapter will be titled "Further Up and Further In" (Lewis 1994b, 185). In both cases the words contain themes of welcome, discovery, and growth.

Doris Myers, one of the more thoroughly literary critics of the Narnian Chronicles, has commented on the importance of the animals' ability to talk. She points out that inside the wardrobe, "the children find the heart's desire, the ability to communicate with Nature" (1994, 129). Lewis first explored the world of talking animals in Boxen, the imaginary world he created as a youth. Later, in *Out of the Silent Planet*, Lewis returned again to the realm of talking nonhumans when Ransom, the protagonist, is taken to Mars, where he struggles with his fears after encountering a seallike biped called a *hross*. In Lewis's description of the meeting, we can find the deep but unspoken feeling behind his creation of Narnian talking beasts, the feeling that talking animals belong to an unfallen paradise and our earliest dreams. Lewis writes:

> [Ransom's fears] arose when the rationality of the *hross* tempted you to think of it as a man. Then it became abominable—a man seven feet high, with a snaky body, covered, face and all, with thick black animal hair, and whiskered like a cat. But starting from the other end you had an animal with everything an animal ought to have—glossy coat, liquid eye, sweet breath and whitest teeth—and added to all these, as though Paradise had never been lost and earliest dreams were true, the charm of speech and reason. (1996f, 59)

Tolkien, in his essay "On Fairy-Stories," made a similar point. "Beasts and birds and other creatures often talk like men in real fairy-stories," he noted, and then suggested that "this marvel" stems "from one of the primal 'desires' that lie near the heart of Faerie: the desire of men to hold communion with other living things" (1966, 43). Readers are not merely surprised but delighted to find that the children can "hold communion" with the other living things in Narnia.

As the Beaver leads the four children to a location deeper in the woods, Lewis again employs his technique of combining fanciful elements—a talking animal guide to an imaginary land—with vivid, tangible descriptions of ordinary objects found in our world. The children are taken to "a dark spot where four trees grew so close together that their boughs met and the brown earth and pine needles could be seen underfoot because no snow had been able to fall there" (65–6).

The first thing the Beaver wants to know is if Peter, Susan, Edmund, and Lucy are "the" Sons of Adam and Daughters of Eve (66), and his use of the definite article can be interpreted in two ways. Are they the particular Sons of Adam and Daughters of Eve which Mr. Tumnus has told him about? Or, alternatively, are they the Sons of Adam and Daughters of Eve mentioned in the prophecy?

As they begin to talk, the Beaver warns them to speak softer for fear that the trees might hear them, for as he explains, while most of the trees are on their side, some are not—a point first made by Mr. Tumnus (21). The trees in Middle-earth share a similar mixed allegiance—the Old Willow which the hobbits encounter is malevolent while the trees in Fangorn generally are not.

Next Edmund asks rather bluntly, "How do we know you're a friend?" (67). In fact Edmund is so blunt that Peter has to explain and partly apologize for his younger brother's distrust which borders on a lack of good manners. The Beaver produces the handkerchief which Lucy had allowed Mr. Tumnus to keep, which he refers to as his "token." In much the same way, in *The Fellowship of the Ring* Strider produces his broken sword, the "blade which was broken" (Tolkien 1994a, 167–8), as his sign to convince Sam to trust him to lead them. Edmund's request for assurance is not met with negativity by the Beaver, but rather with "Quite right, quite right." Why do both Lewis and Tolkien include the need for a physical token of allegiance? In Narnia and Middle-earth, it is taken for granted that appearances may be deceptive and so proof might be needed. Tolkien makes this point explicit as Strider admits that his looks are against him, that even though he may "feel fair" he looks "foul." By contrast, the White Witch may be said to look fair—her face is described as "beautiful" (31)—but feel foul. The need to be on guard against deception will be a primary focus again in *The Silver Chair* and *The Last Battle*.

Joseph Campbell has observed that the heroes of the world's great myths are, more often than not, quite extraordinary people; yet even these uncommon figures need and receive help with their adventure. Campbell finds this element, which he labels supernatural aid, common to hero stories of every culture. The hero encounters a special figure, object, or power that provides assistance, guidance, encouragement, or sometimes simply a push to help him or her along the proper path. Campbell writes, "Having responded to his own call, and continuing to follow courageously as the consequences unfold, the hero finds all the forces of the unconscious at his side" (1968, 72). Aslan, who appears later, will of course represent the most recognizable and most powerful form of supernatural aid, appearing in all the Chronicles and uniting them, but Aslan's representatives also play a major role throughout the stories, providing the heroes with exactly what they need at the precise moment they need it. In *TLWW* the children are provided with a number of these secondary vehicles of supernatural aid at just the right time, among them the robin, the Beavers, and Father Christmas.

The Beaver tells the children that Mr. Tumnus had heard that he was likely to be arrested and so had taken precautions, arranging for the beaver to contact the children if they returned to Narnia and to take them to someone called Aslan, who is said to be "on the move" (67). At the mention of Aslan, the children each experience a strong, inexplicable feeling which the narrator can only describe in terms of a dream. In this dream "someone says something you don't understand" (68), something which nonetheless is felt to have "enormous meaning" which either turns the dream into a nightmare or into a dream "so beautiful that you remember it all your life." While Edmund feels "a sensation of mysterious horror," the other three have positive feelings typical of the second kind of response.

Lewis in using a dream as a comparison was drawing from his own experience. By his own report, at this point in the story Lewis himself did not know exactly where it was going to go. Having started out with only the picture of the character who would become Mr. Tumnus, he got this far in his novel when "suddenly Aslan came bounding into it" (1982a, 53). Lewis explained, "I think I had been having a good many dreams of lions about that time. Apart from that, I don't know where the Lion came from or why He came. But once He was there He pulled the whole story together, and soon He pulled the six other Narnian stories in after Him."

In a letter to a young reader, Lewis would later explain, "I found the name in the notes to Lane's *Arabian Nights*: it is Turkish for Lion. I pronounce it Ass-lan myself" (1995, 29). In America, the name is typically pronounced with a z sound. When Lewis claimed, "I don't know where the Lion came from or why He came," he may not have been thinking about the influence years earlier of reading *The Place of the Lion* by Charles Williams, an author who became one of his best friends and a member of the Inklings. Williams published the supernatural thriller in 1931, and in a letter written February 26, 1936, Lewis told his friend Arthur Greeves, "I have just read what I think a really great book" (1979, 479). Colin Duriez has suggested another possible source for Aslan, noting, "As a child Lewis attended St. Mark's (Anglican) Church in Dundela, on the outskirts of Belfast. The traditional symbol of St. Mark is the lion, a fact reinforced by the name of the church's magazine, *The Lion*" (2000, 23).

This scene, where the mention of Aslan's name causes the children to experience feelings they cannot explain, also had a parallel in Lewis's childhood. In his autobiography Lewis remembers reading Longfellow's *Saga of King Olaf* and coming across the line "I heard a voice that cried, Balder the beautiful is dead, is dead." Lewis describes his feelings after reading this passage: "I knew nothing about Balder; but instantly I was uplifted into huge regions of northern sky" (1955, 17). Similarly, in *TLWW* we read, "None of the children knew who Aslan was any more than you do; but the moment the Beaver had spoken these words everyone felt quite different" (67).

If readers follow the renumbered order for the Chronicles, where *TLWW* is the second book and *The Magician's Nephew* first, the statement about not knowing about Aslan would not hold true. As noted, Peter Schakel builds on this to suggest that *TLWW* should be the book read first, for doing so allows the readers "to share imaginatively" in the children's experiences (2002, 45).

In the Beaver's first words about Aslan, the children learn that he "is on the move" and "perhaps has already landed" (67). Paul Ford notes the "battle-imagery" used here (1994, 19). Given the clash between the two forces which is to come, the choice of military phrases will be appropriate. Exactly how Aslan travels to Narnia will never be explained. Here the use of "landed" suggests that Aslan has either sailed across the ocean, or perhaps, given the way he will later be described as "flying rather than jumping" over the Witch's castle wall (166), Aslan has flown in by some means.

Lucy has not forgotten about the need to do something to help Mr. Tumnus and immediately asks about him. The Beaver warns the children that they are not in a safe place for discussion but promises to bring them to a place where they can have "a real talk and also dinner" (68), and no one objects—particularly to the second part. About an hour later the group is looking down on a valley with a dam across the frozen river. Susan, who is the quickest to remember her etiquette, compliments their guide on his handiwork (69). The particular word she uses to describe his dam, "lovely," is fitting perhaps with her somewhat pretentious aspirations, although British readers would find its use less distinctive than Americans might. The dam, readers are told, is not quite finished, a situation which will help to set up Father Christmas's present to the Beaver in chapter ten (108).

When Peter referred to the beaver earlier, he called him "Mr. Beaver" (67), and now Lewis as narrator will switch to using this somewhat friendlier term and will also switch pronouns, from *it* to *he* (69). By choosing to call the beaver "Mr. Beaver" here and his wife "Mrs. Beaver" a few pages later, Lewis may have unintentionally written himself into what later could be viewed as a problem. These names sound as though these two are the only beavers in Narnia, for what would a third beaver be called, even in a later book? Perhaps it was this difficulty of naming future beavers that led Lewis to the decision to have no other beavers in any of the Chronicles. In *Prince Caspian* Lewis has Nikabrik suggest that the Witch is to blame for their absence, saying, "She stamped out the Beavers, I dare say; at least there are none of them in Narnia now" (1994e, 169). Later in *TLWW* Mr. Beaver will lead the children to "an old hiding-place for beavers in bad times" (104), presumably the bad times of extinction during the reign of the Witch.

Whether or not his use of the names Mr. and Mrs. Beaver had anything to do with the fact that Lewis chose not to have any further beavers in Narnia, two facts remain. Lewis will not name any other creatures in this way—for example, Reepicheep will not be Mr. Mouse, Bree will not be called Mr. Horse—and he will not have any other animal species wiped out by the Witch.

The water below the dam has been frozen in an abnormal way. Instead of being smooth, it is "all frozen into the foamy and wavy shapes in which the water had been rushing at the very moment when the frost came" (69–70), evidence that the Queen's winter was imposed upon Narnia with unnatural swiftness, mirroring the way that she can instantly change living animals into frozen statues.

Over the course of the seven Chronicles of Narnia, Lewis will set out to show the lifespan of a world, from its birth in *The Magician's Nephew* to its death in *The Last Battle*. One of the elements which will make this transition seem real will be the rise and fall of specific, local places, changes which are meant to be indicative of a larger evolution. In *The Horse and His Boy*, a story set during the later years of *TLWW* after the four children have been crowned and are reigning as kings and queens, we find evidence that the area around the Beavers' house has already become a landmark, as Bree and Hwin reminisce about "the grasslands up above Beaversdam" (Lewis 1994a, 34). Much later, in *The Voyage of the* Dawn Treader, the location has become the city of Beaversdam with a thriving marketplace (Lewis 1994g, 123).

At this point in the story, while the other children are noticing the dam and the Beavers' house out on the frozen water, Edmund notices "something else" (70), two small hills "only a mile off or less" which mark the location of the Queen's palace. The sight gets him thinking again about the two rewards which the Witch has tempted him with, "about Turkish Delight and about being a King." As soon as he thinks of the Witch's promise to make him a king, Edmund immediately wonders "how Peter will like that." Edmund, in fact, takes little pleasure in the mere thought of being a king. What he wants is to be a king over his siblings and over Peter in particular. Later Edmund will be described as not wanting his siblings to be put "on the same level as himself" (89).

Smoke is going up from a hole in the house, indicating someone is cooking, and Mr. Beaver tells the children, "It looks as if Mrs. Beaver is expecting us" (70). Presumably the news that the children had arrived in Narnia was somehow first relayed to Mr. Beaver, who then made the trip to meet them near Mr. Tumnus's cave.

At some point the robin would also have been contacted. Mrs. Beaver may have then gotten news that the group was *en route*, or she simply may have made preparations in hopeful anticipation of their safe arrival. When the children enter, Mrs. Beaver is busy sewing, an activity which, like Mr. Beaver's unfinished dam, will create the opportunity for a fitting gift from Father Christmas in chapter ten (107).

"So you've come at last," Mrs. Beaver says as they enter, referring either to her waiting during their long walk, or to the prophecy that one day Sons of Adam and Daughters of Eve would come to fill the four thrones, or to both. "To think that ever I should see this day!" she exclaims (72). Paul Ford has suggested that "the Chronicles are filled with biblical allusions" (1994, 78) and that Mrs. Beaver's statement here may perhaps be an indirect echo of the words spoken in the New Testament by Simeon, who says after seeing the long-awaited infant Jesus, "Now dismiss your servant in peace . . . for my eyes have seen your salvation" (Luke 2:29–30). Besides the similar wording used by both speakers, both have been waiting with longing for the fulfillment of a prophecy, waiting for someone promised who will bring deliverance from evil.

In the very next breath, Mrs. Beaver turns to the everyday details which will be just as much a part of Narnia as the great events which unfold. She mentions that "the potatoes are on boiling and the kettle's singing" (72). Mrs. Beaver concludes by asking her husband to go out and get some fresh fish for the meal.

Paul Ford has described Mr. Beaver as "a cordial, hardworking creature, proud of his dam-building skills and lovingly content with his domestic situation" (1994, 73). In this Ford sees him as "a prototype of the sturdy working-class Englishman." Readers are told that "the Beavers had a very snug little home though it was not at all like Mr. Tumnus's cave," and that there are "no books or pictures" (73), further emphasizing its practical feel.

Next, in one of his longer sentences, Lewis makes a wonderful collage in celebration of the commonplace items around the house. We read: "And there were hams and strings of onions hanging from the roof, and against the walls were gum boots and oilskins and hatchets and pairs of shears and spades and trowels and things for carrying mortar in and fishing-rods and fishing-nets and sacks" (73). Besides Tolkien, one of the writers who had the greatest influence on Lewis was G. K. Chesterton. Lewis mentions this impact in a number of places, including his autobiography, *Surprised by Joy*, where he records how Chesterton made an "immediate conquest" of him (1955, 190). Lewis's description of the Beavers' house here echoes two passages from Chesterton's essay "The Ethics of Elfland" found in *Orthodoxy*. Chesterton mentions the novel *Robinson Crusoe*, maintaining that "the best thing in the book" is simply the list of everyday items saved from the wreck (1994, 65). Certainly Lewis's own list of ordinary things in the Beavers' house here is equally delightful and as enjoyable.

In the same essay Chesterton also claims, "Ordinary things are more valuable than extraordinary things; nay, they are more extraordinary" (1994, 46), a claim which Lewis reinforces in his description here and at numerous other times throughout the Chronicles. Lewis's love of the commonplace began during his youth and was stimulated by his friend Arthur Greeves. In his autobiography Lewis writes about the appreciation for the "homely" which Greeves helped to instill, including a newfound appreciation for drills, the furrows or rows where seeds are planted:

> But for him I should never have known the beauty of the ordinary vegetables that we destine to the pot. "Drills," he used to say. "Just ordinary drills of cabbages—what can be better?" And he was right. Often he recalled my eyes from the horizon just to look through a hole in a hedge, to see nothing more than a farmyard in its mid-morning solitude, and perhaps a gray cat squeezing its way under a barn door, or a bent old woman with a wrinkled, motherly face coming back with an empty bucket from the pigsty. But best of all we liked it when the Homely and the unhomely met in sharp juxtaposition; if a little kitchen garden ran steeply up a narrowing enclave of fertile ground surrounded by outcroppings and furze, or some shivering quarry pool under a moonrise could be seen on our left, and on our right the smoking chimney and lamp-lit window of a cottage that was just settling down for the night. (Lewis 1955, 157–8)

Perhaps one of the most striking and memorable qualities of the Narnia books is that in them Lewis was able to create the "juxtaposition" he loved so well—the homely next to the marvelous, the lowly alongside the exalted.

We are told that Peter goes out with Mr. Beaver in pursuit of the fish, and together they are able to quickly get a "fine catch" of "beautiful trout" (73). Meanwhile the girls help Mrs. Beaver with domestic chores inside. They put more water in the tea kettle, cut bread, put plates in the oven to heat, draw beer from a barrel in the corner, drain the potatoes, and get the frying pan ready. Significantly, perhaps, is that what Edmund does during this time is not mentioned. Of the four children, he is the only one not described as helping with the commonplace preparations of the wholesome meal they will share, further isolating him and indicative of his psychological condition. In addition, filled as he is with thought of being king over his siblings, Edmund may find these ordinary chores to be beneath him.

George Sayer has written that "the most precious moments to Jack" were those times when he "was aware of the spiritual quality of material things, of the infusion of the supernatural into the workaday world" (1994, 317). Lewis may have had additional reason for describing the extensive particulars of the Beavers' home here and earlier at the home of Mr. Tumnus. Lewis will typically encircle the good characters in Narnia by an abundance of detail, an element which helps to give them robust, distinct identities as the profusion in their homes reflects their characters. By contrast, the evil Witch and her followers will be characterized by emptiness, as Colin Manlove points out:

> It is not without significance that the "good" are continually surrounded by a variety of objects—the very detailed description of the interior of Mr. Beaver's house with all its furniture and tackle hanging up and even the tea things is an emblem of this—while the Witch in her spiny castle seems to have nothing about her in her empty rooms, apart from the white statues of the creatures she has frozen by magic. (1987, 133)

good friend, apparently "stumped" Lewis when she "catechized him on how the Beavers could have put on such a splendid lunch for the children in view of the long winter which made it impossible to grow the things they served" (2002, 60).

Walter Hooper has recorded the exchange between Pitter and Lewis (1996, 722) and directs readers to an essay where Lewis points out that "the logic of a fairy-tale is as strict as that of a realistic novel, though different" (Lewis 1982d, 13). In that essay, Lewis describes a similar situation involving the source of the food in Kenneth Grahame's fairy tale *The Wind in the Willows*. Lewis notes:

> Meals turn up; one does not even ask who cooked them. In Mr. Badger's kitchen 'plates on the dresser grinned at pots on the shelf.' Who kept them clean? Where were they bought? How were they delivered in the Wild Wood? Mole is very snug in his subterranean home, but what was he living *on*? If he is a *rentier* where is the bank, what are his investments? The tables in his forecourt were 'marked with rings that hinted at beer mugs.' But where did he get the beer? (1982d, 13)

The logic of the fairy tale calls for readers to suspend their disbelief on other similar occasions. For example, in readers' first encounter with Mr. Tumnus, he was described as carrying several brown-paper parcels "as if he had been doing his Christmas shopping" (10), yet we never see any of the nearby shops he would have been coming from. When Edmund is rescued in chapter thirteen (137), he will be offered a restorative drink of wine, but we are never told about any vineyards.

Finally it might be pointed out that most readers will willingly accept the fact that since the Beavers show a mixture of human and animal qualities, their house does also. Like beavers in our world, they have built a dam on a small river and a house on top of it, but rather than entering underwater, Mr. Beaver leads the children through a human-style door (71), one which opens onto something like a normal English cottage.

Due more to Pauline Baynes's drawings rather than Lewis's explicit descriptions, readers have been led to believe that the Beavers walk upright and are slightly larger than their English counterparts. In *The Magician's Nephew*, we find this description of the talking beasts: "Gradually a change came over them. The smaller ones—the rabbits, moles, and such-like—grew a good deal larger. The big ones—you noticed it most with the elephants—grew a little smaller. Many animals sat up on their hind legs" (Lewis 1994d, 125). In Baynes's first illustration of the Beavers' house already noted (71), we see a tiny shedlike hut with a door so small that even Mr. Beaver must practically walk on all fours to squeeze in. In Baynes's second illustration, now showing the interior (75), the house seems to be bigger on the inside than the outside. Whether intentional or not, the motif of a thing being bigger on the inside than on the outside will be one of Lewis's reoccurring elements—whether the Beavers' hut and the wardrobe in *TLWW* or the stable and the new Narnia found in *The Last Battle*.

After their meal, Mr. Beaver suggests that they get "to business" (75–6), and Lewis ends the chapter with Mr. Beaver's remarks that it has begun snowing again. As has been mentioned, this snow, like the rain at the start of the story which drove the children to play indoors and Lucy to enter the wardrobe, will again be weather that can be viewed as providential. It will hide the tracks the Beavers and the children will soon make as they flee.

EIGHT

What Happened after Dinner

Chapter eight opens, as its title suggests, after everyone has finished with the delicious meal at the Beavers' house. The needs of hospitality having been met, now Mr. Beaver gets down to the business of telling what has happened to Mr. Tumnus, information which has been relayed to him by "a bird who saw it done" (77), presumably some kind of a talking bird and not the robin. The first talking birds readers actually meet in *TLWW* appear in chapter twelve, where a pelican and an eagle will be named in the list of creatures surrounding Aslan (126).

The children learn that Mr. Tumnus has been taken to the Witch's house (for some reason Lewis capitalizes *house* here as well as other common nouns from time to time), where in all probability he was turned into a statue as he had earlier predicted (20). In describing Mr. Tumnus's arrest, Mr. Beaver mentions that "he was taken off by the police" (77). Except for this remark and Mr. Tumnus's brief mention earlier that he had "taken service under" the White Witch and was in her pay, we do not see the full network of spies and "police" which the Witch has instituted to enforce her control over Narnia. Readers may remember that Maugrim's title in the signature on the paper at Mr. Tumnus's cave was "Captain of the Secret Police" (58).

Lewis provided a much fuller description of the workings of a secret police force in *That Hideous Strength* (published in 1945), a force ironically called the N.I.C.E. which has its own malevolent captain, Fairy Hardcastle. Lord Feverstone, one of the leaders of the N.I.C.E., explains the rationale behind the coercion exerted by the N.I.C.E. by stating, "Man has got to take charge of Man. That means, remember, that some men have got to take charge of the rest" (Lewis 2003, 40). In Narnia, the White Witch also intends "to take charge" of the rest of the creatures and so has set up a secret police force to help her accomplish this goal.

Rather than being full of courtiers and nobles as the Witch earlier seemed to promise Edmund (39), Mr. Beaver announces that her house is "all full of statues . . . in the courtyard and up the stairs and in the hall" (77–8) and, as noted earlier, a stark contrast to the other two houses readers have seen which are filled with objects of meaning and delight. The Witch's unique form of punishment is more appropriate to her nature than either torture or execution: all those who oppose her continue to exist but are no longer able to contest her will. They have been sapped of life, like the wintry land of Narnia itself, and stand eternally frozen in stone as monuments to her ability to dominate. This desire to dominate is a defining characteristic of the Witch. When Digory and Polly first meet Jadis in *The Magician's Nephew*, her castle is also filled with statues that she has frozen solid, "hundreds of people, all seated, and all perfectly still . . . like the most wonderful waxworks you ever saw" (50).

Lucy, of course, immediately insists that they *must* do something to rescue Mr. Tumnus. When she declares, "It's all on my account" (78), Lucy is only partially correct, for it is partially on Edmund's account as well. In fact, if he had not told the Witch that Lucy had met Mr. Tumnus (37), their encounter likely would have remained undetected. Mrs. Beaver responds by declaring that she has no questions about Lucy's bravery, a quality that Lewis will give prominence to by having Father Christmas later revisit (109).

Although Lewis frequently describes Edmund's thoughts and feelings in other places, often in depth, from the moment we arrive at the Beavers' he is not mentioned in any way, an approach which is necessary in order for him to exit unnoticed. One of the scenes which it could be argued is missing from the last part of *TLWW* is Edmund's apology to Mr. Tumnus for his role in the arrest. Some measure of resolution can be seen later in *The Horse and His Boy* when Lewis will have Edmund, at that point a reigning king, briefly but harmoniously sharing leadership responsibilities with Mr. Tumnus (1994a, 71–3).

Peter wonders if they might come up with "some stratagem" where they, again like characters in a story, would get into the Witch's house in disguise, pretending to be "peddlers or anything" (78). Peter, with his characteristic deep sense of responsibility, declares, "There must be *some* way. This Faun saved my sister at his own risk, Mr. Beaver. We can't just leave him to be—to be—to have that done to him."

Given what will happen later in the story, Mr. Beaver's response is somewhat problematic, for he tells Peter, "It's no good *your* trying, of all people" (78). Later Aslan will make it clear that the children *are* meant to try, to do whatever they can to defeat the Witch and her forces (130), although ultimately it will be Aslan who does away with her. Perhaps Mr. Beaver here simply means that Peter and the others are not meant to form a plan on their own, or, more likely, that Peter's idea of sneaking into the Witch's castle would face the obvious problem that even if disguised as peddlers, the children would still clearly be humans, the only humans in Narnia and thus the very creatures that the Witch and all her forces are on the lookout for.

Another way to understand Mr. Beaver's claim, "it's no good *your* trying" is to note that he has lived under the Witch's domination and has a firsthand understanding of the awesome power she wields. He rightly knows that the children on their own are no match for her, as will be shown in the battle scene near the end of the book. Mr. Beaver has heard reports of what happens to those who have been arrested. He points out, "There's not many taken in there that ever comes out again" (77). At this point in the story, Mr. Beaver must strongly believe that Mr. Tumnus has already been made into a stone statue, a condition which, without Aslan's help, is irreversible. Given this, his comment to Peter that it is "no good *your* trying" contains the realization that Aslan alone will have the ability to return Mr. Tumnus to life.

Later in the Chronicles Lewis will give Peter another chance to put his disguise idea into practice. In *The Last Battle* Peter and Edmund, dressed not as peddlers but "like workmen" (59), will sneak into the garden of the Professor's former house in London and dig up the magic rings young Digory Kirke had buried there.

Mr. Beaver goes on to suggest that there is hope "now that Aslan is on the move" (78), and his repetition of these words again evokes a mystical response, a "strange feeling" in the children (67). Several voices at once say, "Oh, yes! Tell us about Aslan!" In his use of the term "several voices," Lewis has an economical way to leave out Edmund, who we assume does not experience a feeling anything like "the first signs of spring" or "good news" (78).

"Who is Aslan?" Susan asks (78). "Aslan?" Mr. Beaver replies, "Why, don't you know?" In fact, the children do not know who Aslan is, nor do the readers—and so Mr. Beaver's question includes them as they share the children's wonder and curiosity. As discussed a number of times previously, this aspect of sharing the same lack of knowledge as the children and learning as they do again forms the basis of the argument for reading the stories in their original order.

Aslan, Mr. Beaver explains, is "the King" and "the Lord of the whole wood" (78). Consistent with the suggestion that the unnatural winter imposed by the Witch has lasted a hundred years (Lewis 1994b, 49), Aslan has been away from Narnia for a long time, not appearing in the memory of Mr. Beaver or his father. Now, however, Mr. Beaver has received word that Aslan "is in Narnia at this moment," and Mr. Beaver states that Aslan, not the children, will save Mr. Tumnus. In spite of Mr. Beaver's statement, as noted, the children will find that they must do their part in the battle against evil, and their contributions will play a cooperative role in the defeat of the Witch.

Edmund slips in a question at this point which while seeming innocent to his siblings carries more weight in the minds of readers. When Edmund asks Mr. Beaver, "She won't turn him into stone too?" (79), we may wonder if this is something he is hoping will be possible. Evidence of this can be seen when he quickly assumes that the stone lion at the castle must be Aslan (94). At the end of the chapter, Peter will grasp the significance of Edmund's question here, noting it was "just the sort of thing he would say" (86).

Mr. Beaver, quoting an old rhyme, claims that besides saving Mr. Tumnus, Aslan will "put all to rights" (79). A number of prophecies appear in *TLWW*. In addition to the one about the four thrones, Mr. Beaver now recites prophecies which claim that when Aslan appears wrong will be right, sorrows will end, winter will die, and spring will return. Tolkien used a similar fulfilled-prophecy story within a story in *The Hobbit*. On the final page of the book, Bilbo exclaims, "Then the prophecies of the old songs have turned out to be true, after a fashion!" (Tolkien 1994b, 255). Gandalf answers, "Of course! And why should not they prove true? Surely you don't disbelieve the prophecies, because you had a hand in bringing them about yourself?"

In his essay "On Stories" Lewis describes a class of stories which "turns on fulfilled prophecies" and mentions *The Hobbit* as one of them (1982d, 14). According to Lewis, such stories produce "a feeling of awe, coupled with a certain sort of bewilderment such as one often feels in looking at a complex pattern of lines that pass over and under one another. One sees, yet does not quite see, the regularity" (15). Prophecies, Lewis further explains, allow destiny and free will to be combined in such a way that free will can be "the *modus operandi* of destiny," as it is in *TLWW*.

When Lucy asks if Aslan is a man, Mr. Beaver reveals that Aslan is a lion, not a man, and is the "son of the great Emperor-Beyond-the-Sea" (79). As Paul Ford points out, "In almost every instance where an explanation of Aslan is given, the formula 'the great Lion, the son of the great Emperor-Beyond-the-Sea,' is used," but except for this vague location, "there is no mention in the Chronicles of where the Emperor might live" (167). The White Witch's appropriation of the title of "Empress" establishes her as a rival and enemy not only to Aslan but also to his father the Emperor (58, 140). In actual power, she is not even an approximate match for Aslan or the Emperor-Beyond-the-Sea and, as Peter Schakel has proposed, is perhaps better paired as an evil counterpart to Father Christmas (1979, 10).

Lewis will interchange the terms "Emperor-over-Sea" and "Emperor-Beyond-the-Sea" (1994e, 97; 1994b, 150). While later in *TLWW* there is a brief mention of the Emperor's scepter and the Emperor's magic (141, 142), throughout the Chronicles there will be virtually no information about the Emperor himself. Some readers may later come to see Aslan as a Christ-figure, but as Paul Ford has argued, readers find a relatively small specific presence of anything like a Trinity in the Chronicles (1994, 167). There is no mention of a Holy Spirit, and in *TLWW* Aslan himself mentions his father just once (142), and then only in response to the White Witch having raised the subject.

Susan is the first to mention her concern about the safety of meeting a lion (80), but after Mrs. Beaver tells her she is right to be nervous, even Lucy shows apprehension. Summing up the nature of the adventure, Mr. Beaver responds, "Who said anything about safe?" then adding, "Course he isn't safe. But he's good." In spite of the danger, Peter announces he is "longing" to see Aslan, and as Paul Ford has observed, longing "is one of the most important themes in Lewis's life and thought" and is the term he uses "to express the sort of experience within life that opens us up beyond appearances to the transcendent" (1994, 274–5).

Mr. Beaver tells the children that "word has been sent" that they are to meet Aslan at the Stone Table (80). Lewis never explains Mr. Beaver's use of the passive here. Perhaps this information has come from the same underground network which delivered the news that Aslan was on the move (67), perhaps from the same talking bird who brought the information about Mr. Tumnus (77). Lucy characteristically returns to the plight of Mr. Tumnus, and Mr. Beaver maintains that the quickest way for the children to help the faun is by going to meet Aslan. Mr. Beaver explains, "Once he's with us, then we can begin doing things" (80); however, he immediately adds, "Not that we don't need you too" (80), a complement to his earlier claim "no good *your* trying," and an indication that the children's presence is essential.

Mr. Beaver quotes a second prophecy, one emphasizing the children's role rather than Aslan's as the first prophecy did:

> When Adam's flesh and Adam's bone
> Sits at Cair Paravel in throne,
> The evil time will be over and done. (81)

The connection between Adam's descendants and the Witch is suggested but never made explicit in *TLWW*. If readers go on to read *The Magician's Nephew*, they will learn that it was the young Digory Kirke who was responsible for waking the Witch in Charn and inadvertently bringing her to Narnia. With Digory's help, Aslan will plant a tree which will "protect Narnia from her for many years" (1994d, 154). Aslan states, "As Adam's race has done the harm, Adam's race shall help to heal it" (148), words which may be seen as referring both to Digory's actions in bringing back the apple from which the tree would spring and to the actions of the four Pevensies much later, the "Adam's flesh and Adam's bone" in the prophecy.

Tolkien's parallel use of prophecy in *The Hobbit* has already been mentioned. A closer look at one section of *The Hobbit* reveals how close the parallel is. Tolkien's prophecies focus on the return of one king while Lewis has two interwoven threads: the coming of Aslan, king above kings, and the coming of the children who will be crowned kings and queens. The lines most similar are Tolkien's "all sorrows fail and sadness / at the Mountain-king's return" (1994b, 169) and Lewis's "At the sound of his roar, sorrows will be no more" (79).

When Mr. Beaver quotes the prophecy about Cair Paravel, readers finally get a fuller version of what Mr. Tumnus hinted at in his claim that if the Witch turned him into a statue he would remain one "until the four thrones at Cair Paravel are filled" (20). Clearly Mr. Tumnus has heard of this prophecy, although he seemed to have less faith in it than Mr. Beaver does, as he added, "and goodness knows when that will happen, or whether it will ever happen at all."

In this drawn-out process of revelation—we first hear bits of the prophecy in chapter two and revisit it in its full form here in chapter eight—we again see the gradualness of Lewis's approach. Besides the gradual revelation of prophecy, yet another gradual revelation occurs with the information about Aslan. Next Mr. Beaver says that stories tell of Aslan coming to Narnia "long ago, nobody can say when" but tells the children "there's never been any of your race here before" (81). Both of his statements warrant closer examination.

Walter Hooper has pointed out that "Lewis had no over-all outline of all seven stories in his head when he began" (1996, 419) but after they had been written and published, went back and "for his own convenience" outlined Narnian history "so far as it is known," giving specific years in Narnia and the corresponding year in England. This outline, labeled Lewis MS 51 and originally published in *Past Watchful Dragons* (Hooper 1980, 50), can now be found in several sources (Ford 1994, 454; Hooper 1996, 420; Sammons 1979, 54).

In Lewis's outline, year 1 in Narnia corresponds to 1900 in England, and at that time both the White Witch and the young Digory Kirke first entered Narnia, which was just being created. After being driven out to the North in year 1, the Witch returned to Narnia in the year 898, and in 900 her Hundred Years of Winter began. According to Lewis's outline, the events which transpire in *TLWW* take place in the Narnian year 1000, the English year 1940.

Lewis's outline sheds partial light on Mr. Beaver's statement that Aslan has been in "these parts before—long ago" (81). It is clear that Aslan was in Narnia in the year 1; the next appearance by Aslan which the outline records takes place in a different region,

Telmar, in the year 302. If we discount this appearance in Telmar, a thousand years may have passed since Aslan has been in Narnia. However, Lewis's outline was certainly not meant to be exhaustive, and Mr. Beaver's earlier words "never in my time or my father's time" (78) seem to imply a more recent visit by Aslan, perhaps three or four generations before, a visit which did not have enough historical significance to make it onto Lewis's outline or into any of the other Chronicles.

Mr. Beaver's claim that "there's never been any of your race here before" was correct when Lewis wrote it, but it is made clear in *The Magician's Nephew* that in fact five humans—King Frank and Queen Helen, Digory Kirke and his friend Polly, and Digory's Uncle Andrew—have been to Narnia. Some may argue that this is one of several inconsistencies Lewis did not reconcile in later revisions. On the other hand, one could also argue that any inconsistency here can be explained by the fact that Mr. Beaver, a character with limited knowledge, makes this statement rather than Lewis's narrator. Perhaps the knowledge that a thousand years earlier Sons of Adam and Daughters of Eve had visited Narnia has simply been lost, and thus here Mr. Beaver is speaking the truth as he knows it.

In response to Mr. Beaver's statement, Peter asks, "Isn't the Witch herself human?" (81), a question which leads to another possible area of inconsistency. As Peter Schakel and others have pointed out, "The account of the Witch in *The Magician's Nephew* . . . does not correspond with the details in *The Lion, the Witch and the Wardrobe*" (1979, 140). In *TLWW* the White Witch is described as one-half Jinn and one-half giant, and so although she would like the Narnians to believe otherwise, "there isn't a drop of real human blood" in her (81), again suggesting a counterfeit or false appearance. Mr. Beaver states that the Jinn half of her ancestry "comes from" Lilith, who, Mr. Beaver explains, was Adam's first wife. The use of the somewhat vague phrase "comes from" means that while the Witch is a descendant of Lilith, we do not know if Lilith was the Witch's mother, grandmother, or more distant ancestor. Although Lilith was the White Witch's maternal ancestor, Adam was not her paternal ancestor in any way, Mr. Beaver continues, because she "comes of the giants" on the other side. Peter Schakel's assertion that the Witch "is of human ancestry" (1979, 9), a claim which seems to be true only by marriage, seems at odds with the description found here in *TLWW*.

In his reference to Lilith here, Lewis may have been influenced by the novel *Lilith*, published in 1895 by Scottish author George Macdonald, the writer Lewis viewed as his mentor. Of course, Lewis himself would have been familiar with the stories of Lilith from Jewish folklore and so can also be seen as borrowing from the same sources as MacDonald. Paul Ford notes that Lilith is "a female demon of both Babylonian mythology and the Hebrew tradition, who murders newborn babies, harms women in childbirth, and haunts wildernesses on the lookout for children" (1994, 269). Given this background, Ford observes that "true to her heritage" the White Witch, as Lilith's descendant, spends most of *TLWW* "trying to do away with the Pevensie children."

Two further points might be made about Lewis's choice of the Witch's maternal ancestor here. Another of Lilith's defining characteristics was her refusal to submit to any authority other than herself, or her insistence on being her own authority, and this is a further way that the Witch could be said to be true to her heritage. Finally, by placing the descendants of Adam in opposition to one of the descendants of Lilith, Lewis keeps the mythological conflict between Adam and Lilith alive and in doing so gives *TLWW* a mythological status of its own.

In *The Magician's Nephew* Digory and Polly first meet the Witch when they are magically sent to Charn, the Witch's homeland. There Lewis will refer to her as the Queen, the Witch, and Jadis (1994d, 59, 74, 76). A possible inconsistency between the two novels lies in the fact that there is no direct explanation of how the Witch, an Earthly descendant of Lilith and a giant, could have left our prehistoric world and ended up in Charn. Charn is definitely intended by Lewis to be a world separate from both the Earth and Narnia, and if he did intend for his readers to make the connection between the descendant of Adam's first wife and Jadis the Queen of Charn, he has, at the least, left a gap. In *The Magician's*

Nephew Lewis will offer a hint about a connection between the two accounts, stating, "Some say there is giantish blood in the royal family of Charn" (75). But this is not to say that we need fully understand everything in the fairy tales about Narnia in order to enjoy them. For example, even though in *The Magician's Nephew* Lewis will go on to explain exactly how the lamp-post came to be in Narnia, the fact that its presence is unexplained in *TLWW* should not be considered a fault, and in fact some readers may prefer it to be a mystery.

Following her husband's assertion that the Witch has no human blood in her, Mrs. Beaver states, "That's why she's bad all through" (81). By making the Witch "bad all through," and thus (unlike Edmund) incapable of redemption, Lewis opens the door for her destruction, along with all of her other evil minions, without any qualms. Creatures who have a capacity for good—dwarfs, talking animals, and humans—will not be slain outright in the Chronicles if any possibility that they can be redeemed remains.

Lewis continues his discussion of evil creatures through Mr. Beaver's comments in the next paragraph: "When you meet anything that's going to be human and isn't yet, or used to be human once and isn't now, or ought to be human and isn't, you keep your eyes on it and feel for your hatchet" (82). Certainly these remarks about partial humanness are not meant to be applied to the good half-human creatures which will be part of Aslan's force in *TLWW*—the fauns like Mr. Tumnus, the centaurs (126, 168), or the bull with the head of a man (126). These good creatures are all characterized by having animal bodies but human heads.

The evil half-human creatures in *TLWW*, arguably the creatures referred to by Mr. Beaver here, will always have the reverse—human bodies with animal heads—and this seems to be the physical aspect which distinguishes between the good and the bad half-humans in Narnia. Pauline Baynes captures this distinction well in the contrast between Aslan's forces in chapter twelve (127) and the Witch's forces in chapter fourteen (152) and also in her illustration of the battle between the forces of good and the forces of evil in chapter sixteen, where human-headed creatures can be seen fighting those with animal heads (176–7). In *The Last Battle* Lewis will introduce a different kind of evil creature who, like the White Witch, may in some aspects look human. Shift the ape will dress in human clothing and will tell the animals he attempts to control, "I hear some of you are saying I'm an Ape. Well, I'm not. I'm a Man. If I look like an Ape, that's because I'm so very old. . . . And it's because I'm so old that I'm so wise" (1994b, 35).

Continuing with his warning about "things that look like humans and aren't" (81), Mr. Beaver comments that he has known "precious few" good dwarfs (82) and that these good dwarfs were the ones "least like men." In *Prince Caspian*, Lewis will introduce an exception to Mr. Beaver's general rule here in the form of Caspian's tutor Dr. Cornelius (1994e, 52), who will be half-human and half-dwarf.

Mr. Beaver cites a final prophecy which states that when two Sons of Adam and two Daughters of Eve sit in the four thrones at Cair Paravel, not only will the Witch's reign end but also her life (82). Once again his statement may seem to be somewhat at odds with the account found in *The Magician's Nephew*. There Aslan himself tells the children that the Witch, after stealing and eating a magic apple, will have "endless days like a goddess" (Lewis 1994d, 190). While this may be another of the inconsistencies surrounding the Witch, perhaps in *The Magician's Nephew* Lewis meant to imply that the Witch would be immortal unless killed in battle, a further aspect she would then share with Tolkien's villain Sauron. According to Lewis's outline of Narnian history, the Witch is over a thousand years old in *TLWW*. When Peter battles her later in the novel, his sword against the Witch's stone knife, nothing indicates that she is unkillable (176), and after the battle readers will specifically be told "the Witch was dead" (178).

At this point in the conversation, Edmund's absence is noticed, and everyone immediately rushes outside and calls for him in vain. Susan, always the quickest to despair, exclaims, "Oh, how I wish we'd never come" (83). For "a girl aspiring to adulthood" (Ford 1994, 398), Susan is somewhat of a contradiction—sometimes stronger and older than her years, sometimes, as in this instance, not even as sturdy as her younger sister. Peter, who has learned how to look to others for advice since he last suggested his "stratagem" of dressing like peddlers, now immediately asks Mr. Beaver what should be done. Mr. Beaver, no doubt remembering what happened to Mr. Tumnus, immediately begins putting on his boots, claiming, "We must be off at once."

Peter misinterprets Mr. Beaver's actions and suggests they should split into four search parties. Mr. Beaver replies that they already know where Edmund has gone: to the Witch's house to betray them. When Susan answers back, "Oh, surely—oh really! He can't have done that" (84), Mr. Beaver responds to her assertion with the question, "Can't he?" in a way that forces them to admit to the truth and which may remind readers of the Professor's manner of questioning earlier.

Mr. Beaver astutely asks two more questions, the first about whether Edmund had been in the country before and if he had told the others "what he'd done or who he'd met" (85). After a brief attempt at denial, the children are convinced that Edmund has truly gone to the White Witch to betray them. In spite of this, Peter insists in "a rather choking sort of voice" that they must go and look for Edmund. "He is our brother after all, even if he is rather a little beast," Peter argues, adding, "And he's only a kid." Nowhere in *TLWW* is the suggestion found that the children are too young to know the difference between right and wrong, and except for this appeal by Peter—one which may express more compassion than justification—their youth will not be proposed to excuse their wrongdoing.

Although earlier Mrs. Beaver may have appeared not to be particularly insightful, Lewis brings her to the forefront for the chapter's final pages. Mrs. Beaver is the one who answers Peter, telling him and the girls that the only chance to save Edmund lies in keeping them away from the Witch. Mrs. Beaver is able to see into the Witch's mind and discern her plans to turn the four children into stone, thus preserving her hold on power. Mrs. Beaver comforts Lucy by telling her that the Witch will not kill Edmund since he will be kept alive as bait to get the others—a prediction which turns out to be correct, at least initially. After Mr. Beaver reiterates that more than ever it is important to get the children to Aslan, Mrs. Beaver raises the only question that is crucial—the question of exactly when Edmund slipped away, which will determine how much information about their plans he will be able to relay to the Witch.

Again Mrs. Beaver is able to correctly predict the Witch's actions. When her husband suggests that the Witch is going to try to get between them and the Stone Table to cut them off from Aslan, Mrs. Beaver corrects him, saying, "But that isn't what she'll do first, *not if I know her*. The moment that Edmund tells her we're all here she'll set out to catch us this very night" (87, emphasis added). Everyone agrees with the accuracy of Mrs. Beaver's analysis. She then coolly adds, "And if he's been gone about half an hour, she'll be here in about another twenty minutes." Earlier, when Edmund first caught sight of the two hills marking the locale of the Witch's castle, he had estimated them to be "only a mile off or less" (70). This mile of separation between the Beavers' house and the Witch's castle means that the three children and the Beavers have a little time to spare but not much, heightening the suspense.

Mr. Beaver acknowledges his wife's wisdom, and Lewis ends the chapter with Mr. Beaver asserting that they must leave immediately, stating "There's not a moment to lose" (87), a claim which anyone who has listened carefully to Mrs. Beaver's clear-headed thinking knows is not exactly true. They have another twenty minutes, time which can be put to good use.

NINE

In the Witch's House

Chapter nine opens with a voice which by now is familiar to readers: the voice of Lewis's narrator, who steps in to comment, "And now of course you want to know what had happened to Edmund" (88). At this point the story splits into two parts which will not converge until chapter thirteen when the four children are reunited. In chapter fourteen, the story will divide again when Lucy and Susan separate from Peter and Edmund. This pattern of having a single-stranded narrative divide into separate threads is known as interlace, and it is a technique that Lewis used in an earlier work with great success. As Donald Glover has noted, in *That Hideous Strength* Lewis sets up the narrative structure "by paralleling the lives of his two major characters" (1981, 114). This use of two separate threads will be seen again in *Prince Caspian*, where the two sisters will separate from Peter and Edmund.

Tolkien also used interlace throughout *The Lord of the Rings* as the fellowship split into two and then three separate strands, and the question might be raised, why would an author choose to construct a plot with interlaced stories? In *TLWW* Lewis encountered the same problem Tolkien faced in *The Lord of the Rings*: the problem of developing characters fully in a large ensemble cast. In *TLWW* we find a good number of significant figures besides the four children, including Mr. Tumnus, Mr. and Mrs. Beaver, Aslan, the Witch, her dwarf, and Maugrim her wolf. How can an author provide much in the way of individual character development with such a big cast? One answer is to break the characters off into smaller groups and follow their stories separately.

In fact Lewis already made one separation early in *TLWW* when first Lucy and then Lucy and Edmund went into the wardrobe by themselves. Another separation occurred when Peter and Susan went by themselves to talk with the Professor. While not technically interlacement, since readers are not provided with the details of what happens to the other characters during this separation, these divisions allowed for the kind of individualization that a novel requires. Even when all four children are together, Lewis sometimes breaks off just two of them as he did when the children were following the robin and Peter and Edmund fell back and have a private discussion (61). Some of Lewis's most poignant character development will occur when Lucy and Susan go by themselves with Aslan to the Stone Table. Similarly, some of his keenest insights are provided here as Edmund journeys by himself to the Witch's castle.

For a look at what happens when an author has a large cast and does not use as much interlacement, readers could turn to *The Hobbit*. In that work, Tolkien has Bilbo and Gandalf accompany thirteen dwarfs, a very large ensemble cast, on a quest. Some of the dwarfs not featured in a smaller grouping are never particularly well developed, and in the end, some readers may be left wondering which one was Bifur and which was Bofur.

At this point in *TLWW*, the narrator devotes a good deal of time exploring, but never justifying, Edmund's actions. First, readers are told, Edmund was thinking "all the time" about Turkish Delight (88). Here Lewis continues to make the same distinction highlighted earlier: he is opposed to making food the highest value a person can have but not to the normal pleasure of delicious regular food. Lewis's narrator states, "There's nothing that spoils the taste of good ordinary food half so much as the memory of bad magic food" (88). Besides the "good ordinary food" already seen at the meals provided by Mr. Tumnus and the Beavers, Lewis will also include "something like a plum pudding" provided by Father Christmas for a "merry party" of animals (115).

The pleasures of ordinary food and ordinary sweets will appear at other times in the Chronicles. At the start of *The Silver Chair,* Eustace Scrubb will stumble upon Jill, who has been crying. He first tries to talk to her but unfortunately ends up sounding "rather like someone beginning a lecture" (Lewis 1994f, 4). Then readers are told, "Scrubb saw that she wasn't quite herself yet and very sensibly offered her a peppermint. He had one too. Presently Jill began to see things in a clearer light" (5). In *The Voyage of the Dawn Treader,* Coriakin the Magician will treat Lucy to a dinner of good ordinary food composed of "an omelette, piping hot, cold lamb and green peas, a strawberry ice, lemon-squash to drink with the meal and a cup of chocolate to follow" (Lewis 1994g, 163). Polly and Digory enjoy a bag of toffees in *The Magician's Nephew* (Lewis 1994d, 164), and one of the candies which is planted will produce a toffee tree (167).

Lewis had earlier explored many of the same points about the positive value of good, ordinary pleasures in *The Screwtape Letters.* There the devil Screwtape tells his young nephew:

> Never forget that when we are dealing with any pleasure in its healthy and normal and satisfying form, we are, in a sense, on the Enemy's ground. I know we have won many a soul through pleasure. All the same, it is His invention, not ours. He made the pleasures; all our research so far has not enabled us to produce one. All we can do is to encourage the humans to take the pleasures which our Enemy has produced, at times or in ways, or in degrees, which He has forbidden. Hence we always try to work away from the natural condition of any pleasure to that in which it is least natural. (1996i, 44)

Among the parallels is that concept mentioned earlier that evil cannot create; it can only mock or pervert. Screwtape challenges Wormwood with a goal that fits perfectly Edmund's condition at this point in the story, stating "An ever increasing craving for an ever diminishing pleasure is the formula" (1996i, 44).

Finally, it might be noted that Lewis will return to this idea of the good ordinary in *The Last Battle* where Jill longs for "good, ordinary times" (1994b, 100), when "just walking along" is the only kind of adventure (99). Lewis saw these good, ordinary delights as the antidote for the addictive cravings for the artificially heightened pleasure that the Turkish Delight represents. As Screwtape tells Wormwood after he has allowed his young man to enjoy the simple pleasures of a walk and reading a book, "How can you have failed to see that a *real* pleasure was the last thing you ought to have let him meet?" (1996i, 56).

Lewis next points out that Edmund "kept on thinking that the others were taking no notice of him and trying to give him the cold shoulder" (88). The narrator continues, "They weren't, but he imagined it," making it clear that Edmund's perception of mistreatment is unfounded. How do characters like Edmund who are at least in some ways basically good end up committing horrible deeds—in Edmund's case betraying his siblings? Lewis provides a detailed set of circumstances and motivations which will help readers to understand how Edmund progresses from mere rudeness to full betrayal. As has been mentioned, part of the Witch's magic is that she can "make things look like what they aren't" (138). Here perhaps part of the spell the Turkish Delight has cast over Edmund is to make his siblings' actions "look like what they aren't." This spell may be contributing to Edmund falsely perceiving that he is being slighted, a perception which he uses to justify his actions against his siblings.

Lewis clearly understood this idea of a person taking offense where none was intended when he or she makes neutral words or actions look like what they aren't. Earlier he explored this issue in *The Screwtape Letters*. There Screwtape advises Wormwood to make sure that his "patient" demand that all the things he says "be taken at their face value and judged simply on the actual words, while at the same time judging all his mother's utterances with the fullest and most over-sensitive interpretation" (1996i, 26). So too here with Edmund, Lewis again lets readers see the subtlety of self-justification and projecting fault in others to cover a person's own deficiencies.

Continuing with his pattern of building his descriptions out of specific, concrete details, Lewis next gives us a short paragraph explaining exactly when and how Edmund was able to slip away (88). Readers who have looked at Pauline Baynes's drawing of the Beavers' dinner in chapter seven (75) may wonder how could Edmund have gotten up and left with no one noticing. Lewis describes a "curtain which hung over the door" that Edmund was able to edge himself under (88), the rare occurrence of a significant detail which Baynes left out of her drawing.

Next Lewis returns once more to Edmund's motivations. While *TLWW* is a fairy story, Lewis avoids making his main characters one-dimensional, a complaint sometimes leveled against stories for young people. In a review of *The Fellowship of the Ring*, Edwin Muir complained of a lack of "human discrimination and depth" in Tolkien's characters (1954, 7). Muir asserted that Tolkien's "good characters are consistently good, his evil figures immovably evil." In his own essay, "Tolkien's *The Lord of the Rings*," Lewis responded to Muir's charge of one-dimensionality, writing of "one piece of false criticism which had better be answered: the complaint that the characters are all either black or white" (1982g, 87). Lewis went on to distinguish between a clear right and wrong and perfectly good or perfectly evil characters. He noted, "I think some readers, seeing (and disliking) this rigid demarcation of black and white, imagine they have seen a rigid demarcation between black and white people."

As if anticipating that future reviewers might complain that his characters in *TLWW* were "consistently good or immovably evil," Lewis tells us here, "You mustn't think that even now Edmund was quite so bad that he actually wanted his brother and sisters to be turned into stone" (89) and then goes on to explain that yes,

Edmund did want Turkish Delight; and yes, he did want to be a prince; and yes, Edmund did want to pay Peter back for calling him a beast. But while Edmund does not want the Witch to be "particularly nice" to his siblings and certainly does not want her "to put them on the same level as himself," he manages to convince himself that she will not do anything "very bad" to them.

At the end of his long discussion of Edmund's rationalization, Lewis concludes with an observation which has been central to his thinking about moral decisions throughout *TLWW*: while all these factors help us to understand Edmund's actions and may even give us a certain compassion for him, they do not justify his wicked behavior. What Edmund does is wrong, and he knows it is wrong. As Lewis observes, "That was the excuse he made in his own mind for what he was doing. It wasn't a very good excuse, however, for deep down inside him he really knew that the White Witch was bad and cruel" (89). In spite of the fact that there will often be complexities, extenuating circumstances, and many factors to be weighed, as Paul Ford notes, "Lewis believed there was a clear distinction between right and wrong; between morality and immorality; and between good acts and bad acts" (1994, 351). As Peter Schakel has pointed out, the very fact that Edmund attempts to excuse his actions here shows that "he is aware of a standard of conduct he is violating" (1979, 23).

In *The Magician's Nephew* when Digory asks if there was something wrong with Mrs. Lefay, Uncle Andrew will reply, "Well, it depends on what you call *wrong*" (Lewis 1994d, 19). Lewis's point here is not that right and wrong are relative—quite the opposite. His point is simply that people will frequently try to justify actions which they know to be evil.

Lewis chooses to have Edmund leave his coat behind—perhaps partly out of necessity as his departure from the Beavers' has to be rather quick and secretive, but perhaps also partly to make the descent into evil unpleasant and uncomfortable, rather than agreeable and enjoyable as may sometimes be suggested in other works. As fallen tree trunks, rocks, and steep banks cause Edmund to become "bruised all over" (91), Edmund's psychological discomfort is even worse than his physical woes, as Lewis concludes: "The silence and the loneliness were dreadful." For Lewis, one of the key by-products of evil is isolation. In *The Great Divorce*, Lewis's satirical novel about the afterlife, the inhabitants of hell continue to move further and further away from each other, making their isolation greater and greater. A passenger on the bus ride to Heaven explains the reason for the empty neighborhoods that can be seen in the gray town below:

> "They've been moving on and on. Getting further apart. They're so far off by now that they could never think of coming to the bus stop at all. Astronomical distances. There's a bit of rising ground near where I live and a chap has a telescope. You can see the lights of the inhabited houses, where those old ones live, millions of miles away. Millions of miles from us and from one another. Every now and then they move further still." (1974, 21)

At this point in *TLWW* Edmund becomes isolated by his treachery, mirroring the Witch who is largely alone in her great castle.

Edmund is, by this point, quite miserable. Lewis's narrator jumps in with an observation which adds to the believability of Edmund's character, telling readers, "In fact I really think that he might have given up the whole plan and gone back and owned up and made friends with the others, if he hadn't happened to say to himself, 'When I'm King of Narnia the first thing I shall do will be to make some decent roads'" (91). Unfortunately, this thought leads Edmund to think about all sorts of other things that he will do when he is king, including "schemes for keeping Peter in his place," and any thoughts of reconciliation with his siblings are quickly forgotten. At the end of the novel when Edmund actually does become a king in Narnia, his achievements will not include the roads, cars, private cinema, or railways he dreams about here. Nor will he enact any laws "against beavers and dams."

Lewis turns next to a somewhat lengthy description of the weather. The snow stops, a wind springs up, and the moon comes out, a full moon which makes everything "almost as bright as day" (91). Lewis makes a point of telling us that Edmund "would never have found his way if the moon hadn't come out." On the next page he will note once again, "He could not have managed it at all in the dark" (92). What should we make of these comments? One way to approach the detail of the moon coming out is simply to see it as another one of Lewis's concrete descriptions which add realism to his imaginary land. From this perspective, the moon's appearance here is simply an answer to the practical question, how could Edmund have found his way at night through an unfamiliar wood?

However, since in other places Lewis has given weather providential overtones, exploring the same possibility here seems worthwhile, particularly since Lewis tells us not once but twice how critical it was. We might ask, What would have happened if the moon had not just happened to come out when it did? How could the moonlight be seen as providential for Edmund? Without the full moon, Edmund might never have found his way to the Witch's house, and so may never have seen her for what she really was, and so might never have come to his total rejection of her and her evil. Colin Manlove makes this very claim about Edmund here, arguing that "only the shock that is administered to him by his experience of evil, and Aslan's subsequent mercy, save him" (1987, 135) and that without the "extraordinarily difficult journey" to the Witch's castle and the "cruel treatment" that ensues, his change might seem "rather abrupt."

Evan Gibson also identifies a providential aspect in Edmund's encounter with the Witch. Gibson sees Edmund as "a small boy whose tendency to selfishness and bullying needs to be checked before it colors his whole life" (1980, 136). Gibson continues, "And this is one reason why he has found his way into Narnia. . . . All that Edmund needs is a glimpse of what true meanness is like in order to start the process of repentance. The lesson in misery he learns at the hands of the Witch does its proper work" (137). Later, in chapter thirteen, readers will be told that "Edmund had got past thinking about himself" (141), and part of the reason given for this change will be "all he'd been through."

As Edmund stoops under branches, "great loads of snow" fall on him (92), making him wetter and wetter. Every time this happens, we are told that Edmund thinks "more and more of how he hated Peter—just as if all this had been Peter's fault." The Witch's magic and Edmund's jealousy have finally succeeded in completely making something seem like what it isn't. How could Peter have caused the snow to fall on Edmund? In Edmund's mind somehow the connection is perfectly clear, and in his seeking to blame his sibling, he resembles the Witch herself. When Digory and Polly first meet her in *The Magician's Nephew*, Lewis gives the Queen a line nearly identical to Edmund's here: "It was my sister's fault," she says, referring to the total destruction around her (1994d, 66).

Regardless of whether readers see the full moon here as providential or not, Lewis makes good use of it as Edmund finally arrives at the Witch's castle and sees its "long pointed spires" that shine "in the moonlight" and cast "long shadows" which look "strange on the snow" (92).

The Witch's castle is, like the Witch herself, quite terrifying, and Lewis notes that from his first sight of it, "Edmund began to be afraid of the House" (92). The most essential qualities are its narrowness, silence, and isolation. Colin Manlove observes that the Witch's castle "is set in a hollow among hills, shut in on itself" (1993, 38), a place where she "lives alone."

Edmund's first encounter at the castle is with a lion that the Witch has turned to stone. Edmund falsely concludes that this statue must be Aslan, a thought which gives him pleasure for a number of reasons, one of which is that Edmund wants to become the ruler of Narnia and not, at this point, a king under "the true king," as Aslan will later be called (109). Edmund's relief that the lion is a statue comes at the same time as his assumption that the statue must be Aslan, and with this realization we are told that he "suddenly got warm all over right down to his toes" (94). Earlier in chapter three, when Edmund drank the Witch's magic drink, readers were informed that it "warmed him right down to his toes" (36). The similarity of these descriptions suggests that Edmund's hateful reaction to the

IN THE WITCH'S HOUSE

stone lion here is part of the same spell cast over him by the Witch at their first meeting.

After drawing a mustache and a pair of spectacles on the statue, Edmund is described as "gloating" and "jeering" at it (96), actions which reflect his debased spiritual condition. Later, in chapter fourteen, when the Witch's troops shave, muzzle, and beat Aslan, they too will be described as jeering (154).

Since, as Mr. Beaver has told the children, the lion is "the King of Beasts" (79), Lewis creates a slight consistency problem here in introducing a non-Aslan lion in Narnia—for what, if any, title or authority should it have? At the end of TLWW when Peter and Edmund are crowned as kings, no mention is made of any subordinate kingship for lions. Perhaps sensing this incongruity, Lewis has the stone lion seen here make only a few brief appearances in TLWW: when Aslan changes him back to life (167–8), when the army rescued from the Witch's castle heads off to join the battle (174–5), and when the children give out honors at the end (182). After these minor instances in TLWW, a non-Aslan lion will not appear in the Chronicles, thus avoiding the problem of additional kings. In The Last Battle, the final book of the series, Lewis makes use of the fact that no lions besides Aslan have been present in any of the stories. When Shift the ape disguises a donkey as a lion, the Narnians are fooled into thinking that this must be Aslan. King Tirian has his doubts, though as readers are told, "He had never seen a common lion. He couldn't be sure that what he saw was not the real Aslan" (47).

As Edmund passes dozens of creatures who have been made into statues, not once are readers told that he feels any compassion or pity for them. In fact, Edmund is glad that, as it appears to him, a dwarf is about to be attacked by the lion, because he hopes to make his escape while the lion's attention is directed elsewhere (94). As has been discussed earlier but is now seen vividly, turning anyone who will not obey her into stone is the ultimate act of domination for the Witch, for now the statues have not even the slightest amount of free will. Turning rebellious subjects into statues is the final step in reducing people to possessions.

In contrast to the diverse multitude that will surround Aslan later when Peter, Susan, and Lucy meet him (126), the White Witch is guarded by a single wolf, just as a single dwarf drives her sledge. Community will be associated with Aslan, isolation with the Witch.

From the moment of Edmund's arrival, we see clearly that his welcome is not going to be as he had hoped or imagined. Maugrim, whom readers may remember as the signer of the note left at Mr. Tumnus's cave (58), refers to Edmund as "Fortunate favorite of the Queen—or else not so fortunate" (98). The Witch's very first words reveal her true character, a side that Edmund had not seen before, or at least a side he has chosen not to see: "How dare you come alone?" she snarls (99). After learning Edmund's news about his siblings, the chapter ends with the Witch ordering her dwarf to prepare her sledge so she can immediately go after them.

TEN

The Spell Begins to Break

Lewis's narrator opens the interlacing story in chapter ten with a transition similar to the one that started chapter nine: "Now we must go back to Mr. and Mrs. Beaver and the three other children" (100). Donald Glover has pointed out that in *That Hideous Strength* the prime effect of Lewis's use of interlacement is contrast, how at one point in the novel, for example, "Jane meets Ransom and feels a flood of warmth and joy" (Glover 1981, 114) while in the corresponding scenes, "Mark meets the Head and vomits, awaking to a sense of his captivity." In *TLWW* Lewis's interlaced stories produce this same element of contrast. As Edmund journeys further and further into evil, he becomes more isolated and miserable. As his siblings make their way to the Stone Table and Aslan, they become more connected and more contented.

In the second sentence of chapter ten we find what is supposed to be a direct quote of Mr. Beaver's words from the end of chapter eight: "There's no time to lose"

(100). Mr. Beaver's last words were actually, "There's not a moment to lose" (87). Certainly the misquote is a minor quibble, and most readers, even those who have reread the series many times, may even fail to notice the discrepancy. Lewis was aware of inconsistencies in the Chronicles, and just a few days before his death he met with Kaye Webb, the editor of the Puffin books edition of the Chronicles, and promised to edit the books and "connect the things that didn't tie up" (Green and Hooper 1994, 307), a task he was not able to complete. Readers may wonder what, if anything, Lewis might have done with minor problems like this one or with the possible inconsistencies in the differing accounts of the White Witch in *TLWW* and *The Magician's Nephew*.

Next we are told that everyone immediately begins putting on their coats "except Mrs. Beaver" (100), who keeps her head and realizes that they have at least fifteen minutes before the Witch could possibly arrive and that some of this time should be used to pack food for their journey. Allowing her fear to push her to near-rudeness, Susan exclaims, "What *are* you doing, Mrs. Beaver?" Readers can hear a number of emotions in Lewis's uses of italics here: urgency, exasperation, even an implication of superiority. While the other four allow panic to cloud their thinking, Mrs. Beaver points out that even if they were to leave immediately without any supplies, they would have no chance of reaching the Stone Table before the Witch. Susan, often quick to despair, asks, "Then—have we no hope?" (101).

"We can't get there *before* her," Mrs. Beaver says, "But we can keep under cover and go by ways she won't expect" (101). As noted earlier in chapter eight, Mrs. Beaver is able to foresee what the Witch will do, but the Witch will not be able to "expect" the actions that the forces of good—the children and beavers, and later Aslan—will take. Paul Kocher has referred to this difference in awareness as the "basic epistemological superiority of the good over the evil" (1972, 59). As Kocher points out, "Lacking imaginative sympathy an evil intelligence cannot by understanding penetrate a good one, which does have that power in reverse. The former is too involved in self."

Feminist critic Kath Filmer has classified Lewis's attitude to women as "anachronistic and annoying" (1993, 3). In a chapter titled "Masking the Misogynist in Narnia and Glome," Filmer raises objections about Lewis's portrayal of a number of female characters in the Chronicles, including Mrs. Beaver, who according to Filmer "fusses and bullies Mr. Beaver as they prepare to leave the hole" (107). To share Filmer's negative evaluation of Mrs. Beaver's character requires that readers see the preparations that Mrs. Beaver insists upon as unnecessary. Certainly during the long walk from the lamp-post, the lack of anything to eat was brought up a number of times as a serious problem (59, 62, 65, 68). The food packed here will be eaten for breakfast the next morning (110), and the wisdom in Mrs. Beaver's preparations will be clear, as this and the hot tea provided by Father Christmas will be the only nourishment which the children will have for the entire day until they meet Aslan (129). One might also note that in the early chapters of the very next Narnia book, *Prince Caspian*, Lewis will present readers with a look at how difficult a journey without provisions can be.

In addition, Filmer's use of the word *fusses* runs counter to the fact that Lewis makes a point of telling readers that Mrs. Beaver responds "very coolly" to Susan's alarm (100) and that it is Mrs. Beaver who must remind her husband to "think it over" (101). Despite the protests of those around her, Mrs. Beaver remains unruffled, as is seen in her sensibly making sure that Lucy's pack will be light enough for her to carry. Later that night, after they are safe in the beavers' hideaway, Mrs. Beaver will refer to the reactions of the others during this time as "a plaguey fuss" (104).

Despite the good thinking Mrs. Beaver shows in this scene, Filmer asserts that she is not "intellectually well-endowed" (1993, 107) and as evidence cites the fact that Mrs. Beaver "wants to bring her sewing machine on the flight." Readers must decide for themselves if they think Mrs. Beaver is making a serious proposition or merely expressing regret when she says, "I suppose the sewing machine's too heavy to bring?" (102–3). A few sentences later, Mrs. Beaver explains the reason for her reluctance to leave behind something she values, saying, "I can't abide the thought of that Witch fiddling with it and breaking it or stealing it, as likely as not." Readers who remember the devastation at Mr. Tumnus's cave might see the opposite of a lack of intelligence in Mrs. Beaver's worry over what might happen to their home and their cherished possessions. Mr. Beaver, perhaps brought back to reason by his wife's clear-headedness, thinks of locking the door as they leave, in the hope that this will delay the Witch or her minions at least briefly and thus buy the group a little more time.

When Lewis states "everyone began bundling themselves into coats, except Mrs. Beaver" (100), whether Mr. Beaver is supposed to be included in this grouping is not clear. Lewis seems to be using "everyone" here as a shorthand for the three children. For Mr. Beaver to wear a coat now would make little sense unless he had one on before. Pauline Baynes's earlier illustrations of him, which Lewis approved of, do not show a coat (66, 71). In chapter twelve when we are told that the coats are abandoned, the passage does not indicate if the Beavers are wearing them or not (123). Lewis explicitly states that Mrs. Beaver wears "snow-boots" (101) but does not mention the snow shoes which Baynes portrays Mr. Beaver as wearing (102). Instead Lewis earlier had described Mr. Beaver as "putting on his snow-boots" (84). Although the talking beasts in Narnia are anthropomorphized in many respects, Lewis will typically not have them dressed in human clothes. Shift the Ape from *The Last Battle* is the notable exception to Lewis's pattern, and his desire to dress in human clothing is clearly meant to be interpreted as indicative of a wrong turning on his part.

After the little group has walked along for a while, Lewis tells us that the moon which had previously come out to guide Edmund disappears once more and that the snow begins to fall (103). At this point in the story, Lewis does not point out the result that the falling snow will have. But when the wolves later arrive at the house, he will note the providential effect this second change in weather has had. We will be told: "It would have been a dreadful thing for the Beavers and the children if the night had remained fine, for the wolves would then have been able to follow their trail—and ten to one would have overtaken them before they had got to the cave. But now that the snow had begun again the scent was cold and even the footprints were covered up" (113).

As mentioned earlier, Joseph Campbell has described the "supernatural aid" which the hero always receives in some form during his adventure. He goes on to describe how "Mother Nature herself supports the mighty task" (1968, 72). Mother Nature, which in the form of the rainy weather had supported the children's "mighty task" when they were at the Professor's, continues to do so after their arrival in Narnia, here in the form of snowy weather.

The Beavers take the children on an escape march that may remind readers of a parallel scene early in *The Lord of the Rings* where Frodo, Sam, and Pippin—childlike characters themselves and as inexperienced as Lewis's three children here—are fleeing the Black Riders. Tolkien's Black Riders are on horseback and, like the White Witch in her sledge, are much faster than their prey. Both fleeing groups take refuge on lower paths which are impassable to their pursuers. Mr. Beaver tells the children, "Best keep down here as much as possible. She'll have to keep to the top, for you couldn't bring a sledge down here" (103). Sam makes a very similar comment about the Black Rider who is after them, stating, "I don't fancy he would try bringing his horse down that bank" (Tolkien 1994a, 87). In both tales smaller, weaker good characters are forced to elude more powerful evil characters, and to do so they must rely on their wits and stealthiness rather than on strength or speed.

Lewis describes Lucy as being "so tired that she was almost asleep and walking at the same time" (103). Although readers now see Lucy bravely facing certain death as she flees for her life, they are also reminded through this detail that she is still just a young girl who is up way past her bedtime. In contrast to the beds at the Professor's where they had slept only the night before, the children are led to a snug little cave that Mr. Beaver describes as "an old hiding-place for beavers in bad times" (104). As noted earlier, for some reason the Witch apparently has set out to exterminate all beavers from Narnia, and despite the existence of secret hideouts like this one, we learn in *Prince Caspian* that her efforts will prove successful (Lewis 1994e, 169).

Mrs. Beaver passes round a flask containing a drink that makes them all feel "deliciously warm" (104), and afterwards, we are told, "everyone went straight to sleep" (105). Lucy wakens to the sound of "jingling bells," the same sound which had preceded the White Witch's first appearance to Edmund (30). Exactly why the children and the Beavers had been listening for the Witch's bells during their walk the night before is not perfectly clear, because there is no record of anyone but Edmund knowing about the Witch's harness, and he certainly never told any of his siblings about it. Perhaps readers are supposed to assume that either this was something the Beavers had told the children about or simply that bells might naturally be associated with a sledge. While the children and the Beavers fear that the jingling signals the Witch's approach, careful readers would remember that the Witch had ordered her dwarf to use "the harness without the bells" (99). And so this becomes one of the few times in *TLWW* when we know more than the children do and thus do not share their feelings. While the children are anxious that the bells signal the Witch's arrival, readers already know this is not the Witch and are merely curious about who else it might be.

Mr. Beaver scurries outside and soon calls for the others to follow him. He tells them, "It's all right! It isn't *Her*!" (106). Caught between using the correct subject-case pronoun as a model for young readers—*it isn't she*—and having his dialogue seem natural, Lewis tries to have it both ways by having his narrator add, "This was bad grammar of course, but that is how beavers talk when they are excited." Father Christmas, not the Witch, has arrived, and Mr. Beaver notes that this is an indication the White Witch's power "is already crumbling," for her spell had made it "always winter and never Christmas." As mentioned before, an earlier but less direct indication that the Witch's power was weakening was the presence of the robin (60), typically seen as a harbinger of spring.

Lewis's inclusion of Father Christmas in this chapter has raised a number of eyebrows as well as objections from some adult readers and critics. Chief among them was J. R. R. Tolkien, who was deeply disturbed by what he saw as not only a mixing of mythologies but a mixing of two worlds. As mentioned earlier, Tolkien described the writer of fairy stories as a sub-creator of a secondary world (1966, 68–75). With this in mind, Joe Christopher has phrased Tolkien's objection to the appearance of Father Christmas in Narnia in this way: "What is a symbol tied to a Christian celebration in the Primary World doing in the Secondary?" (1987, 119).

Lewis, in a letter where he gives some advice on the writing of fairy tales, points out, "In a fantasy every precaution must be taken never to break the spell, to do nothing which will wake the reader and bring him back with a bump to the common earth" (1993, 468). Whether or not Lewis's decision to include Father Christmas here breaks the spell and creates exactly the kind of a bump which he warned against seems to depend upon the reader.

Roger Lancelyn Green, Lewis's friend and biographer, remembers "reacting against the appearance of Father Christmas" and "urging Lewis to omit him somehow as breaking the magic for a moment" (Green and Hooper 1994, 241). Clyde Kilby, one of the first scholars to write about Narnia, had a similar reaction, calling the appearance of Father Christmas "incongruous" (1964, 145).

Peter Schakel, another of the Father Christmas critics, takes a somewhat different tack. Schakel holds that it is "the inclusion of Christmas itself" which is "the more basic inconsistency" (1979, 140). Schakel argues that since the Christmas holiday "celebrates the birth of Christ in his earthly incarnation," in order to be faithful to his fantasy world Lewis should have come up with "a Narnian equivalent to our Christmas instead of taking it into Narnia."

Donald Glover is yet another objector, complaining that "Father Christmas, for all Lewis's attempts at his rehabilitation as a Christian figure, strikes the wrong note, reminding us all too forcefully of childish pleasures and frivolous fantasies" (1981, 141). Somewhat unclear is why Glover finds the reminders of "childish pleasures" or even "frivolous fantasies" to be such a misstep in a children's book, although in this he may be distinguishing between *childish* and *childlike* pleasures, and between *frivolous* fantasies and those which are *nonfrivolous*. However, it should be noted that Lewis has chosen to include the more reserved Father Christmas here rather than Santa Claus. To underscore his intention to evoke more than "frivolous fantasies," Lewis becomes almost repetitious here, using the word *solemn* three times within two pages (107–8). He also points out that in Narnia, Father Christmas does not seem "funny and jolly" as he does in our world.

Green and Hooper take a position about Father Christmas with a foot on each side of the argument, claiming, "He still does not seem to fit quite comfortably into his place, but the rightness of introducing him seems more certain on each re-reading" (1994, 241).

Other critics have fully supported Lewis's decision. Colin Manlove writes, "Where those whose allegiance is to the witch take, those whose allegiance is to Aslan give. . . . Right at the center of the narrative, not the anomaly he has sometimes been seen, is the arrival of Father Christmas, with a sackful of gifts for everyone" (Manlove 1993, 36). According to Manlove, Lewis sought a contrast for the White Witch who, vampirelike, takes all the life from Narnia and thus turned to Father Christmas, a character whose very identity is associated with giving and generosity.

A. N. Wilson sees Lewis's inclusion of Father Christmas as following in the tradition of Edmund Spencer in *The Faerie Queen*. Wilson writes, "The appearance of a familiar figure like Father Christmas among so much that was new and strange is precisely the effect which Spenser achieved by juxtaposing old friends like St. George with new monsters of his own invention" (1991, 221).

Earlier it was noted that *TLWW* is a cornucopia of many differing ingredients and that even the title itself reflects this mixture of divergent elements. If a faun from classical Greece can exist alongside a dwarf from Northern Europe, why not the mythological figure of Father Christmas? As Evan Gibson has observed about Lewis's practice, "From the folklore and fables of many cultures he invites creatures of all sorts—dryads, dragons, giants, and talking animals. And as they enter through the magic portals, the Narnian air works a change in their natures. The Greek centaurs, German dwarfs, British witches, become Narnian through and through" (1980, 132).

Finally, one could point out that from the moment Lewis penned the wonderful line "always winter and never Christmas" (19), he had written himself into a literary corner. When the Witch's power is broken, readers expect to find not only the return of spring but also the return of Christmas; and in keeping with his motif of gradualness, Lewis would have to bring Christmas back first. For Lewis to have eliminated the character of Father Christmas from the story, he would also have needed to eliminate his magnificent line.

Joseph Campbell writes that "for those who have not refused the call, the first encounter of the hero-journey is with a protective figure (often a little old crone or old man) who provides the adventurer with amulets against the dragon forces he is about to pass" (1968, 69). The children have fit this aspect of Campbell's hero-myth pattern not once but three times, as they have received protective assistance on their journey from each of the characters they have encountered—the robin, the Beavers, and now Father Christmas. Lewis makes his Father Christmas more awe-inspiring than he is frequently depicted and certainly more serious than the Santa Claus figure which American readers might know, causing the children to feel not only "very glad, but also solemn" (107). With this added gravity, which causes Lucy to feel "a deep shiver of gladness" the kind which only comes from "being solemn and still" (107), Father Christmas becomes a precursor of Aslan, who produces a similar effect.

Father Christmas immediately passes out his presents. Mrs. Beaver is given "a new and better sewing machine," while Mr. Beaver is told that when he returns home he will find his dam completed and all the leaks fixed (107–8). Mr. Beaver's "present" here may strike readers as being a somewhat unusual gift unless they are aware of the conditions under which Lewis himself lived during the time he was writing *TLWW* and the long list of household chores which Mrs. Moore, the woman who became somewhat of an adopted mother to Lewis after he returned from the war, always had for him to do. In a letter written during this time Lewis complained that he had to be "Nurse, Kennel-Maid, Wood-cutter, Butler, Housemaid and Secretary all in one" (1993, 390). Having all his household tasks finished for him might have been Lewis's own Christmas wish on many occasions.

Near the start of *Prince Caspian*, a story set over a thousand years after *TLWW*, Caspian and Doctor Cornelius are meeting in secret on the roof of a tower and hear "the sound of the waterfall at Beaversdam, a mile away" (Lewis 1994e, 49). Lewis does not explicitly say so, but since the children's presents are still in existence then, perhaps it is not too far-fetched to imagine that the finishing and mending Father Christmas performs on the dam gives it a magical longevity and that the waterfall sound Caspian will hear ten centuries later is the sound of water still going over it.

Next Father Christmas gives the children the "amulets against the dragon forces" they soon must face (Campbell 1968, 69). As Peter receives his gifts of a shield and a sword from Father Christmas, he, like Lucy, is described as being "silent and solemn" (108). Before the day is over, Peter will need this sword in his first battle as he encounters the wolf Maugrim (131). In addition to a bow and a quiver of arrows, Father Christmas gives Susan an ivory horn which holds the assurance of "help of some kind" when blown, a promise which will be kept that very day when Susan is attacked by the wolf and then kept again in *Prince Caspian* (100). Lucy is presented with a small bottle filled with a healing elixir that will be used in *TLWW* to heal Edmund (179) and in later books to heal Trumpkin, Reepicheep, and finally Eustace (Lewis 1994e, 109, 207; 1994g, 27, 98). Although Lucy is also given a dagger, Father Christmas says that the girls are to use their weapons only in self-defense, instructions which some critics find sexist (Ford 1994, 368; Schakel 1979, 14; Filmer 1993, 106).

What these critics do not seem to object to, however, is the fact that Peter does not receive a bow or a healing cordial. Is Lewis saying males cannot be archers or healers? Not at all. What Lewis is illustrating, here in this scene and elsewhere, is that in Narnia all are called upon to put their unique abilities and inclinations to use. If Peter is better suited to use a sword and shield in the service of Narnia, Lucy is better suited to serve as a healer and, as we see in *Prince Caspian*, Susan is better suited to serve as an archer (Lewis 1994e, 33, 108).

In *The Horse and His Boy*, Lewis will return to this same point when he has Shasta explain that in times of war, "Everyone must do what he can do best" (1994a, 209). As noted earlier, readers find a similar incident in *The Last Battle* when Jewel, Tirian, Eustace, and Jill must travel through dense thickets which make it hard to get a bearing. Jill is clearly "the best pathfinder" (Lewis 1994b, 69), and Tirian puts her in front to lead.

Lucy wants to know why Father Christmas does not want her in the battle, and her response shows both humility and self-awareness. She tells him, "I think—I don't know—but I think I could be brave enough" (109). Father Christmas does not question Lucy's bravery, and readers as well think Lucy indeed could be as brave as either of her brothers. As mentioned earlier, in chapter seventeen Lewis will show explicitly that Lucy is certainly "brave enough" by choosing to have her known as "Lucy the Valiant" (184).

Father Christmas offers as his reasoning the claim that "Battles are ugly when women fight" (109), a claim which could be said to tell only half the truth. Truth be told, battles are ugly when men fight also—a fact which Lewis, a veteran of the trenches of World War I, would have known well. Here Lewis, or at least Father Christmas, may be guilty more of glorifying men's role in warfare than of being sexist. In chapter twelve Lewis will realistically describe the climax of Peter's first battle as "a horrible, confused moment like something in a nightmare" (131). The personal revulsion that Lewis had for war can be clearly seen in a letter he wrote near the start of World War II to his friend Dom Bede Griffiths in which he stated, "My memories of the last war haunted my dreams for years. . . . I think death would be much better than to live through another war" (1993, 320).

One further point which might be added here has to do with the ages of the children at this point and the use that Lewis makes of his readers' willing suspension of disbelief. No precise ages for the children are given in *TLWW*, but Lewis's outline of Narnian history indicates they entered Narnia in 1940 and gives the following years of birth: Peter 1927, Susan 1928, Edmund 1930, and Lucy 1932, making them 13, 12, 10, and 8 years old respectively. Even without these dates, Lucy is clearly not a woman, and so Father Christmas's admonition might more accurately have been that battles are ugly when young girls fight, rather than women.

Lewis will take the opportunity to return to the issue of having young people in battle in *The Horse and His Boy*. Near the end of the novel King Edmund gives orders that Corin, a young prince at the time, is not to take part in the upcoming conflict. Corin's guardian, the dwarf Thornbut, will tell him, "You will be allowed to see it, and that's treat enough for your Highness's little years" (1994a, 179). Corin in fact goes to battle anyway, taking his untrained twin brother Shasta with him. As the Hermit gazes into his magic pool which allows him to see Shasta trying to fight, he will expand Father Christmas's point by claiming, "It's mere murder sending a child into battle" (190).

Over the course of the Chronicles, Lewis's position on the role of children, young girls, or women in battle is neither clear nor consistent. A couple of days after this scene in *TLWW*, Edmund, without seeming to have aged at all, will play a major role in the clash against the Witch and her forces (178). In *The Horse and His Boy*, Lucy, who has by then become "a fair-haired lady," is shown riding off to battle wearing "a helmet and a mail shirt" with "a bow across her shoulder and a quiver full of arrows at her side" (1994a, 176). Readers are told that she is going to be "with the archers" (179). In *The Last Battle*, Lewis will give Jill an active role in the fighting, and the battle he depicts will not seem to be any more "ugly" because of her involvement.

In fact, in *The Last Battle* Lewis will reverse the position presented by Father Christmas here, or at least will suggest that the issue of the role of young girls and boys in battle may be more complicated. There Tirian will focus on their youth rather than their gender as he tells Eustace and Jill, "You are too young to share in such a bloody end as we others must meet tonight. . . . I entreat you—nay, I command you—to return to your own place. I should be put to shame if I let such young warriors fall in battle on my side" (1994b, 105). Jill is the first to reply, and she defies the king, saying, "I don't care what you say. We're going to stick with you whatever happens."

Both Eustace and Jill participate in the fighting which follows, and Jill uses her bow and arrows to hit a wolf (141), a fitting reversal to Susan's running from the wolf in chapter twelve of *TLWW*. Jill will also appear to kill at least two men (134, 141).

Later in *TLWW* Aslan will seem to have specific knowledge about the gifts the children receive here, a detail which strongly suggests he may have played some role in what they each are given. When Susan blows her horn for the first time, Aslan will identify it for Peter and will imply that Peter is to use his new sword against the wolf (130). After the final battle, Aslan will remind Lucy about her healing cordial (179). Aslan's knowledge of the gifts casts Father Christmas in the role of acting as the lion's agent here.

Peter does not give his sword a name in *TLWW*, but in *Prince Caspian* when the children return to Narnia hundreds of years later, Peter will find the sword still in perfect condition in Cair Paravel's treasure chamber. Drawing it from its sheath, he will declare, "This is my sword Rhindon; with it I killed the Wolf" (Lewis 1994e, 29). In *Prince Caspian* when Lucy retrieves her cordial, it is still "more than half full" (Lewis 1994e, 27). Susan's gifts are also magically preserved. Readers will learn in *Prince Caspian* that the quiver is made of ivory, matching her horn.

We get only a small glimpse of Peter's sword with its gold hilt and his silver shield with its red lion in the drawing of the final battle at the end of chapter sixteen (176). To get a much better look at Peter's gifts and Lucy's cordial, readers can turn to the drawing Baynes provides near the close of the second chapter of *Prince Caspian* (Lewis 1994e, 28). In this second illustration, Baynes captures the blend of familiar and fantastic which has been the distinctive trademark of Narnia. Peter has retrieved his sword, sheath, and shield, but he is still wearing the clothes of an English schoolboy, not a knight's armor.

After passing out each person's presents, Father Christmas has one last gift. He brings out a great teapot full of "piping hot" tea to complement the breakfast that Mrs. Beaver will serve from the supplies she brought the night before (109). Whether one accepts the presence of Father Christmas in Narnia or not, his departing wish of "Merry Christmas" seems a bit out of place, and perhaps Lewis realized this himself, for it is a wish no one else echoes. Father Christmas has come, but if this is supposed to be Christmas morning, the holiday is not celebrated or even noted by the children beyond receiving their gifts. As the chapter closes, the group turns to its next task of eating their sandwiches and continuing their march.

ELEVEN

Aslan Is Nearer

Chapter eleven opens with the contrast Lewis intended to produce by interlacing the two narratives. While Edmund's three siblings have been getting their Christmas presents and enjoying ham sandwiches and tea, Edmund has been having "a most disappointing time" with the White Witch (111). The Witch's promise of more Turkish Delight turns into "an iron plate with a hunk of dry bread," meager rations given by the Witch only reluctantly so that "the brat" will not be "fainting on the way." The contrast is not just with what the children receive but also in how they are welcomed. While the Beavers and Father Christmas have been warm and encouraging, the Witch's second dwarf grins "in a repulsive manner" as he serves Edmund the bread and water and then takes the opportunity to add the taunt, "Turkish Delight for the little Prince. Ha! Ha! Ha!" (112).

In writing the Chronicles, Lewis drew on his extensive literary and biblical background in three distinct ways. First, Lewis sometimes included *borrowings*. These are occasions where he took a creature or character from another tradition and included it in his own story, often with modifications. Mr. Tumnus and the other fauns in the Chronicles are a borrowing from Greek and Roman mythology. Lewis kept their characteristic half-human, half-goat composition as well as their flute-playing ability and love of dancing but, for example, made Mr. Tumnus more domestic and somewhat anglicized. Father Christmas, seen in the last chapter, is another example of one of Lewis's borrowings, but one modified to be not "only funny and jolly" as he is often depicted but bigger, gladder, and more solemn (107).

Borrowings can also be made in a more general sense. For example, Lewis was not the first author to include dwarfs, unicorns, and talking animals in his stories. Borrowing elements from earlier traditions and adapting them as desired is a normal practice of the mythic tradition. Tolkien also chose to borrow dwarfs, magicians, and knights in *The Lord of the Rings*. Green and Hooper have defended Lewis's practice of borrowing from earlier works. They argue that in the Narnia stories Lewis made "a new mythology that grew out of and embraced the old and gave it a new life in another world," and they assert that Lewis "could no more be accused of plagiarism for introducing fauns and centaurs, dryads and hamadryads, Bacchus and Silenus and satyrs, than Homer could" (1994, 251–2).

Besides borrowings Lewis also included *allusions* in the Chronicles. These are places where we find a brief, unexplained mention of a literary, historical, or biblical character or event. An allusion seeks to draw upon a commonly shared background knowledge—perhaps one less present in readers today than it was during Lewis's time—to economically evoke an emotional resonance. For example, the use of the terms "Son of Adam" and "Daughter of Eve" are allusions to the creation story found in the first four chapters of Genesis. Lewis's mention of these names may elicit a number of responses from readers who are familiar with the story. They might be reminded of another time when life was lived in a gardenlike world, a time when humans and animals were closer. Or they may remember another world which was created good but which fell under the power of evil.

In an allusion found in *The Voyage of the* Dawn Treader, Edmund compares Reepicheep's plan to tie Caspian up to what the crew "did with Ulysses when he wanted to go near the Sirens" (Lewis 1994g, 239). With this allusion to *The Odyssey*, Lewis can evoke a wide range of responses from readers, again assuming they are familiar with the work. They may think of the similarities between Ulysses's journeys and the journeys of the crew of the *Dawn Treader*. They might think of the themes of duty and responsibility which are present in both stories. They might see Caspian as a figure who is in some ways like Ulysses—both are on a quest, and in both cases the sea journey will be the making of them, will be instrumental in determining what kind of men they become.

Readers can find a third type of connection between Lewis's fiction and the literary or biblical tradition. *Echoes* or *parallels* are places where the connection is not as direct as a borrowing or an allusion but where we nevertheless can see similarities with an earlier source. At this point in *TLWW*, the Witch orders Maugrim to go to the Beavers' house and "kill whatever you find there" (113). Readers may find a parallel or an echo between the Witch's attempt to kill the children here before they can take the throne from her as has been prophesied and the biblical account of King Herod's effort to kill the young Jesus, who was also prophesied to become king. In both cases the ruler's henchmen are instructed to carry out widespread killing, and both attempts to stop the prophecy's fulfillment fail. This similarity, too indirect to be called a borrowing or an allusion, is better labeled as a parallel or echo.

Lewis himself wrote about yet another way an author might draw upon his literary background: those times when an author may be said to be *influenced* by a previous work. Lewis used the term *influence* to mean "that which prompts a man to write in a certain way," for example in the way "that *Paradise Lost* is influenced by Homer and Virgil" (1962, 38–9). While *TLWW* is in many ways unlike any book written before it, one can also see that it was influenced by earlier stories from a number of authors. Chad Walsh provides a list of authors who had an influence on Lewis, among them Edmund Spencer, George MacDonald, J. R. R. Tolkien, Roger Lancelyn Green, Kenneth Grahame, and E. Nesbit (1979, 12).

Next readers learn that Edmund, without a coat and without the welcome from the White Witch or the Turkish Delight he had expected, must travel in the Witch's sledge all through the night on what the narrator calls "a terrible journey" during which he is "miserable" (114). As his misery continues, Edmund comes to realize he has made a terrible mistake. Paul Ford, writing about Edmund's reversal, claims that "it is only when the Witch shows her real cruelty on their journey to the Stone Table that he begins to experience a change of heart: he wants to be a loving and beloved brother again" (162). While this claim about when Edmund's reversal occurs is for the most part true, readers should remember that earlier, during Edmund's long walk to the Witch's castle, he nearly gave up his whole plan and went back and "owned up and made friends with the others" (91).

To be realistic, Edmund's descent into evil needed to be gradual. Now readers must also see a gradual, step-by-step climb back toward goodness. As if to underscore the need for a gradual change in Edmund, one that is not accomplished in a moment but slowly over a period of time, Lewis's narrator tells how Edmund's miserable journey went on "hour after hour" (114), finally adding, "This lasted longer than I could describe even if I wrote pages and pages about it." Realistic characters do not act one way and then a completely different way seconds later. Drastic change, when it happens at all, requires time, motivation, and the potential for change—three elements which Lewis has been careful to provide for Edmund.

After hours and hours of driving through the night and into the morning, suddenly the Witch orders the sledge to stop. To contrast the attitude of the White Witch with not only Mrs. Beaver's prudence but also her kindness in taking the time to bring provisions for the journey, Lewis then turns to the topic of food, writing, "How Edmund hoped she was going to say something about breakfast!" (114). In fact, food is what has caused the Witch to stop, but not food for Edmund. The Witch stops because of what seems to be a party, complete with "decorations of holly" and "something like a plum pudding" (115).

Notice what exactly the Witch objects to here as she demands, "What is the meaning of all this gluttony, this waste, this self-indulgence?" (115). From the readers' point of view, the festivities Lewis depicts here are nothing like gluttony, waste, or self-indulgence. They are simply a continuation of the celebration and delight taken in good food and fellowship seen first at Mr. Tumnus's, then at the Beavers', and finally at the breakfast after Father Christmas's appearance. The real problem is not gluttony, waste, or self-indulgence, for these are all vices the Witch was seen to encourage in her first meeting with Edmund. It is the fact that the Witch can not bear to see anyone enjoying a simple, wholesome pleasure. Perhaps to emphasize the Witch's dual nature of evil and dominance, Lewis here for the only time refers to her as "the Witch Queen."

Concerned primarily with domination and not with the truth, the Witch denies that Father Christmas has been there and tells the group, "Say you have been lying and you shall even now be forgiven" (116). When the merrymakers, led by one of the young squirrels, refuse to make the scene seem like what it is not, the Witch turns them all into statues. Edmund cries out, "Oh, don't, don't, please don't," and we are told that Edmund "for the first time in this story felt sorry for someone besides himself" (117). This compassion will mark a tipping point for Edmund. From this moment on, he will be more aligned with the forces of good than the forces of evil.

Readers might take careful note of Lewis's words "for the first time *in this story*" (117, emphasis added) which seem to imply that Edmund has felt sorry for someone besides himself at some point before the story opened. Later, Lewis's narrator will briefly mention Edmund's "first term at that horrid school" as the point "where he had begun to go wrong" (180). And so Edmund's wicked behavior in *TLWW* may be best seen as a phase he is going through and his gradual transformation as a return to his former self and thus not as surprising.

Paul Ford has pointed out that Lewis uses the words *for the first time* several times in the Chronicles to "signal that an enormous change is taking place in a character" (192). Ford goes on to provide several examples. When Eustace is off by himself on Dragon Island in *The Voyage of the* Dawn Treader, readers are told that he feels lonely "for the first time in his life" (Lewis 1994g, 79). Before facing an adventure late in *The Silver Chair*, Jill and Eustace mark a change in their relationship by calling one another by their first names for "the first time" (Lewis 1994f, 191). In *The Horse and His Boy*, Aravis also has a turning point when she realizes "for the first time" that traveling with Shasta was "more fun than fashionable life in Tashbaan" (Lewis 1994a, 103).

Even critics who may feel that Lewis's Narnia stories are sometimes overly moralizing acknowledge the craftsmanship they display. The stories are always well-paced, clear, and inviting. In addition, at the end of each book Lewis is typically careful to tie up any loose threads. In what seems to be a rare exception to this rule, we never learn what becomes of the members of the tea party who are made into statues here, an omission which is even more conspicuous since Lewis makes a point to tell us, "It seemed so pitiful to think of those little stone figures sitting there all the silent days and all the dark nights, year after year, till the moss grew on them and at last even their faces crumbled away" (117).

Edmund's gradual change mirrors the gradual transformation from winter to spring that we see at this point, and both are in keeping with Lewis's overall theme of gradualness, which Manlove has pointed out (1993, 31–3). The magical change from deep winter to glorious spring is made believable by Lewis's characteristic use of familiar, concrete details. Here in the first stage of the transformation, the melting snow splashes; streams chatter, murmur, and bubble; and a steady "drip-drip-drip" comes from the tree branches (118). Through the growing fog, Edmund sees "the dark green of a fir tree" free of snow.

Soon the Witch's sledge becomes mired in the mud and must be abandoned. Edmund is forced to walk rapidly with his hands tied behind him. Each time he slips, we are told, "the dwarf gave him a curse and sometimes a flick with the whip" (119–20). As Edmund, the Witch's captive, is driven on and on through the mud, Narnia, in contrast, is released from the Witch's hold and goes from a thaw into full spring. The mist turns from "white to gold" and then gives way to "a blue sky between the tree tops" (120). A single bird chirps, it is answered by another a little ways off, and soon there is "chattering and chirruping" from every direction (121). Snowdrops are followed by primroses. Finally larches, birches, laburnums, and beech trees "come fully alive" as Lewis provides accurate details of their differing leaf patterns (122). Donald Glover argues that "Lewis's descriptive power is at its height in the noises and sights of spring. Symbolically the turning point, the thematic shift of power from the Witch to Aslan, it is the heart of the book's beauty, and significantly it is Edmund who, tied to the dwarf and driven along, first sees it" (141).

Lewis's depiction of the change from winter into spring is the longest descriptive passage in *TLWW*, and in it we can find the three characteristics which Evan Gibson has claimed make Lewis's descriptions so powerful. First, as has been mentioned, Lewis will always use the concrete. As Gibson notes, Narnia is real for its readers, not a land of "dim shadows and indistinct forms" (1980, 39). Secondly, Lewis will keep his descriptions short and make as much use of the reader's imagination as he can; as Gibson has observed, "When a hint will spur the reader to employ his own imagination, Lewis does not drown us with details." Finally, the descriptions we find here and elsewhere in *TLWW* are never description for description's sake, the type young readers might skip over looking for where the plot begins again. As Gibson points out, "Lewis does not introduce setting simply as pictures to decorate the walls of his story. It is always joined to the action or the theme. The melting snow slows down the Witch so that the Beaver party gets to Aslan first. The bird songs and crocuses are evidence that her magic has been overcome by a greater magic."

Note also that, as Martha Sammons has observed, the "celandines, crocuses, primroses, laburnums, and bluebells" seen here all begin to bloom "in the very same order as they bloom in our world" (1979, 32), providing an additional measure of realism to the magical transformation. As the evidence becomes overwhelming, the dwarf states, "This is no thaw. This is *Spring*. What are we to do? Your winter has been destroyed, I tell you! This is Aslan's doing" (122).

Lewis closes out chapter eleven with the Witch forbidding the mention of Aslan's name (122). When we return to Edmund's story in chapter thirteen, the Witch's dwarf will be careful to use a pronoun in place of the name *Aslan*, and there readers will be told, "He did not dare, even now, to mention the name of Aslan to his mistress" (135). In her attempt to prohibit anyone speaking about Aslan, the Witch continues her pattern of dominance and her pattern of seeking to make things seem like what they are not. Throughout the Chronicles, evil will frequently be seen in opposition not only to good but also to truth.

In addition, another likely reason the Witch forbids the mention of Aslan's name is because it elicits the same unpleasant response in her as it did earlier in Edmund (68), not the delightful feelings the other children experienced. Lewis will give a later character a similar response in *Prince Caspian*. When Caspian mentions Aslan to his uncle, Miraz commands, "Stop that noise. Stop it. And never let me catch you talking—or *thinking* either—about those silly stories again" (1994e, 43–4).

The Witch's final command is, "If either of you mentions that name again, he shall instantly be killed" (122), and with these words in mind, the way Lewis will describe Aslan's work at the Witch's castle near the end of the book in chapter sixteen is worth noticing. As Aslan and the recently transformed statues rush into the castle's interior, readers will be told:

> For several minutes the whole of that dark, horrible, fusty old castle echoed with the opening of windows. . . . But at last the ransacking of the Witch's fortress was ended. The whole castle stood empty with every door and window open and the light and the sweet spring air flooding in to all the dark and evil places which need them so badly. (171)

In this description of the Witch's castle and in her attempts to silence first the Christmas revelers and later Edmund and the dwarf, Lewis characterizes the Witch's reign over Narnia as stifling, confining, and dark.

TWELVE

Peter's First Battle

As chapter twelve opens, Peter, Susan, Lucy, and the Beavers have been walking "hour after hour" (123), similar to Edmund. But in contrast to Edmund's nightmare, they journey into what seems "a delicious dream." Like Edmund, they look on in surprise as Narnia passes "from January to May" in a few hours, and like Edmund they become tired. But unlike Edmund, they are not "bitterly tired" (124), only "dreamy" and "quiet inside." Part of this dreaminess results from the fact that with the snow gone they are able to relax a bit, knowing that the Witch "would no longer be able to use her sledge."

As Paul Ford has noted, dreams and dreamlike states play "a large part" in the Chronicles (1994, 149), appearing in each of the seven stories. Earlier in *TLWW*, the narrator compared the feelings that came with the first mention of Aslan's name to a dream (68). During his long miserable march with the Witch, Edmund tried to pretend "the whole thing was a dream and that he might wake up at any moment" (114). At the end of the novel, Edmund as a grown king of Narnia will remember the lamp-post as "in a dream, or in the dream of a dream" (186). In *Prince Caspian*, when Lucy claims to have seen Aslan, Susan will tell her, "You've been dreaming" (Lewis 1994e, 145). In *The Voyage of the* Dawn Treader, the crew sails to an island where dreams come true (Lewis 1994g, 183). In *The Silver Chair*, Jill will have a dream in which Aslan appears (Lewis 1994f, 116). Later in the same story, the Queen of the Underland tries to convince the adventurers that the world on the surface where they came from is "all a dream" (176). After Aslan appears in *The Horse and His Boy*, Lewis will have Shasta wonder, "Was it all a dream?" (1994a, 167). And when Queen Helen first arrives in Narnia, she will think she is dreaming (Lewis 1994d, 150).

Lewis gave the idea of dreams a prominent place not only throughout the Narnia books but in nearly all of his imaginative writing. Both *The Pilgrim's Regress* and *The Great Divorce* were framed as dreams of the author. In the second chapter of *Out of the Silent Planet*, Ransom has a dream which turns out to be precognitive (1996f, 20). The clairvoyant dreams of Jane Studdock play a central role throughout *That Hideous Strength*, as do the dream-visions of Orual in *Till We Have Faces*.

Lewis might have included dreams and dreaming in his fiction for a number of reasons. One may have been the dreamlike longing for something inexplicable just beyond his reach which haunted him from his youth (1955, 16–18). Another reason may have been his own active dream life. In describing how *TLWW* came to be written, Lewis noted, "I had been having a good many dreams of lions about that time" (1982a, 53). Finally, Lewis saw the relationship between the dream world and the real as a perfect metaphor for the connection between the reality of this world and the greater reality of the next. In a letter Lewis observed, "I suppose that our whole present life, looked back on from there, will seem only a drowsy half-waking. We are here in the land of dreams. But cockcrow is coming" (1967, 119–20). This same sentiment is found in Aslan's very last words in the series: "The dream is ended: this is the morning" (Lewis 1994b, 210).

Next we are told that "long ago" the group had needed to shed the fur coats from the wardrobe (123). At the end of the story, Lewis will use this detail to provide the children with a reason to tell the Professor about their adventures (187). Strictly speaking, the coat Edmund took was not left along the path but hanging in the Beavers' snug house, and one could argue that there it might have been expected to be preserved almost as well as if it had been in the wardrobe.

After walking all day, the three children and the Beavers climb a great hill as the sun is getting low. In the "very middle of this open hilltop" the children have their first view of the Stone Table (125). It is described as "a great grim slab of gray stone" that has been placed upon four upright stones, perhaps causing readers to think of the ancient standing stones in Britain and Europe. Given that the Stone Table has from the start of the story been associated with Aslan, Lewis's inclusion of the word "grim" here adds a somewhat paradoxical emotional coloring. Why should the Stone Table be grim? The negative connotations associated with this word, left unexplained here, will resonate later in the Witch's comments about the previous killings in this location.

In the next chapter, the Witch will indicate that the Stone Table is an altar for sacrifice and will state that she would prefer to kill Edmund on the Stone Table since it is "the proper place" (135), the location "where it has always been done." However, at this point in the story, Lewis has provided only Mr. Beaver's few unexplained references to this object (80), adding to its mystery.

Next readers are told that the Stone Table looks "very old" (125), apparently having been created some time early in the thousand years between Narnia's creation in *The Magician's Nephew* and the events which take place in *TLWW*. The strange lines and figures on the table are not explained here, and Lewis's narrator will only venture a guess that they "might be the letters of an unknown language" and add only that "they gave you a curious feeling when you looked at them." In the next chapter, the Witch will reveal that these letters on the Stone Table tell of "the Deep Magic" which states that every traitor belongs to the Witch as her "lawful prey" and that for every treachery she has "a right to a kill" (141–2). Exactly what "unknown language" might be used is never explained. From the start, English is the only language used in Narnia.

In *Prince Caspian*, the four children will return to Narnia thirteen hundred years later, a time when the ruins of Cair Paravel will evoke the same mystery and awe, the same "curious" feeling, that the Stone Table does here. At that point in time, the Stone Table will have been covered by a hill referred to as Aslan's How, described by Doctor Cornelius as "a huge mound which Narnians raised in very ancient times over a very magical place, where there stood—and perhaps still stands—a very magical Stone" (Lewis 1994e, 91). The stone mentioned is a piece of the Stone Table, which cracks into two pieces at the end of *TLWW* (161). Nikabrik, indicating the stone, will observe, "Do not the stories say that the Witch defeated Aslan, bound him, and killed him on that very stone which is over there, just beyond the light?" (Lewis 1994e, 168). What has happened to the other piece of the Stone Table will be left unexplained.

Off to the side of the hilltop's open space, the children see a "wonderful" yellow silk pavilion which has been set up under the lion's banner (125). Donald Glover observes that as the children reach Aslan, he is "portrayed as a medieval king in his cloth of gold pavilion and surrounded by his courtiers" (1981, 142). In stark contrast to the seclusion seen at the Witch's castle, Aslan stands "in the center of a crowd of creatures" (126)—dryads, naiads, centaurs, a bull with the head of a man, a pelican, an eagle, a dog, and leopards. Colin Manlove finds this scene to be the conclusion to an earlier progression, pointing out:

> The book conveys a gradual increase of population—first one faun, then two beavers, then a party of Narnians at a table; by the time the children and the beavers reach the hill of the Stone Table where a pavilion is pitched, the pace of creation seems suddenly to leap, as they find Aslan surrounded by a whole group of Narnians as though they had been begotten by him—which, since he has released them from the Narnian winter, is in part true. (1993, 40)

The leopards are reported as carrying Aslan's crown and standard. Some readers might not know that a standard is a banner which has been mounted on top of a long pole to mark a rallying point in battle. Exactly how four-legged animals with paws might carry these items is not made clear by Lewis's narrator or by Pauline Baynes's illustration of this scene, in which she has hidden the leopard with the standard behind Aslan (127). Similar anthropomorphic occurrences can be found from time to time throughout the Chronicles. For example, at the end of this chapter Aslan will somehow use his paws to accept Peter's sword and make him a knight by striking him with the flat of the blade (133). Another un-animallike action occurs when Peter and Aslan are said to shake "hands" in the final chapter (178). Presumably Aslan uses the humanlike hands which seem to be present in Baynes's rare un-lionlike illustration of Aslan near the end of chapter thirteen (143).

In spite of these brief lapses, Lewis's intention throughout the Chronicles is that the talking animals are real animals, not humans with animal faces. In *The Horse and His Boy*, Bree will try to argue that it is "absurd" to think Aslan is a "real" lion (1994a, 200), for if he were "he'd have four paws, and a tail, and *Whiskers!*" When Aslan appears, he will dispute Bree's claim, saying, "Here are my paws, here is my tail, these are my whiskers. I am a true Beast" (201). Paul Ford has observed that the talking animals in Narnia are not simply humans in animal bodies but that Lewis intended they "retain their animal natures" (1994, 405). Readers are expected to simply assume that from time to time certain physical activities requiring hands are somehow possible for the four-pawed creatures in Narnia, whether they are beavers, leopards, or Aslan himself.

Among the many creatures that surround Aslan in this scene are "Dryads and Naiads," creatures that Lewis feels the need to explain are "Tree-Women and Well-Women" (126). They are responsible for the music that the children heard as they arrived, playing "stringed instruments" which can be seen in Baynes's illustration (127). Back in chapter two, Mr. Tumnus told Lucy stories of "how the Nymphs who lived in the wells and the Dryads who lived in the trees came out to dance with the Fauns" (15). The Dryads and Naiads will play only a minor role in *TLWW*, but Lewis will give the spirits of the trees a larger part in *Prince Caspian* (1994e, 138–9, 157, 189, 196).

Some readers may have trouble identifying with the Dryads and Naiads as well as they do with the other Narnians which Lewis introduces. One reason for this may be that Lewis is sometimes inconsistent with the names he uses to refer to them and sometimes inconsistent with their qualities. In Baynes's illustration of them here, no discernable difference appears between the four creatures who represent the Dryads and Naiads (127). A second reason that readers, particularly young readers, may have trouble identifying with these characters is that unlike the mice, beavers, horses, dwarfs, wolves, or lions that inhabit Narnia, Dryads and Naiads are very unfamiliar mythical creatures. While the same argument could seem to be made for Mr. Tumnus, who is probably the first faun that many readers have encountered, at least he is made up of familiar components, being half goat and half human.

In a letter to Arthur Greeves, Lewis himself highlighted a third reason why modern readers may not identify as well with these creatures, one which can be traced to our general lack of a deep relationship with a specific section of land. Lewis wrote:

> Tolkien once remarked to me that the feelings about home must have been quite different in the days when a family had fed on the produce of the same few miles of country for six generations, and that perhaps this was why they saw nymphs in the fountains and dryads in the wood—they were not mistaken for there was in a sense a *real* (not metaphorical) connection between them and the countryside. What had been earth and air and later corn, and later still bread, really was *in* them. We of course who live on a standardized international diet (you may have had Canadian flour, English meat, Scotch oatmeal, African oranges, and Australian wine today) are really artificial beings and have no connection (save in sentiment) with any place on earth. We are synthetic men, uprooted. The strength of the hills is not ours. (1979, 363–4)

If Lewis is correct in his portrait of today's society as being "synthetic" and "uprooted," one of the functions of the make-believe world of Narnia may be to give back to readers this sense of a connection to a particular countryside, even if it is an imaginary one.

Next Aslan is described as being "good and terrible at the same time" (126), so that the children find it difficult to look at him and go "all trembly." This dual and paradoxical nature will be characteristic of Aslan. As Mr. Beaver has already told the children, "he isn't safe. But he's good" (80). At the end of the story, Mr. Beaver will emphasize this aspect in a slightly different way, claiming that Aslan is not "a *tame* lion" (182). Paul Ford has noted this occurrence of "simultaneous awe and delight" that we find in *TLWW*, a unique experience he labels as "numinous" (1994, 301). Earlier, after Peter first heard about Aslan, his way to express these dual feelings was, "I'm longing to see him, even if I do feel frightened" (80).

In *The Problem of Pain*, Lewis had discussed this experience of the numinous (1996h, 14–20) and provided several examples from literature, including the following passage from *The Wind in the Willows* where Rat and Mole approach Pan on the island. In this passage, which Lewis quoted, readers may see an attitude which also appears in the children's feelings towards Aslan in *TLWW*:

> "Rat," he found breath to whisper, shaking, "Are you afraid?"
>
> "Afraid?" murmured the Rat, his eyes shining with unutterable love. "Afraid? of Him? O, never, never. And yet—and yet—O Mole, I am afraid." (Lewis 1996h, 16)

Because of Aslan's "terrible" side, none of the group wants to go first to meet him. Peter prods Mr. Beaver, who whispers back, "Sons of Adam before animals" (126). Peter suggests, "Ladies first" (127), but Susan also defers, arguing that Peter should go first since he is the eldest. In the end, we are told that Peter "realized that it was up to him" and leads the group forward (128).

Most readers will probably accept Peter's decision without pausing; however, exactly why or how Peter realized that he should go first is not explained here. Clearly the strongest argument would be that, as Susan points out, he is the oldest. However, it bears pointing out that age was not a factor in coming to Narnia. In fact Lucy, who is the youngest, came first, and Edmund, the next youngest, came second. Throughout the Narnia books Lewis will typically go out of his way to avoid imposing limits on his characters because of their age. Lucy has already been the group's leader on their journey to Mr. Tumnus's cave (57). In *Prince Caspian*, despite Susan's complaint "It's four to one and you're the youngest" (Lewis 1994e, 148), Lucy will again be put at the head of the group.

When Edmund arrived at the castle, the White Witch's first words were, "How dare you come alone?"—words spoken in a "terrible voice" (99). The Witch's two subordinates there were identified as only "the first dwarf" and "another dwarf" (111–2). Here, by contrast, Aslan's first words are to welcome each of the five newcomers, calling them individually by name in a voice that is "deep and rich" and "somehow took the fidgets out of them" (128).

After his greeting, Aslan inquires, "Where is the fourth?" which raises the question of whether he has special knowledge or not. While Aslan in many ways is supposed to be a regular lion, he also possesses a somewhat vague set of extraordinary powers. In *TLWW* his roar will bend trees over (164). He will run twice as fast as the fastest racehorse (165) and will leap over castle walls (166). In addition, with his breath he will change the Witch's statues back into living creatures (167). In the other Narnia books, Aslan will display further special abilities including the power to appear in dreams (Lewis 1994f, 116), to change into other creatures such as a lamb and a cat (1994g, 245; 1994a, 89), and to blow characters through the air (1994f, 28).

The White Witch's powers are also somewhat vaguely delineated. In *The Magician's Nephew* readers will be told that she has "unwearying" though perhaps not unlimited strength and "endless days like a goddess" (Lewis 1994d, 190). With her wand she can turn creatures into stone, but she cannot, for example, simply wave it and cause her sledge to fly after it gets stuck in the mud. With a drop from her copper bottle, she is able to make the magic Turkish

Delight candy which casts a spell over Edmund (36). But once he breaks free from its enchantment, she is not able to simply cast another spell that would force him to obey her. In addition, she has demonstrated the power to impose a never-ending winter upon all of Narnia and later will be able to turn herself into a boulder and her dwarf into a tree-stump (138). In *The Magician's Nephew* the Witch has the power to turn the palace gates to dust by uttering a magic word (Lewis 1994d, 64), but this ability is lost when she comes to London (87), implying she has somewhat differing powers in different worlds.

To what extent Aslan possesses ordinary knowledge or something more is left unclear here and elsewhere throughout the Chronicles. From his question here about Edmund's location, one might argue that Aslan seems limited to knowing only what a normal lion might know—although how exactly he had learned the children's names is left unexplained. Alternatively, one could argue that Aslan might know exactly what has happened to Edmund—through normal or supernatural means—but asks the question in order to give Peter the opportunity to comment on his own role in Edmund's downfall. Later in *TLWW* a more significant question about possible limits to Aslan's knowledge will come up: Does Aslan know whether his sacrificial death for Edmund will be permanent?

When Mr. Beaver answers Aslan's question by telling him of Edmund's treachery, readers are told that "something" makes Peter confess that he was partly to blame for Edmund's downfall, and here Lewis becomes somewhat ambiguous (128). Presumably this "something" is Peter's conscience, stirred by being in Aslan's presence. Aslan neither excuses Peter nor blames him but responds by "merely looking at him with his great unchanging eyes," and readers are left to speculate on what point Lewis is trying to make by this silence.

One likely interpretation for Aslan's disinclination to talk about Edmund involves a theme which appears later in *TLWW* and will run throughout the Chronicles, that no one is told "any story but their own" (Lewis 1994a, 165, 202). In chapter thirteen when Edmund and Aslan have their conversation, the narrator will comment, "There is no need to tell you (and no one ever heard) what Aslan was saying" (139). So perhaps here, in Aslan's silence, he is simply following his own principle not to discuss other characters' "stories." He may just be letting Peter's words express the truth.

A different kind of clue about Lewis's stance here may be found in *Letters to an American Lady* where Lewis would later write, "I am rather sick of the modern assumption that, for all events, 'we,' the people, are never responsible: it is always our rulers, or ancestors, or parents, or education, or anybody but precious 'us'. We are apparently perfect and blameless. Don't you believe it" (1967, 15). While the silence following Peter's comment may be ambiguous here, in the next chapter when Edmund is reunited with his siblings, it may be significant that we find an apology from Edmund but not one from Peter (139). From this readers might conclude that the best way to interpret Peter's statement here is to see him as not truly responsible for Edmund's misdeeds but merely as exemplifying Lewis's pattern of showing compassion and understanding for those who commit mistakes. In addition, here we might see Peter, who on the following page is told that he will become High King, assuming some measure of special accountability for those he leads.

Paul Ford takes a middle position on Aslan's silence here, one which sees Peter as not wholly at fault, stating, "In his silent gaze, Edmund's absence and Peter's partial guilt need only acknowledgement, not explanation" (1994, 20). If, as Ford argues, Peter was partly to blame, the question arises as to exactly what he might have done differently to change things. In the end Lewis leaves readers to speculate about what effect, if any, Peter's different behavior may have had on his younger brother.

Aslan tells Lucy that "all shall be done" for Edmund, adding, "But it may be harder than you think" (129), suggesting that even before his meeting with the White Witch, Aslan is fully aware of the law that every traitor rightfully belongs to the Witch as her "lawful prey" and that for every treachery in Narnia, she has "a right to a kill" (142). Still, readers may not see clearly how they are supposed to understand Aslan's use here of the words *all* and *may*. Perhaps Aslan, if he is not omniscient, is not completely sure how the debt which is owed to the Witch is going to be paid, although he may be thinking that paying the debt is not optional. When the Witch declares that unless she has blood "as the Law says," all of Narnia "will be overturned," Aslan will not only concur but also view anyone who disagrees with this as working "against the Emperor's Magic." So when Aslan says here that it *may* be harder than Lucy imagines, the implication is that it *will* be harder, and when he says "all shall be done," he truly means *all*, even to the extent of giving his own life in exchange for Edmund's.

If readers go on to *The Magician's Nephew*, they will find a very brief but highly significant clue as to how to interpret Aslan's statement "all shall be done" here. After creating Narnia and its talking beasts, Aslan explains to them the Witch's presence there: "Before the new, clean world I gave you is seven hours old, a force of evil has already entered it; waked and brought hither by this son of Adam. . . . Evil will come of that evil, but it is still a long way off, and I will see to it that the worst falls upon myself" (Lewis 1994d, 148). From the Witch's entrance into Narnia, Aslan has foreseen the consequences and has vowed that he would bear the most suffering in bringing about her elimination.

Lewis follows with another of the paradoxical descriptions of Aslan which make him such an unforgettable character. A few pages before, Aslan was portrayed as "good and terrible" (126). Now he is not only "royal and strong and peaceful" but "sad as well" (129), though only for a moment. Colin Manlove has described Aslan's multidimensional nature: "No simple, single thing he: he contains and reconciles some of the most energetic opposites" (1987, 134). Significantly, readers see this sad side of Aslan here through the eyes of Lucy, who is the most sensitive of the children.

While Susan and Lucy are sent to a pavilion to get ready for a feast, one which happens outside the narration of the story, Aslan takes Peter aside to show him distant Cair Paravel, where he is to be "High King over all the rest" (130). Paul Ford notes that the name Cair Paravel is used for both the castle and the city surrounding it and suggests the designation comes from *kaer*, an old British word meaning *city*, and from *par aval*, Old French for *down*, and *ad vallem*, Latin for *to the valley*, and so Cair Paravel is "city in the valley" (1994, 90–1). In support of this reading, Ford cites a letter sent by Lewis to his friend Arthur Greeves in which Lewis mentions learning older vocabulary through his reading of Geoffrey Monmouth's *History of the Kings of Britain*. In the letter Lewis wrote, "One learns a little too. *Kaer* apparently is British for *city*. Hence Leil builds Kaer-Leil (Carlyle) and Kaer-leon is the city of legions" (Lewis 1979, 263). If readers have Pauline Baynes's map of Narnia, they can find Aslan's How labeled (rather than the Stone Table) and can see how far away Cair Paravel is on the seacoast.

Martha Sammons offers an alternative explanation for *Paravel*, stating: "A 'Paravail' is one in a position below another but who holds another beneath like a tenant. Lewis is thus implying that while the Kings and Queens rule over Narnia, they, in turn, are in submission to Aslan and the Emperor-Over-Sea" (1979, 141).

Peter's appointment to the position of high king here in *TLWW* comes about not because of any special merit, although he has proved himself a good leader. Rather, as Aslan explains, Peter is made high king simply because he is the "first-born" (130), and in this pattern of responsibility, Lewis built a particularly medieval view into the authority structure in Narnia. Edmund and the two sisters will be subject to their older brother not because he is never wrong, as seen in *Prince Caspian* (Lewis 1994e, 153), but simply because of their birth order.

In fact, Peter will turn out to be a rather democratic high king. In *TLWW* Peter never issues any orders to his siblings, perhaps because Aslan is present most of the time, so his special position is never seen other than when Aslan goes over battle plans with him (145). In the children's further adventures in *Prince Caspian* when Edmund hesitates to follow Peter's lead, Lucy whispers, "Hadn't we better do what Peter says? He is the High King, you know" (Lewis 1994e, 103). But then, undercutting this, she also adds, "And I think he has an idea." Later when they must decide which way to go and can reach no consensus, Edmund will state, "There's nothing for it but a vote" (127). The children do vote, and Trumpkin is the only one who suggests that Peter's opinion should count more than the others (128).

Chapter thirteen of *Prince Caspian* will be titled "The High King in Command," and there readers will find the clearest indication of Peter's position of authority above King Edmund and Prince Caspian. In *The Last Battle* Peter will play a special role as high king when he is the one Aslan calls on to shut and lock the door to Narnia (Lewis 1994b, 181).

Evan Gibson has offered this summary of Peter's kingly character:

> Peter, the oldest, is a natural leader. As he is to be the High King of Narnia in its Golden Age, he shows, as we would expect, some royal qualities even as a boy. . . . He acts with courage when Susan is in danger, and does not flinch when Aslan leaves the conduct of the battle in his hands. He rebukes the spiteful tongue of Edmund, is kind to Lucy even when he thinks she is out of her mind, and apologizes to her when he discovers that her story is true. We are not surprised that he grows up to be a tall, deep-chested ruler of Narnia, known as King Peter the Magnificent. (1980, 135–6)

At the end of *The Horse and His Boy*, when Cor says he does not want to become king, he will be told he has no choice because he is the oldest (Lewis 1994a, 222). As King Lune tells him, "The king's under the law, for it's the law makes him a king. Hast no more power to start away from thy crown than any sentry from his post" (223). In the two cases of primogeniture in Narnia, the eldest sons, Peter and Cor, also happen to be the best leaders among the siblings. The case of whether younger family members would be required to follow a consistently poor older leader is left unexplored, as is the question of whether an older sister, had there been one, could have served as High Queen. Caspian, Rilian, and Tirian, the other prominent Narnian kings, will have no siblings—older or younger.

When Aslan points out "Cair Paravel of the four thrones" (130), a castle reflecting in the sunlight like "a great star" and the place where the children will be kings and queens, it is as much a mystery to readers as it is for Peter. Readers may wonder who built the castle and if anyone else has ever reigned there or if it has sat empty for years and years waiting for them—questions which Lewis leaves unanswered. In purposely leaving out this kind of background material here and at other times throughout *TLWW*, Lewis enhances, rather than diminishes, the experience of the reader. By surrounding certain elements—Cair Paravel, the lamp-post, the Witch, the Stone Table, the wardrobe, and Aslan himself—with an aura of mystery instead of explanation, Lewis increases the reader's sense of wonder.

Aslan opens his remarks about Cair Paravel by referring to Peter with the phrase, "O Man" (130). Besides the formality and the sense of pronouncement which comes through this method of address, perhaps Aslan is suggesting that Peter has grown up significantly during his night journey from the wardrobe to the Beavers' and then to the Stone Table. The question of how quickly the four children age in Narnia or how quickly their skills develop is left somewhat open in *TLWW*. The next day, after the battle with the Witch, Peter will seem to Lucy to be "so much older" (178), a comment which may refer to a physical change, a psychological change, or both.

Suddenly Susan's horn is heard, calling for help to save her from the wolf's attack. Certainly Aslan could have stepped in and killed the wolf himself. Alternatively, he could have had one of the more powerful creatures save Susan, perhaps a unicorn or a centaur. But Aslan makes clear that this is something Peter needs to do himself (130), somewhat in contrast to Mr. Beaver's statement when Peter wanted to save Edmund, "It's no good *your* trying" (78). As mentioned earlier, the children will have a cooperative role in saving Narnia: Aslan will play his part, and they must play theirs. And the tasks they must undertake will in many ways be the making of them. In *Prince Caspian*, Lewis will have Peter make this observation about Aslan's role and the role that the other characters must play: "We don't know when he will act. In his time, no doubt, not ours. In the meantime he would like us to do what we can on our own" (1994e, 175).

Readers may remember that when Father Christmas gave Susan her magic horn, he promised her, "When you put this horn to your lips and blow it, then, wherever you are, I think help *of some kind* will come to you" (108, emphasis added). In fact the horn will characteristically always bring help—both here where it brings only Peter, who has never wielded a sword before, and in *Prince Caspian* when it calls the four young children back to Narnia (Lewis 1994e, 103)—but never exactly the type that the one blowing the horn may have expected. In *Prince Caspian* Lewis will have Doctor Cornelius point out this unpredictability as he tells Caspian, "It is said that whoever blows it shall have strange help—no one can say how strange" (1994e, 62). He will later remind the council, "We do not know what form the help will take" (96).

Susan's horn is described as making "a strange noise" like "a bugle, but richer" (130). In *Prince Caspian* Lewis will give its distinctive sound more prominence, including its ability to carry over a great distance. The dwarf Trumpkin will describe it this way: "I'd been plugging away for many hours when there came a sound that I'd never heard the like of in my born days. Eh, I won't forget that. The whole air was full of it, loud as thunder but far longer, cool, and sweet as music over water, but strong enough to shake the woods" (1994e, 100). Tolkien includes a similar call for help at the start of *The Two Towers* where Boromir's horn sounds, calling Aragorn, Tolkien's version of a high king, to rush in and help. Tolkien writes: "Then suddenly with a deep-throated call a great horn blew, and the blasts of it smote the hills and echoed in the hollows, rising in a mighty shout above the roaring of the falls" (1994d, 403). Boromir's horn also calls help of a somewhat different form than expected. Boromir had hoped for help in fighting the orcs. Instead Aragorn arrives after the battle is over but just in time to accept Boromir's confession of wrongdoing so he can die in peace (404).

Peter stands, saying nothing, as he attempts to figure out what the "strange noise" is (130), for he has never heard the horn before. Then Lewis adds what may seem to be an odd detail. Aslan tells Peter, "It is your sister's horn," with a voice that is "so low as to be almost a purr." We might take this just to mean that it was a quiet, soft voice, except Lewis adds the comment "if it is not disrespectful to think of a Lion purring," his way to say that, in fact, Aslan is purring here. As a lion, Aslan will roar and growl from time to time, but Lewis will have Aslan purr very rarely in the Chronicles. In *The Voyage of the* Dawn Treader, Aslan will purr with happiness when Lucy meets him at the Magician's (Lewis 1994g, 158), and so we might ask, what might Aslan be happy about when he purrs at the sound of Susan's horn?

Perhaps he purrs because the plans he has made for the maturation of the four children are turning out as he had planned. For Peter to be able to face the Witch in battle, he first must face a lesser foe, the wolf. Perhaps he is purring because the wolf's attack represents an act of disobedience to her order to wait for her, and Aslan certainly would not be unhappy that the Witch cannot count on her captain to carry out her commands. Perhaps Aslan is purring here because Maugrim's disobedience and the subsequent flight by the second wolf to find the Witch are the first steps in rescuing Edmund. Finally, perhaps Aslan is purring because he was the one behind Father Christmas's gift of the horn and now, as he had somehow known, it is being put to good use.

In spite of the "brave and adventurous" feelings Peter experienced earlier at the sound of Aslan's name (68), he now feels he is "going to be sick" as he faces Maugrim in his first battle (131). Here we see Lewis portraying realistic and gripping action in relatively few words. Lewis once gave the following advice about writing: "Never use adjectives or adverbs which are mere appeals to the reader to feel as you want him to feel. He won't do it just because you ask him: you've got to *make* him. No good *telling* us a battle was 'exciting.' If you succeeded in exciting us the adjective will be unnecessary: if you don't, it will be useless" (Lewis 1993, 468).

In his description of Peter's first battle, we see Lewis practicing what he preached. Peter comes to a "horrible, confused moment like something in a nightmare" (131), and then he plunges his sword "as hard as he could, between the brute's forelegs into its heart." Peter is described as "tugging and pulling" as the wolf seems "neither alive nor dead." Finally, in Lewis's marvelous concluding description, the wolf's bared teeth knock against Peter's forehead and readers are told "everything was blood and heat and hair" (132). It is an account which suggests, as a complement to Father Christmas's statement about battles being ugly when women fight (109), that battles are not pretty no matter who is fighting.

Worth noting before moving on, here in the first battle scene in the story the two females are shown attempting to flee while a male steps in to save the day. Perhaps also worth noting is that the girls are younger than Peter here, and so their different responses could and should be at least partially attributed to their age. After the battle is over, in a more gender-balanced portrayal, Peter is described as "shaky" as he and Susan greet each other with "kissing and crying on both sides" (132). As noted earlier, Lewis will have Jill slay a wolf in *The Last Battle* (1994b, 141).

The wolf's attack here has seemed chaotic and ill-planned. Why indeed would he try to kill the children so nearby to Aslan, who certainly could have stopped him if Peter had failed to? Readers may remember that here Maugrim was acting against the orders of the Witch, who had sent him to the Beavers' house with the specific instructions: "If they are already gone, then make all speed to the Stone Table, but do not be seen. Wait for me there in hiding" (113). That the Witch's first-in-command disobeys her clear orders suggests that obedience may not be a widely held virtue among her minions, particularly when she is not around to enforce her wishes.

Perhaps the wolf is trying to earn extra favor with the Witch. Or perhaps his attack is simply an expression of his malevolence. In either case, the fact that he attacks rather than waiting in hiding makes Edmund's rescue possible. With no attack, the second wolf would not have needed to retreat. With no retreat, he would not have been followed, and Edmund would not have been rescued but would have been killed by the Witch there in the woods. And so in this attack, Maugrim, like Gollum in *The Return of the King*, will "do good that he does not intend" (Tolkien 1994c, 797). In this aspect both Lewis and Tolkien were following in the footsteps of an earlier writer, John Milton. In *Preface to Paradise Lost*, Lewis observes that in Milton's epic, "whoever tries to rebel against God produces the result opposite to his intention" (1961b, 67). Lewis points out how at the end of the poem Adam is astonished at the power "that all this good of evil shall produce."

Aslan sends centaurs, eagles, and other creatures who are naturally gifted with speed to follow the second wolf back to the Witch and rescue Edmund. Here again we see a task given to those with the appropriate talents—again one which Aslan could have easily performed himself.

After sending the rescue party, Aslan turns to Peter and reminds him to clean his sword. This done, Aslan makes Peter a knight. Although Aslan renames Peter as Sir Peter Wolf's-Bane, this is a title which is never used again. After his own first battle, Edmund will be knighted in a similar fashion (180), as will Caspian, Trufflehunter, Trumpkin, and Reepicheep in the following book (Lewis 1994e, 210). Perhaps Lewis felt that the renaming part of the knighting ceremony rang a bit false, as it is not included for these later characters.

Paul Ford has suggested that Aslan's final words in the chapter, "And whatever happens, never forget to wipe your sword" (133), should be taken simply as useful advice. Ford states, "Lewis's inclusion of practical notes helps to make the fantasy world of Narnia quite real" (1994, 331) and goes on to note similar examples of helpful advice which occur throughout the Chronicles, such as that the best way of getting to sleep is to stop trying (Lewis 1994e, 115) or that when thrown into deep water, a person should kick off his shoes (Lewis 1994g, 12).

In commenting about the end of chapter twelve here, Ford claims, "Reminding Peter to clean his sword after every fight is one in a whole series of practical notes that the avuncular Lewis adds throughout the Chronicles" (1994, 46). Coming as it does after a series of moments of high drama—the slaying of the wolf and Peter's knighting—perhaps, as Ford suggests, Lewis wanted to use Aslan's words to end the chapter on a lighter note. In this sense Aslan's statement could be said to have the same jocular tone as the Professor's final words at the end of the book: "Bless me, what *do* they teach them at these schools?" (189).

That Lewis may be using this instance of the first blood-taking in the story to make a fundamental point about violence also seems possible. When Aslan first tells Peter he has forgotten to clean his sword, we are told that Peter "blushed" as he looked at the bright blade "all smeared with the Wolf's hair and blood" (132), details which inject elements of shame and then gravity into the scene. So in Aslan's final words, "never forget to wipe your sword," we may hear Lewis saying that while grim violence may sometimes be a necessary part of life in Narnia, it is not the only part and certainly not the central part. Violence is not to be glorified or reveled in. And when it is over, it is not to impede on the tranquil part of Narnia which is primary.

Yet another alternative reading of this incident suggests the need for readiness. Aslan could be warning Peter that while he has won a battle, the war is not over and he must always be prepared to fight against the forces of evil, forces which may appear unexpectedly. However readers interpret Aslan's final words of the chapter here, they may note that Lewis will choose to revisit this particular topic again in *The Last Battle* where Eustace puts his sword "back in the sheath all messy from killing the Calormene" and gets "scolded for that and made to clean and polish it" (1994b, 87).

THIRTEEN

Deep Magic from the Dawn of Time

Chapter thirteen opens with the narrator providing an update on Edmund's condition, and Lewis's descriptive technique here is worth examining. Far more effective than just telling us *Edmund was exhausted*, Lewis provides details that lead us to conclude ourselves how tired he is (134). We learn the following: (1) that Edmund has been made to walk "further than he had ever known anybody *could* walk," (2) that he sinks down and lays "on his face" as soon as the Witch calls a halt, (3) that he does not care what happens next as long as they "let him lie still," and (4) that he is even too tired "to notice how hungry or thirsty he was," a detail which Lewis uses to say much about Edmund's tiredness and at the same time to comment about his spiritual state. Remember, only hours before Edmund had reentered Narnia totally dominated by his craving for Turkish Delight. Now, although he is under the physical control of the Witch, he is free of her domination of his will.

The Witch and her dwarf discuss the fact that by now the other three children will have reached the Stone Table and Aslan and thus are out of their reach. They contemplate killing Edmund and then falling upon the other children after Aslan is gone, for as the Witch correctly points out, Aslan "may not stay long" (135). For reasons Lewis does not directly tell us, Aslan will seem to spend relatively little time in Narnia over the course of the 2555 years the Chronicles cover. Granted, not every appearance by Aslan is recorded in the seven novels; yet as Mr. Beaver has pointed out, Aslan has not appeared in Mr. Beaver's time or his father's and is "not often" in Narnia (78). It certainly seems unlikely that Aslan has been in Narnia since the Witch initiated the perpetual winter which, as already noted, in *Prince Caspian* will be stated as lasting one hundred years (Lewis 1994e, 169). In later Narnia books, Lewis establishes that Aslan can be *present* in Narnia without *appearing* (1994g, 159), but this is not a distinction which is seen in *TLWW*. Back in chapter seven when Mr. Beaver told the children that Aslan "perhaps has already landed" (67), the implication is that Aslan was not present in Narnia prior to this.

In *TLWW* Aslan is in Narnia for only around seven days before "quietly" slipping away (182). Through Mr. Beaver, Lewis will offer two suggestions for Aslan's very limited presence, but neither seems to tell the whole story. Mr. Beaver will claim Aslan "doesn't like being tied down" and also that "he has other countries to attend to" (182). A more satisfying explanation, one which is reflected in Aslan's diminishing presence in each successive Chronicle, is that the Narnians and the humans who enter Narnia are supposed to gradually come to be able to do things for themselves, to themselves act as Aslan's agents.

In the end, fearing that Edmund may be rescued, the Witch decides to kill him immediately, although as she states, she would have preferred "to have done it on the Stone Table" since "that is where it has always been done before" (135). What is this *it* the Witch mentions twice here? A practice which appears to be a blend of sacrifice and execution—not human sacrifice, for there have not been humans in Narnia during the Witch's reign, but presumably the sacrifice of the other sentient creatures, the lawful punishment, as we learn later, for "treachery" (142). Exactly what agreement the Emperor-Beyond-the-Sea has made with the White Witch that not only allows but seems to require her to kill all traitors is never made explicit. Some contradiction may be seen in that here Aslan orders his forces to stop the Witch from taking her rightful prey, but then later he will frown at Susan when she urges him to do something to work against the Emperor's magic. Aslan's later statements almost seem to imply that in saving Edmund, the members of the rescue party, while obeying Aslan, are actually behaving contrary to the Emperor's design. The possible inconsistency here can be reconciled by assuming that Aslan has intended all along to fulfill the magic's requirements himself.

In the Witch's announcement that the Stone Table is "where it has always been done before" (135), we are led to believe that she has killed many others in the past. Whether these other victims were traitors she had a right to kill or simply creatures she wanted dead is another aspect Lewis leaves unexplained. Nor does he make clear exactly what makes the dwarf reply that "it will be a long time now before the Stone Table can again be put to its proper use," since he and the Witch have just agreed Aslan probably will not be staying long. Whatever the reasons for the dwarf's claim about the Table, the Witch concurs with him.

In his autobiography, *Surprised by Joy*, Lewis records a turning point which came when he was learning how to write. He recalls: "Up to then, if my lines rhymed and scanned and got on with the story I asked no more. Now . . . I began to try to convey some of the intense excitement I was feeling, to look for expressions which would not merely state but suggest. . . . I had learned what writing means" (1955, 74). Throughout *TLWW*—here in the discussion of the Witch's role as an executioner, earlier in the description of the children's passage through the wardrobe, and later in Aslan's resurrection because of the Deeper Magic—Lewis will typically not *state* exactly how the magic works but rather will *suggest* a means which is never fully made plain. Tolkien employed a similar technique in *The Lord of the Rings* and in a letter briefly summarized it.

Tolkien claimed that, in his opinion, "A part of the 'fascination' of *The Lord of the Rings* consists in the vistas of yet more legend and history, to which this work does not contain a full clue" (2000, 185). Throughout *TLWW*, Lewis too will provide many "clues" to "more legend and history" than is fully described, partial clues which will shed partial light.

As discussed earlier, perhaps the clearest example of a time when Lewis suggests rather than states, and by doing so elicits a wonder which would have otherwise been lost, is when Lucy first emerges from the wardrobe to discover a lamp-post shining in the middle of the woods. Readers are told that Lucy stood "wondering why there was a lamp-post in the middle of a wood" (9), but she never finds out. Readers of *TLWW* never find out either, and not until *The Magician's Nephew* will Lewis turn to the lamp-post's origins (1994d, 100, 116, 119).

Suddenly the second wolf arrives to report Maugrim's slaying. Significantly, this second wolf is never named, nor is the dwarf. In fact, the only one of the Witch's minions who seems to posses a name is Maugrim, suggesting a loss of identity when one enters her service, the opposite to those serving Aslan, who are all known and called by name. The wolf makes a point to tell the Witch, "I was hidden in the thickets" (135), indicating that unlike his captain, he obeyed her instructions not to be seen and to wait "in hiding" (113). He urges the Witch to fly without saying anything about being followed, leaving open the question of why he thinks the Witch should flee immediately.

The Witch orders the wolf to "summon all our people" (135) and then recites a list of eleven types of creatures, nearly all of them borrowings. Some of the creatures, such as giants, werewolves, and ogres, should be familiar to readers. A ghoul is an evil spirit that robs graves and feeds on the dead, an entity which Lewis refers to again in *The Horse and His Boy* (1994a, 45). A boggle is a general term from dialectical British for a goblin, specter, or bogeyman. A minotaur is a creature with the body of a man and the head of a bull, one of the "bull-headed men" who appear later (151) and the kind of creature Mr. Beaver was perhaps referring to when he warned the children against things which are only partially human (82).

After reciting her catalogue of evil forces, the Witch declares, "We will fight" (136), and she asks, "Have I not still my wand? Will not their ranks turn into stone even as they come on?" In the final battle, Edmund will succeed in smashing the Witch's wand (178), which has been the key factor in her military supremacy. Edmund's heroic act may be both prompted and assisted by the fact that he overhears the Witch's strategy here and was witness to what she did to the merrymakers earlier (116). At the battle, Edmund will be the only one who has actually seen the wand in action.

Uncertain of what exactly is happening, Edmund finds himself being pushed to have his back up against a tree, where he is tied fast. In a vivid detail here, Lewis describes how it is "so dark in this valley under the dark trees" that Edmund can see very little except for the Witch's bare arms which are "terribly white" (136). The dwarf undoes Edmund's collar and pulls his head back as the Witch sharpens her knife, an action which we hear before we see, preparing the weapon which will also play a role later when she slays Aslan. There her knife will be described as being "made of stone, not of steel" and having "a strange and evil shape" (155). The Witch will also use this special knife in her battle with Peter, who will use the sword he was given (176).

In his description of the Witch's knife here, Lewis uses the same technique of gradual revelation he used earlier in introducing Mr. Beaver and Maugrim, and by doing so he heightens the suspense. Initially Mr. Beaver was described as "something moving among the trees" and then as "something that doesn't want to be seen" (63–4). When Maugrim attacked Susan, Peter saw him first only as "a huge gray beast" and then as possibly a bear or a dog before finally realizing that he was a wolf (131). Here we read, "Edmund heard a strange noise—whizz—whizz—whizz. For a moment he couldn't think what it was" (136). Readers have not seen the stone knife before and so are able to share Edmund's terror of the unknown. Finally Edmund recognizes that the mysterious sound is "a knife being sharpened."

In *The Magician's Nephew*, when the Witch is in London, she will be described as having "a long, bright knife" (Lewis 1994d, 98), presumably one made of steel, not of stone. This suggests that she may have acquired the stone knife, like her wand, not in Charn but during the years she is "away into the North" of Narnia where she is described as "growing stronger in dark Magic" (189).

The forces sent by Aslan arrive in the nick of time to save Edmund. The specific creatures are not identified at first, presumably because we are seeing the world through Edmund's eyes and the night is dark and "confusion" is "all round him" (137). We hear through Edmund's ears "shouts from every direction" and, after "strong arms" untie him, "big, kind voices" that bring comfort. In spite of being given wine to steady him, Edmund passes out.

Two paragraphs later, the members of the rescue party are listed as centaurs, unicorns, deer, and birds (137–8), presumably the eagles Aslan had called on earlier to help (132). In Pauline Baynes's illustration of the rescuers (137), we see two unicorns and two birds—creatures listed in the text. We also see what appears to be a winged horse, a creature mentioned earlier as one of the statues that Edmund saw (96) but not specifically named as having been sent by Aslan, though possibly one of the "dozen or so of the swiftest creatures" referred to in the previous chapter (132). This is not the first time readers have seen a winged horse. In the illustration of Aslan's troops back in chapter twelve (127), Baynes included two winged horses—which had not been specifically mentioned by Lewis there either. Lewis will later give a winged horse prominence in *The Magician's Nephew*, where Fledge helps Digory and Polly bring back the apple seed for the tree which keeps the Witch out of Narnia for many years (1994d, 156). But here in *TLWW* the only winged horse Lewis mentions in the text is one turned to stone at the Witch's castle (96).

In the chaos surrounding the rescue, the Witch and the dwarf appear to have fled. However, after Aslan's forces leave, the reader sees that the Witch has used her power to disguise herself as a boulder and the dwarf as a stump. Readers are told "it was part of her magic that she could make things look like what they aren't"

(138). After this single example, readers will not see the Witch directly use this particular power again, and they might wonder why she did not use it during the final battle—for example, why did the Witch not make the clouds appear like attacking dragons? Readers are told that the knife was knocked out of the Witch's hand, but Aslan's rescue forces apparently leave it behind, as she will later still have it.

The scene shifts to Aslan's camp, where the children wake to the good news that Edmund has been rescued during the night. They find their brother walking with Aslan apart from the rest, having a conversation which neither the readers nor the other children hear, but one we are told "Edmund never forgot" (139). As Aslan presents Edmund, he makes a point of telling the children, "There is no need to talk to him about what is past." Paul Ford has noted, "Respect for the privacy of 'one's own story' is important in Narnia. Lewis himself had an intense sense of privacy, and this theme is apparent in the Chronicles" (1994, 333).

As mentioned earlier, in *The Horse and His Boy* Aslan will reiterate this point, stating, "No one is told any story but their own" (Lewis 1994a, 165, 202). In *The Last Battle*, Aslan will whisper something to Puzzle which causes the donkey's ears to turn down, but then he will add something which makes them perk back up. Readers will be told, "The humans couldn't hear what he had said either time" (Lewis 1994b, 210), leading to a good deal of speculation about the two things Aslan might have said. In *Reflections on the Psalms* Lewis mentions one reason why "no one is told any story but their own." There he notes that "the itch to be a busybody," to know other people's failings, their "stories," can often tend to obscure our awareness that we ourselves are fallen, perhaps in God's eyes "far more so" than the person whose business we are making our own (1986, 69).

In the adventures which follow, none of Edmund's siblings will subvert Aslan's instructions about Edmund by bringing up "what is past," although Edmund, apparently being under no such restriction, will twice do so himself. In *Prince Caspian* when Trumpkin implies that the children will not be much help, Edmund will reply, "I suppose you don't believe we won the Battle of Beruna? Well, you can say what you like about me because I know—" (Lewis 1994e, 103), and then is stopped by Peter, presumably as he was about to make reference to his treachery in *TLWW*. In *The Voyage of the* Dawn Treader, Edmund will make a clearer mention of what is past when he tells Eustace, "Between ourselves, you haven't been as bad as I was on my first trip to Narnia. You were only an ass, but I was a traitor" (Lewis 1994g, 110).

In a single sentence of twenty-four words, we have Edmund's apology and his siblings' acceptance. Readers are told: "Edmund shook hands with each of the others and said to each of them in turn, 'I'm sorry,' and everyone said, 'That's all right'" (139). We find no excuses from Edmund nor any further incrimination from Peter, Susan, or Lucy. Lewis will use an identical exchange in *Prince Caspian* where Susan apologizes to Lucy for not believing her about seeing Aslan. "I can see him now," Susan will say, simply adding, "I'm sorry" (1994e, 153). Lucy will accept Susan's apology with the same three words the siblings say to Edmund here—"that's all right"—words which in both instances fully finish the matter.

Readers might remember that one of Edmund's defining characteristics has been that he "did not like to admit that he had been wrong" (30). And so his willingness and what even seems to be his eagerness here to say "I'm sorry" can be seen as an indication of a major internal change. As mentioned earlier, no apology comes from Peter here for whatever role he may have played in Edmund's downfall. Since this moment would appear to be the perfect place for Peter to say that he too was sorry, perhaps we are meant to understand that he was not truly at fault in any direct way.

The happy reunion lasts for less than a paragraph. Suddenly the Witch's dwarf appears, announcing that "the Queen of Narnia and Empress of the Lone Islands" has requested a guarantee of safe conduct to speak with Aslan (140). When Mr. Beaver objects to her appropriation of the title "Queen of Narnia," Aslan promises him that "all names will soon be restored to the proper owners." Although not made explicit here, the proper owners of the title Queen of Narnia, and thus the direct rivals of the Witch, are Lucy and Susan. In this vein, readers may see a parallel between Lucy's bottle containing the healing cordial and the "small bottle which looked as if it were made of copper" that the Queen used earlier to magically produce Edmund's enchanted warming drink (35). One should also note, though, that just as Lucy is no match for the Witch in physical power, Lucy's healing cordial is not powerful enough to undo the power of the Witch's wand.

In *Prince Caspian*, Peter will refer to himself not only as "High King over all Kings in Narnia" but also as "Emperor of the Lone Islands" (Lewis 1994e, 176–7). However, except for the Witch's claim to it here, the latter title of Emperor or Empress of the Lone Islands is not mentioned again in *TLWW*. In later books Lewis will provide more details about this separate region. The *Dawn Treader* will sail to the Lone Islands, and the narrator will comment, "By the way I have never yet heard how these remote islands became attached to the crown of Narnia; if I ever do, and if the story is at all interesting, I may put it in some other book" (Lewis 1994g, 98). In *The Last Battle*, Lewis keeps his promise as Jewel will tell the story of King Gale, the ruler ninth in descent after King Frank. Early in Narnia's history, Gale delivered the Lone Islanders from a dragon and in return was given the Lone Islands "to be part of the royal lands of Narnia forever" (1994b, 100).

In this exchange, Lewis has Aslan twice refer to the Witch's dwarf as "Son of Earth" (139–140), highlighting a distinction between dwarfs and humans and further emphasizing the fact that except for Maugrim, the Witch's forces are not named and have little individuality. Perhaps Lewis, in this use of *Earth* here, was already thinking that his dwarfs, like Tolkien's, would be known for their mining, as he later portrayed them to be (Lewis 1994f, 220). Dwarfs in Narnia, though humanlike in many ways, including the ability to mate with humans (Lewis 1994e, 52), are not "Sons of Adam" and will always be subordinate to them, like the talking animals.

As the Witch and Aslan converse, the Witch is not able to look Aslan "exactly in his eyes" (141). Readers might remember Mr. Beaver's earlier response to Edmund's question about whether the Witch would turn Aslan into stone: "If she can stand on her two feet and look him in the face it'll be the most she can do and more than I expect of her" (79). Paul Ford has pointed out a stark difference between the two rulers here: "In Aslan's parlay with the Witch, Lewis intends to contrast his serenity with her villainy: his golden face, her death-white face; his calm strength, her agitation; his looking her in the face, her avoiding eye contact" (1994, 20). Readers are told, "The only two people present who seemed to be quite at their ease were Aslan and the Witch herself" (141). Perhaps Lewis's use of *seemed* here should be taken literally—perhaps the Witch only seems to be at her ease here, as she displays fear in her interaction with Aslan at other times (144, 151).

The discussion of the Deep Magic which follows leaves several questions unanswered, and perhaps Lewis intended to make this issue more suggestive than explicit, as might be appropriate for a fairy tale. When Aslan suggests that Edmund's offence was not against the Queen, is he suggesting the possibility that Edmund might have gone unpunished? If the rules of Deep Magic were established by the Emperor-Beyond-the-Sea, and if without a kill all of Narnia would have been overturned, why does Aslan take the stance of having forgotten the Deep Magic, allowing it to come up only when the Witch raises the point? If the Witch had not pursued Edmund, could Aslan simply have forgiven him, as he appeared to do?

These are questions which the story leaves open for speculation. All that readers know is that when Susan speaks up for her younger brother, asking if there is something Aslan can do to work against the decree, Aslan frowns at her and replies in a way that prevents any further discussion, "Work against the Emperor's Magic?" (142).

On the topic of Deep Magic, even Paul Ford has offered little further clarification. Ford notes that Deep Magic is "a complex term," one used by the White Witch and well-known to Aslan, "connoting the demands of justice" (1994, 132). Since, as we learn, it was something put into Narnia at its beginning, Ford argues that "it is not eternal justice as we understand it, but the effects of justice in a created world." Donald Glover observes that later in *TLWW*, "the Deeper Magic of mercy" will triumph over "the Deep Magic of the law of justice" (1981, 142).

As will be explored later in the discussion of chapter fifteen, Lewis did not intend for Aslan to be an allegory for Jesus. However, in *TLWW* Aslan is certainly a Christ-figure in much the same way that Gandalf is a Christ-figure in *The Lord of the Rings*. Both characters, like Christ, sacrifice their lives so that others may live. So with this caveat—that Aslan is *not* an allegory for Jesus—to be discussed further later, we might take a look at what Lewis has written about Christ's atonement to see if it can shed some light on the issue of Deep Magic here in *TLWW*.

In *Mere Christianity* Lewis writes, "We are told that Christ was killed for us, that His death washed out our sins, and that by dying He disabled death itself" (1996c, 59). If we substitute *Aslan* for *Christ* and *Edmund* for *us*, we would have a nearly perfect statement of what takes place in *TLWW*. Lewis never makes explicit how the Deep Magic, or the Deeper Magic found later in the novel, works. Again in *Mere Christianity* Lewis argues, "A man can accept what Christ has done without knowing how it works."

Having said this, if the Emperor is inclined to forgive Edmund's treachery, what purpose is found in requiring Aslan to substitute his life? Another passage from Lewis's nonfiction may provide further understanding about the agreement that Aslan secretly makes here to give his life in exchange for Edmund's and so to fulfill the requirement of the Emperor-Beyond-the-Sea. In *Mere Christianity* Lewis addresses the issue of "our being let off because Christ had volunteered to bear a punishment instead of us" (1996c, 59). As Lewis explains: "If God was prepared to let us off, why on earth did He not do so? And what possible point could there be in punishing an innocent person instead? None at all that I can see, if you are thinking of punishment in the police-court sense. On the other hand if you think of a debt, there is plenty of point in a person who has some assets paying it on behalf of someone who has not."

In the end, Lewis never intends for us to fully understand the mechanism behind the Emperor's Deep Magic. His intention once again to suggest rather than to state can be seen in the fact that in

The Magician's Nephew Lewis will choose not to mention the topic of Deep Magic, even though, as this chapter's title states, it comes "from the Dawn of Time" and as we are told was "put into Narnia at the very beginning" (1994d, 142–3) and so would have been created during the time period covered in that story.

Lewis's descriptive powers are in finest form in the short scene where Aslan and the Witch talk by themselves. He achieves a powerful result from very sparse details (143–4). Lucy says, "Oh Edmund!" and begins to cry. Peter looks out to the sea. The Beavers bow their heads and hold paws. The centaurs stamp uneasily. The silence grows and so does the tension until, as the narrator tells us, "You noticed even small sounds like a bumble-bee flying past, or the birds in the forest down below them, or the wind rustling the leaves." Finally, just as the waiting is about to become unbearable, Aslan tells everyone that they can come back because he has "settled the matter" and that the Witch has renounced her claim on Edmund's "blood."

How exactly did Aslan settle Edmund's debt while still upholding the Emperor's Deep Magic? At this point neither the children nor readers have any idea, although the Witch's final question indicates that Aslan has made her some kind of "promise" (144). Aslan answers her question about how she can be sure he will keep this promise with a loud roar, "half-rising" from a throne which Lewis seems to have neglected to first put him on. Lewis ends the chapter with a final view of the Witch in a panic as she "picked up her skirts and fairly ran for her life."

FOURTEEN

The Triumph of the Witch

Lewis begins chapter fourteen by having Aslan de-clare, "We must move from this place at once, it will be wanted for other purposes" (145), but Aslan will say no more about what these other purposes are. This adds to the mystery of the secret agreement made with the Witch at the end of the preceding chapter. As readers later learn, the area around the Stone Table will be needed for Aslan's sacrificial death that evening to release Edmund from the Witch's claim on his life. We read that among Aslan's forces "everyone was dying to ask him how he had arranged matters with the Witch," but because of his "stern face" and the deafening roar he made at the departing Witch, no one dares. At this point in the story, Lewis gives no hint of what the deal was, of why they must move, or of what is to come other than the sadness which begins to color Aslan's mood and also, if readers remember, Aslan's initial response to Lucy's request to help Edmund: "All shall be done, but it may be harder than you think" (129).

In the previous chapter, Edmund and Aslan were portrayed as walking together "in the dewy grass" (139). Now before they break camp, Aslan's troops take a meal together "in the open air on the hill-top," and Lewis adds the realistic note that "the sun had got strong by now and dried the grass" (145). By two o'clock they have finished packing up and are on their way. Aslan's next words are instructions to Peter, and he begins them by saying, "As soon as she has finished her business in these parts. . . ." Here we have another vague allusion to the deal that Aslan has made. Lewis uses these veiled hints to increase our anticipation of something to come.

Careful readers will notice that Aslan does not speak with complete confidence here about the movements of the Witch and her army. He says only that they will "almost certainly" fall back to her House (145), and this lack of certitude suggests that Aslan does not have any special powers to foresee the future, only the normal predictive powers any experienced war leader might have, at least in this instance.

In fact, in this prediction Aslan seems to have even less than a normal leader's power to foresee what will happen, as he is proven to be completely wrong. After the Witch finishes her "business" at the Stone Table—after she finishes killing him—she does not fall back to her house to prepare for a siege but does the exact opposite, immediately calling upon her troops to follow her into battle (156). Given the military superiority she appears to have, an obvious dominance which is reflected in the way that the battle goes until Aslan's arrival (176), it is unclear exactly why Aslan would have predicted here that the Witch would retreat to her castle or why he would have suggested that Peter should attempt to engage her army—unless, of course, we assume that Aslan somehow thought he would very soon be rejoining the combat. The resurrected Aslan's immediate rush to the castle to release the stone prisoners and their immediate journey to the battle might support this idea.

Later in the Chronicles Aslan makes predictions which do come true, and this suggests that he does have something more than ordinary knowledge about the future, something like omniscience, at least in those cases. In *The Magician's Nephew* Aslan correctly foresees that the Witch "will come back to Narnia again" (Lewis 1994d, 154). He also foretells that King Frank and Queen Helen will be "father and mother to many kings that shall be in Narnia and the Isles of Archenland" (187). Perhaps the clearest instance of Aslan having extraordinary knowledge will occur in *The Silver Chair* where he is able to correctly predict four future events involving the signs that Jill is to memorize (Lewis 1994f, 25).

Aslan outlines battle plans for the next day with Peter, giving one plan if Peter is able to catch the Witch in the woods and one plan for assaulting her at the castle. Finally Peter asks what readers themselves have been wondering—whether Aslan himself is going to be at these battles.

In Aslan's response "I can give you no promise of that" (146), a number of issues are raised. Does Aslan know if he is going to come back to life? That is to say, at this point is he aware of the Deeper Magic which says that "when a willing victim who had committed no treachery was killed in a traitor's stead, the Table would crack and Death itself would start working backward" (163)? And if Aslan is aware of this Deeper Magic, does he know exactly what the process will be like and when he might return? About this issue Paul Ford has written:

> The fact that the Lion makes two plans with Peter for the course of the coming battle with the Witch and her forces and that he cannot guarantee to Peter that he will assist Peter in the battle is an allusion to the "humanness" of the Lion. Lewis is aligning Aslan with what some Christian theologians believe of Christ in his earthly life: that he did not, as man, know the future, that he did not see the resurrection on the other side of his death, and that, therefore, he had to suffer and die like all of his fellow humans, trusting that his Father had a plan even for dying. (1994, 21)

Taking a somewhat different approach, Colin Manlove has proposed that at this point in the story Aslan *knows* he will return to life but perhaps cannot *feel* this truth (1987, 136).

When he later rescues the statues at the Witch's castle, Aslan will ask the other animals "who are good with their noses" to help "us lions to smell out where the battle is" (174). The second lion will remark on Aslan's use of the phrase "us lions," saying, "Did you hear what he said? *Us Lions*. That means him and me." Throughout the Chronicles, Aslan is certainly something more than a real lion, but at the same time, he is always meant to be a real lion, and so he must retain the traits and qualities of a real lion. One of these traits, arguably, would be at least some of the limitations of what a real lion might and might not know.

Lewis was aware of a similar question raised about Christ's nature, a topic known as the *kenosis* of Christ, a term meaning *to empty* (see Phil. 2:7). Christ was at all times a man and yet at all times the Son of God, so to what extent did Christ need to "empty himself" of certain supernatural qualities in order to be a man? In *The Problem of Pain*, Lewis in describing Christ's nature suggests, "It might be argued that when He emptied Himself of His glory He also humbled Himself to share, as man, the current superstitions of His time. And I certainly think that Christ, in the flesh, was not omniscient—if only because a human brain could not, presumably, be the vehicle of omniscient consciousness" (1996h, 119–20).

In the end, what we can say is that in *TLWW* Lewis does not intend to make clear exactly what Aslan knows beforehand about his possible return to life. As mentioned earlier, Lewis sometimes sought in his writing to suggest rather than to state. When Aslan tells Peter, "I can give you no promise," readers may hear two suggestions: that Aslan is not certain he will return to life, but neither is he certain he will remain dead. Alternatively, readers may conclude that Aslan knows what will happen but cannot tell Peter, possibly because Peter is meant to act without knowing for certain what the outcome will be, a way of further developing his courage and confidence.

When Aslan gives orders to stop on the near side of the Fords of Beruna, Peter wonders if it would not be better to camp on the far side in case the Witch decides to attack that night. Aslan replies, "No. She will not make an attack tonight" (147), providing another hint that he knows something about the Witch's immediate plans that we do not. Peter's question here almost seems to ignore Aslan's earlier statement to him that the Witch "will almost certainly fall back to her House and prepare for a siege." Perhaps his phrasing of the question about the possibility of a "night attack *or anything*" is Peter's attempt to avoid seeming like he is contradicting Aslan, or perhaps he is still wondering what Aslan might have meant by "as soon as she has finished her business in these parts."

As the children go to bed after a quiet and moody supper, we find one of the rare instances where Lewis chooses to view the scene from Susan's perspective. Two other times Lewis does this are during the conversation Susan and Peter have with the Professor (48) and briefly during the mention of Aslan's name (68). Here Lewis writes, "This feeling affected Susan so much that she couldn't get to sleep when she went to bed. And after she had lain counting sheep and turning over and over she heard Lucy give a long sigh and turn over just beside her in the darkness" (147). While Lewis will often experience events through a specific child, typically this will be Lucy. Two significant instances of seeing the world through Lucy's perspective occur during the nighttime march with the Beavers (103) and at the arrival at the battle (175).

So why choose Susan in this scene when Lucy might have been the logical choice? What effect does choosing Susan's perspective here have? One answer may be that although Lewis gives Lucy the prominent position throughout the novel, from his first decision to make this a story about "four children whose names were Peter, Susan, Edmund, and Lucy" (3), he had the responsibility to bring each of them to life. Of the four children, Susan has been given the least development so far, and when the opportunity came up to show more of her character, Lewis took it. A second answer may have to do with a direction Lewis will go in the book's final chapter. There Susan as an adult queen will be known as "Susan the Gentle" (184). If she is going to be known by her gentleness later, to be realistic we need to see some indication of it earlier, as we do here.

Both sisters admit to feeling "a most horrible feeling—as if something were hanging over us" (147). Lucy worries that "something dreadful" is going to happen to Aslan or that he is going to do something dreadful (148), and both intuitions are accurate. Susan comments that "there's been something wrong with him all afternoon." But then—as she has been worried about her personal safety since the start—Susan is afraid that Aslan may be "stealing away" and leaving them. Fears about safety are Susan's besetting problem in *TLWW*, and in *Prince Caspian* this problem continues, as Aslan himself will point out to her, "You have listened to your fears, child" (Lewis 1994e, 153–4).

Lucy suggests that they go outside and "have a look around" in the hope they might see Aslan (148). Susan agrees but with a comment that indicates she does not have quite as much compassion as Lucy, saying, "We might just as well be doing that as lying awake here." The concern the girls share turns out to be valid, for on the far side of the camp they see Aslan slowly and sadly walking away into the woods, retracing the same route they took earlier that day back to the Stone Table.

When Aslan reaches a clearing and notices them, Susan, not Lucy, is the one who takes the initiative and asks if they can come with him (149). As their journey continues, Lucy asks what is wrong and Susan asks Aslan if he is ill. Aslan replies that he is not ill but is sad and lonely, and he asks the sisters to lay their hands on his mane so he can feel their presence. This sad side of Aslan, though a very real aspect of his character, is seen rarely in the Chronicles. Earlier in *TLWW* when Aslan told Lucy, "It may be harder than you think," she noticed that he "looked sad" (129), but "the next minute that expression was gone." At the end of *The Silver Chair* Jill and Eustace will take a similar walk with Aslan to a stream where King Caspian lies dead. There we read, "All three stood and wept. Even the Lion wept: great Lion-tears, each tear more precious than the Earth would be if it was a single solid diamond" (Lewis 1994f, 237–8).

In *The Magician's Nephew* we find another instance where this sad side of Aslan is revealed. As Digory expresses his worries for his ill mother, suddenly he will look up at Aslan, and readers are told:

What he saw surprised him as much as anything in his whole life. For the tawny face was bent down near his own and (wonder of wonders) great shining tears stood in the Lion's eyes. They were such big, bright tears compared with Digory's own that for a moment he felt as if the Lion must really be sorrier about his Mother than he was himself. (Lewis 1994d, 154)

Next we learn that Lucy and Susan "did . . . what they had longed to do ever since they met him—buried their cold hands in the beautiful sea of fur and stroked it and, so doing, walked with him" (150). First mentioned in the prophecy at the Beavers' (79), Aslan's mane has a prominence throughout the Chronicles. Here in *TLWW* the sisters stroke Aslan's fur to comfort him. In *Prince Caspian* Lucy will bury her head in Aslan's mane, but this time it is a comfort to her, as we read, "There must have been magic in his mane. She could feel lion-strength going into her" (143).

In *The Horse and His Boy*, Shasta is comforted twice by Aslan through his fur. The first time, Aslan will appear as a cat which sleeps next to Shasta during the cold and lonely desert night. Lewis writes, "And he at once lay down again, back to back with the cat. . . . The warmth from it spread all over him" (1994a, 90). Later, after Shasta arrives in Narnia, Aslan will appear to him again, this time in a way that inspires awe. Readers will be told, "The High King above all kings stooped toward him. Its mane, and some strange and solemn perfume that hung about the mane, was all round him" (166). Later in *TLWW* after Aslan returns to life, Susan will be concerned that Aslan is a ghost. She will be reassured by the warmth of Aslan's breath and also by "a rich sort of smell that seemed to hang about his hair" (162).

One of the first things readers were told about Lucy was that she liked nothing so much "as the smell and feel of fur" (7), and that as soon as she first stepped into the wardrobe, she "rubbed her face against" the furs hanging there. Here as Lucy buries her hands into Aslan's fur, she can be seen as fulfilling her earlier desire—but magnified by the fact that the fur is on a living creature, one whom she dearly loves. Lewis once wrote in a letter about the topic of furs, stating, "I like them *on* the beasts of course" (1967, 46). At the end of *The Voyage of the* Dawn Treader, readers will find a scene with some parallels to this one in *TLWW*. As Reepicheep the mouse prepares to leave, we read that Lucy "for the first and last time, did what she had always wanted to do, taking him in her arms and caressing him" (Lewis 1994g, 244).

As Aslan leaves the two girls at the last tree and prepares to go on to the Stone Table alone, Lewis is careful to add a realistic touch, telling us that the tree "was one that had some bushes about it" (150) so that we are convinced that Lucy and Susan will not be seen by the Witch's forces. Lucy and Susan's presence is essential to Lewis's description of Aslan's suffering and death because we will see the events which unfold through the girls' eyes. In this way we will also come to share their horror and grief.

The inventory of evil creatures who are waiting around the Stone Table closely resembles the catalogue of the forces the Witch called upon in the previous chapter (136). Some names from the earlier list—giants, ghouls, boggles, specters, and people of the toadstools—are missing here (151), and several new ones have been added, including three beings which also appear in *The Lord of the Rings*. The Wraiths which Lewis lists here have their counterpart in Tolkien's Ringwraiths, who are the disembodied spirits of former men. Lewis spells *Wooses* slightly differently than Tolkien. In *The Return of the King* Elfhelm offers Merry this description: "You hear the Woses, the Wild Men of the Woods: thus they talk together from afar. They still haunt Druadan Forest, it is said. Remnants of an older time they be, living few and secretly, wild and wary as the beasts. . . . Let us be thankful that they are not hunting us: for they use poisoned arrows, it is said, and they are woodcrafty beyond compare" (Tolkien 1994c, 813). Tolkien's Woses are not the evil creatures we find here in *TLWW*. While not full allies of the forces of good, the Woses in Middle-earth are definitely enemies of Sauron and offer to aid the Rohirrim, guiding Theoden's troops by secret paths to Minas Tirith, which may raise the question of whether there might be some Wooses in Narnia who are not bad.

Finally, Paul Ford has noted that the Orknies mentioned here in *TLWW* are also mentioned in line 112 of *Beowulf* and that here Lewis "is content to allude to them in order to add an atmosphere of horror surrounding Aslan's death" (Ford 1994, 306). Ford also notes that with Lewis's Orknies, "the allusion to Tolkien's *orcs* is inescapable."

Partway through the list of the Witch's troops, the narrator jumps in to say that he will name the remaining creatures but will not describe them, claiming, "If I did the grown-ups would probably not let you read this book" (151). Lewis is half-joking but half-serious here. He was aware of critics who thought stories for children should never be frightening. While he was sympathetic to their concerns, he did not agree with their arguments. In his essay "On Three Ways of Writing for Children," Lewis discussed the need for courageous knights in stories for young people:

> A far more serious attack on the fairy tale as children's literature comes from those who do not wish children to be frightened. I suffered too much from night-fears myself in childhood to undervalue this objection. I would not wish to heat the fires of that private hell for any child. On the other hand, none of my fears came from fairy tales. . . . Since it is so likely that [children] will meet cruel enemies, let them at least have heard of brave knights and heroic courage. . . . Let there be wicked kings and beheadings, battles and dungeons, giants and dragons, and let villains be soundly killed at the end of the book. Nothing will persuade me that this causes an ordinary child any kind of degree of fear beyond what it wants, and needs, to feel. (1982e, 39–40)

Paul Ford has observed that "one of the chief objections to the Chronicles is their violence" (1994, 434). He argues that Lewis took the position "that life is violent, and to deny that would be wrong." Ford then cites G. K. Chesterton, who "anticipates" Lewis's position and wrote:

> A lady has written me an earnest letter saying that fairy tales ought not to be taught to children even if they are true. She says it is

cruel to tell children fairy tales, because it frightens them. . . . All this kind of talk is based on that complete forgetting what a child is like. . . . Exactly what the fairy tale does is this: it accustoms [the child] for a series of clear pictures to the idea that these limitless terrors have a limit, that these shapeless enemies have enemies, that these strong enemies of man have enemies in the knights of God, that there is something in the universe more mystical than darkness, and stronger than fear. (Ford 1994, 454)

In a letter written shortly after the publication of *TLWW*, Lewis noted one kind of reaction to the book, stating, "A number of mothers, and still more, school mistresses, have decided that it is likely to frighten children, so it is not selling very well. But the real children like it, and I am astonished how some *very* young ones seem to understand it. I think it frightens some adults, but very few children" (1993, 406).

The question of whether *TLWW* frightens children and, if so, whether it frightens them in a bad way may depend more on the specific child. Some people, given the relatively restrained violence in *TLWW* compared to other types of graphic images that young people are now exposed to, may wonder what all the fuss was about.

Aslan was first seen in *TLWW* in the center of "a crowd of creatures who had grouped themselves round him in the shape of a half-moon" (126). Lewis provides a parallel setting for the Witch "right in the middle" of the creatures summoned by the second wolf (151). As Aslan approaches the Stone Table, the Witch is temporarily "struck with fear" until she realizes that he has come to keep his bargain, that he is going to be a "willing victim" (163). Four great centaurs were described as standing near Aslan in his first appearance (126). Here their counterparts among the Witch's forces are four "grinning and leering" hags who, with the help of evil dwarfs and apes, rush in to bind Aslan (151). Four hags, presumably these same four, will also be mentioned as standing at the corners of the Stone Table, holding four torches during the execution (154). Since hags are the first creatures to attack Aslan here, they will perhaps fittingly be one example of "foul brood" specifically mentioned as being "stamped out" in the final chapter (183). However, they are apparently not completely stamped out, as Lewis will have one appear in *Prince Caspian* (1994e, 171). If readers look closely at Baynes's illustration (152), they can find at least three of the hags pulling on the rope which binds Aslan.

The contrast between the two leaders and their followers, between the stately serenity which encircled Aslan and the menacing chaos which surrounds the Witch, is clearly depicted in the two corresponding illustrations which Baynes provides (127, 152). Colin Manlove has made this observation about the Witch: "She can only reduce things—Narnia to stasis, the rational creatures of Narnia to stone, Aslan to a shorn cat" (1993, 40). And so after having Aslan tied up, the Witch orders his mane to be shaved off. This causes him to seem to Lucy at first "all small and different" but, paradoxically, after the first shock is over, "braver, and more beautiful, and more patient than ever" (153–4). This shaving of Aslan serves no real purpose in the death besides humiliation and may remind readers of Edmund's drawing a mustache on the stone lion he thought was Aslan and "jeering at it" (96).

After binding and shaving, the third order given by the Witch is to muzzle Aslan. During all the insults, Aslan has not moved. Now the forces of the Witch complete their abuse by "kicking him, hitting him, spitting on him, jeering at him" (154). Finally the Witch's "rabble" has had enough and lifts Aslan upon the Stone Table. Readers are told that he is "so huge that even when they got him there it took all their efforts to hoist him," raising the question of just how big Aslan really is.

Besides being referred to twice in this scene as huge (151, 154), we find no definitive answer of whether Aslan is larger than a normal lion at this point before his death. When Aslan reappears to the girls after his death, he will be described as "larger than they had seen him before" (162). In Pauline Baynes's drawing of him next to the regular lion in chapter sixteen, an illustration which Lewis approved of, the resurrected Aslan appears slightly larger than the other lion (170). In *Prince Caspian* one of the first things Lucy will say to Aslan is "You're bigger" (Lewis 1994e, 141), and it will be his nature to appear bigger as characters themselves grow. In *The Voyage of the* Dawn Treader, Aslan will appear to everyone in a vision as "the hugest lion that human eyes have ever seen," although afterwards Lucy will not be able to decide if he was "the size of an elephant" or "the size of a cart-horse" (Lewis 1994g, 128). When Aslan appears to Shasta, who is on horseback, he will be described as being "taller than the horse" (Lewis 1994a, 166).

In the same way that Lewis leaves Aslan's exact size somewhat vague, he is also content to be imprecise about the exact dimensions of the Stone Table. After Aslan's death, we are told that Lucy and Susan are able to kiss his face and stroke his fur as they kneel in the grass (157), which suggests that while the top must be wide and deep enough to accommodate Aslan's great bulk, the table is not particularly high, just a "great grim slab of gray stone" set on four upright stones which are not particularly tall (125). Baynes's illustration of the broken table would fit this description (162).

Lewis describes the "great crowd of people" as "standing all round" the Stone Table (150) and the Witch as being "right in the middle," standing "by the Table" (151). Some readers, in looking at Baynes's illustration of the taunting of Aslan (152), may believe that the Witch is shown actually standing on top of the Stone Table, which in the picture appears long enough to hold her and seven of her followers and tall enough to allow others to stand underneath.

After even further "tying and tightening of cords" (154), the Witch goes through the same ritual she began with Edmund the day before, first baring her arms and then whetting her knife, which has a mysterious and unexplained "strange and evil shape" (155). At the end of *The Voyage of the* Dawn Treader, Lucy will come upon this same knife again at Aslan's table, where it has been brought "to be kept in honor while the world lasts" (Lewis 1994g, 201). As Ford comments, "like the cross of Christ, the ugly instrument of Aslan's death has become a revered symbol of the atonement" (1994, 394). The two Baynes's illustrations which show the Witch's knife do not shed any light on what might be strange about its shape other than it appearing to be long and thin (152, 176), a shape associated with the Witch from the start.

A number of critics have outlined the biblical parallels found in this chapter (Ford 1994, 21; Hooper 1996, 429–38; Sammons 1979, 127–9). Joe Christopher writes, "Aslan's sadness on the afternoon before his death suggests Christ's prayer that the cup may pass from Him; the binding, shaving, and vilifying of Aslan, the arrest, beating, and mocking of Christ" (1987, 113). However, as Colin Manlove has noted, "If we then proceed to see similarities between Aslan's sacrifice and that of Christ in our world, we at once see that they are also quite different" (1993, 39). For example, as Manlove observes, "The special sordid intimacy of Aslan's stabbing by the Witch is quite different from Christ's more solitary and drawn-out bodily pain on the cross."

The Witch's face is "working and twitching with passion," in contrast to Aslan's face which readers are told "looked up at the sky, still quiet, neither angry nor afraid, but a little sad" (155). As Manlove has suggested, "Aslan finds dying no easy matter: the choice is hard, the pain of the soul very real, the shame and indignity very great" (1987, 136). Finally, just before the final blow, the Witch taunts Aslan, saying, "When you are dead what will prevent me from killing him as well?" And she concludes, "You have lost your own life and you have not saved his." Besides the Witch's comments here, the fact that Aslan is dying in the very spot the Witch would have preferred to kill Edmund (135) reinforces the fact that Aslan is giving his life in exchange for Edmund's.

Here in *TLWW* Aslan is clearly vulnerable, able to be hurt and certainly able to be killed. By contrast, in *The Magician's Nephew* when Lewis will have the Witch hit Aslan with an iron bar, he seems to be completely unaffected (1994d, 116). A few pages later, Digory will say to his uncle, "Do you still think *that* Lion could be killed by a gun? He didn't mind the iron bar much" (118), which raises the question of whether Aslan might be omnipotent generally but here *allows* himself to be killed, somewhat in the same manner as Christ may have done. As the stroke comes down, Lucy and Susan hide their eyes, and so readers do not see "the actual moment of the killing" (155). Besides seeing what the sisters see, readers also feel what they feel. As the chapter closes, we share the girls' despair, for neither we nor they have any real reason to not believe the Witch's final words.

FIFTEEN

Deeper Magic from Before the Dawn of Time

Lewis opens chapter fifteen with the girls still hiding in the bushes, their hands over their faces, fearful of what is to come. Lewis uses this position, where they cannot see, to highlight the perceptions from their other senses. They hear the Witch calling her forces to follow her into battle (156). They feel something like "a cold wind" as the specters go by and sense "the ground shake beneath them" as the minotaurs gallop past. Overhead is the sound of "a flurry of foul wings."

The Witch summons her army "to crush the human vermin" and "the traitors" (156), and here Lewis intends us to see the thinness of the vocabulary she uses to describe those who oppose her. All she seems to be able to do is label them as vermin or traitors over and over. Mr. Tumnus was accused in the note left at his house of "High Treason" (58), a crime which simply means he would not obey the Witch's commands. Earlier the Witch used the term "vermin" to label the partygoers that she then turned to stone (115). Here the Witch uses the term "traitors" to describe the Narnians who have joined Aslan, since from her way of seeing things they have abandoned their rightful ruler. Readers may recall that she also called Edmund a traitor (141). Never reluctant to bend the truth in whatever manner suits her, the Witch wants to have it both ways. She claims here that the members of Aslan's army are traitors because they do not obey her and also claimed that Edmund, in obeying her, was a traitor to his siblings.

In her final words before departing, the Witch lets the sisters and the readers know for certain that Aslan now "lies dead" (156). As the Witch's "vile rabble" races off to find and destroy Aslan's army, they go "right past" the girls' hiding place. Pauline Baynes's picture depicting this scene—one of her least clear drawings, presumably to evoke the darkness and the chaos of the setting—seems to show a specter, a minotaur, a vulture, and a giant bat passing near to a girl who is very hard to see as she crouches by a bush, someone we may assume is supposed to be Susan because of her dark hair (157). However, one should note that in most of the drawings of the two sisters in *TLWW*, Baynes typically does not make Lucy's blond hair look any different from Susan's black (71, 75, 83, 188). The two exceptions where the girls' hair is clearly different are in the illustration of the mice nibbling at Aslan's cords (159) and in the drawing of the sisters as older Queens hunting the White Stag (185).

While Donald Glover has suggested that Lewis's descriptive powers are at their height in the passages where winter changes into spring (1981, 141), perhaps no descriptive scene in all the Chronicles is done better than the one which follows the departure of the Witch's army. First, Lewis gives us vivid insight into the shock of "sadness and shame and horror" which fills the girls by simply telling us that they "hardly thought of" the terrifying horde as it rushes past them (156–7). Next Lewis offers his characteristic concrete details of familiar images, details which will contrast with the fantasy elements set against them: once again the wood is silent, the moon is getting low, and thick clouds pass across it as the girls get up and see "the Lion lying dead in his bonds." The grass is wet as they kneel. His face is cold as they kiss it. They stroke Aslan's fur, or "what is left of it," and then we are told that they "cried till they could cry no more." Finally the sisters simply look at each other and hold each other's hands "for mere loneliness" and cry again, and then again are silent. In a certain type of story for young people, pain, if it occurs, does not hurt very much. *TLWW* is not that type of story.

Lucy suggests that they try to remove the muzzle. After "a lot of working at it" (158), the sisters are finally able to get it off, and then they break into tears once again. The girls try to wipe away "the blood and the foam." Finally after all these powerful, specific details—and only after them—Lewis turns to the special voice of the first person narrator to say, "It was all more lonely and hopeless and horrid than I know how to describe." After the girls make a brief but unsuccessful attempt, initiated by Susan, to untie the cords, the voice of the narrator returns for a longer comment, and its ring of authenticity assures us that Lewis himself was well acquainted with the kind of grief described. Lewis as narrator says, "I hope no one who reads this book has been quite as miserable as Susan and Lucy were that night; but if you have been—if you've been up all night and cried till you have no more tears left in you—you will know that there comes in the end a sort of quietness. You feel as if nothing was ever going to happen again."

Lewis may have been drawing from memories of his own grief as a young boy following the death of his mother. Of that time in his life, he wrote, "With my mother's death all settled happiness, all that was tranquil and reliable, disappeared from my life. . . . It was sea and islands now; the great continent had sunk like Atlantis" (1955, 21). In 1960, ten years after *TLWW* appeared, Lewis would revisit these feelings again following the death of his wife, Joy Gresham, and would find them just as painful. In describing this loss in *A Grief Observed*, Lewis would begin with the famous opening statement: "No one ever told me that grief felt so like fear" (1961a, 19).

It seems like "hours and hours" to the girls before not light but the promise of light begins to grow in the eastern sky (158). Readers are told that all this time the sisters have been getting "colder and colder," possibly due to the normal chill which comes before dawn but also perhaps a hint that with Aslan now dead the Witch's eternal winter may be creeping back into Narnia. The suggestion that winter may be returning to Narnia here may not be too far-fetched. In chapter thirteen when the Witch first came over to the Stone Table to speak with Aslan, readers were told, "Though it was bright sunshine everyone felt suddenly cold" (141).

Lucy becomes aware of "some tiny movement" in the grass (158), but stricken by grief, she takes no interest in it, thinking, "What did it matter? Nothing mattered now!" The movement grows more pronounced and turns out to be a troupe of mice climbing the upright pillars of the Stone Table. Susan responds with her characteristic "ugh" (159), the same response she had to the cold when they first left the wardrobe what now seems like much more than three days before (55). She wants to shoo the mice away, but Lucy is quick to see that they are gnawing at the ropes the girls had been unable to loosen.

While it is not made explicit in *TLWW*, these are regular, non-talking mice. We learn elsewhere that Aslan did not make any talking mice at the creation of Narnia. Near the end of *Prince Caspian* we learn that Aslan later will give mice the gift of speech in reward for their assistance here in this scene. In *Prince Caspian* when Aslan decides to grant Reepicheep's wish to have his tail restored, he will tell the mouse that he does so, "Not for the sake of your dignity, Reepicheep, but for the love that is between you and your people, and still more for the kindness your people showed me long ago when you ate away the cords that bound me on the Stone Table (and it was then, though you have long forgotten it, that you began to be *Talking* Mice)" (Lewis 1994e, 209). Just as with the robin who appeared early after the children's first entrance into Narnia, these mice, while not being able to talk, seem to understand more than ordinary animals would. A number of years earlier, Lewis had included a delightful scene with mice in *That Hideous Strength*, one where Jane Studdock shares Susan's revulsion before Ransom helps her to see them from a different perspective (2003, 146–7).

The dawn breaks gradually upon the two grief-stricken sisters, much as spring progressively arrived. As the girls walk back and forth to warm themselves, Lewis adds more details to the scene. The birds begin to sing, the last star of the night fades, and far off in the distance the pale sea is visible. The dawn's stillness is suddenly shattered by "a great cracking, deafening noise as if a giant had broken a giant's plate" (161). "What's that?" Lucy and the readers wonder together, but as this will be the most climactic scene in the novel, Lewis will answer this question somewhat gradually.

Susan is afraid to turn around, but Lucy worries, "They're doing something worse to *Him*" (161). Immediately—in what is either great courage or great rashness, given who or what might be waiting there—Lucy turns, pulling Susan with her. Next Lewis tells us, "The rising of the sun had made everything look so different—all the colors and shadows were changed—that for a moment they did not see the important thing. Then they did." The Stone Table has been broken in two pieces and Aslan's body is missing.

Lucy complains that someone has done something with the body, and Susan wants to know who has done it and if it is more magic. Behind them, "a great voice" answers (162), "Yes! It is more magic." The girls turn, and Aslan is standing before them, "shining in the sunrise," looking larger than before and shaking his golden mane which has been restored.

With Lucy's comment about Aslan's missing body and the resurrection which follows, readers can find parallels with the story of Christ found in the New Testament. However, before looking at the areas of comparison between Christ and Aslan, note again that these two figures can also be seen as being unlike in a number of significant ways. For example, some readers may agree with Colin Manlove that "Aslan's voluntary death as a substitute for Edmund is not the same as Christ's less-chosen Crucifixion" (1993, 39), since Aslan is specifically portrayed as "a willing victim" (163), whereas Christ requested that he not have to die, praying, "Father, if you are willing, take this cup from me; yet not my will, but yours be done" (Luke 22:42). Having said this, other readers may disagree with Manlove's distinction because (1) Christ, though preferring not to die, ultimately fully accepted his sacrificial death, and (2) Aslan, though he was a willing victim, certainly was saddened by the fact of his upcoming death.

Another area of possible difference between the two figures is that throughout the Chronicles, Aslan never claims equal status with the Emperor as Christ did with God, though of course it might be argued that nothing he says ever specifically excludes this equal status either. Yet a third area of difference may be seen in the fact that in *TLWW* there is no indication that Aslan was something else which became incarnate as a lion—he *is* a lion. As Paul Ford has written,

> Lewis is not writing a Christology in the *Chronicles*; if he were, then he would have to indicate somewhere that Aslan is the pre-existent son of the Emperor and became a lion through a miraculous and at the same time natural birth. But there is no precise analogue of the Incarnation of Jesus Christ, as Christian theology understands it, in the figure of Aslan: he comes on the Narnian scene already and always a lion; he did not become lion to save Narnia. (1994, 19)

Following this reasoning, the relationship is not a simple equation where Aslan equals Jesus. We can, as pointed out earlier, see that there are numerous parallels between Aslan and Christ.

Peter Schakel has proposed a valid way to view the "religious" elements in the Narnia stories. Schakel has noted that readers will encounter elements in the Chronicles that they have met in religious experience. He explains, "Some readers, when they encounter such elements . . . seek biblical equivalents to every character and detail. To do so, however, violates the stories as examples of Story: that is, as fiction intended to appeal to and work on readers' imaginations. . . . It also limits and lowers Lewis's mythic achievement" (2002, 67–8). Schakel claims that "to take the Chronicles as allegory . . . raises the danger of breaking their spell" because we destroy "the independence of the imaginary world, as we begin looking outside it for the completion of its meaning" (1979, 3–4).

One of the defining qualities of an allegory is that all of its major elements will point to a consistent secondary interpretation, and this secondary interpretation will be one that can and will be agreed on by most readers. Following this thinking, one can easily see why *TLWW* is not an allegory. As Chad Walsh has pointed out, "If the Chronicles of Narnia were a straight allegory, in the manner of *The Pilgrim's Progress* (or *The Pilgrim's Regress*) the reader would expect every event to have a precise correspondence with some proclamation of Christian doctrine" (1979, 132), a condition which does not hold true. For example, if Peter Pevensie is supposed to represent the disciple Peter because both are leaders, what about the disciple Peter's denial of Christ? If, because of his betrayal, Edmund is supposed to represent the disciple Judas, then what do we do with the prominent role Edmund has in the battle with the Witch?

While *TLWW* is not an allegory, as Joe Christopher has argued, "the biblical parallels are obvious" (1987, 112–3). Besides the ones already mentioned relating to the events leading up to Aslan's death, Christopher contends that "the cracking of the Stone Table, [suggests] the tearing of the curtain of the Temple as well as the earthquake at the rolling away of the stone from Christ's tomb . . . Aslan's resurrection at sunrise and his appearance to Lucy and Susan at the Stone Table, [suggests] the angel's appearance to the two Marys who came at sunrise to the empty tomb" (1987, 113). Manlove also has observed: "Of course there are similarities. The process whereby Aslan dies only to rise again transfigured, is like Christ's death and resurrection. The breaking of the great Stone Table on which he is sacrificed is perhaps like the breaking of the power of the grave" (1993, 39).

No topic surrounding the Narnia stories has been so misunderstood or has had so much written about it as the question of whether they are allegory. With this in mind, perhaps a few final words on this subject are warranted from two additional sources—Walter Hooper and Lewis himself. Walter Hooper has made his opinion clear, writing, "It is often asked if the Narnian stories are 'allegories.' The answer is 'No'" (1996, 423).

This same answer comes from Lewis as well. In a letter written in 1958, Lewis would state:

> If Aslan represented the immaterial Deity in the same way in which Giant Despair represents Despair [in *The Pilgrim's Regress*], he would be an allegorical figure. In reality however he is an invention giving an imaginary answer to the question, "What might Christ become like if there really were a world like Narnia and He chose to be incarnate and die and rise again in *that* world as He actually has done in ours?" This is not allegory at all. (1993, 475)

In this same letter, Lewis coined a word for what he was trying to do in the Chronicles—not allegory but *supposal*.

Because this difference often confuses readers, Lewis clarified it several times in letters, including one written to a fifth grade class in Maryland, where he would later say:

> You are mistaken when you think that everything in the books "represents" something in this world. Things do that in *The Pilgrim's Progress* but I'm not writing that way. I did not say to myself "let us represent Jesus as He really is in our world by a Lion in Narnia": I said "Let us *suppose* that there were a land like Narnia and that the Son of God, as He became a Man in our world, became a Lion there, and then imagine what would happen." If you think about it, you will see that it is quite a different thing. (1995, 44–5)

In his essay "Sometimes Fairy Stories May Say Best What's to Be Said," Lewis makes the same point about his intentions, writing, "Some people seem to think that I began by asking myself how I could say something about Christianity to children; then fixed on the fairy tale as an instrument; . . . then drew up a list of basic Christian truths and hammered out 'allegories' to embody them. This is all pure moonshine" (1982f, 46).

Writing in a different context, Lewis made an observation about the interest, and perhaps even the obsession, that many readers have in finding allegorical meanings in works where authors never intended them. He noted, "Where [the critic] seems to me most often to go wrong is in the hasty assumption of an allegorical sense. . . . No story can be devised by the wit of man which cannot be interpreted allegorically by the wit of some other man. . . . The mere fact that you *can* allegorise the work before you is of itself no proof that it is an allegory" (1982c, 140–1).

In *Reflections on the Psalms*, a work published in 1958—two years after the final volume in the Narnia series had been published and after the books had been subject to numerous reviews—Lewis took a moment to touch on this same topic, writing: "As we know, almost anything can be read into any book if you are determined enough. This will be especially impressed on anyone who has written fantastic fiction. He will find reviewers, both favorable and hostile, reading into his stories all manner of allegorical meanings which he never intended" (1986, 99).

Tolkien faced a similar problem with readers who persisted in seeing *The Lord of the Rings* as an allegory for the Second World War, the One Ring for the atomic bomb, Sauron for Hitler, and so on. So much talk spread about possible allegorical interpretations that Tolkien used his foreword to the second edition to make the point that his work was not allegory, writing: "I should like to say something here with reference to the many opinions or guesses that I have received or read concerning the motives and meaning of the tale. . . . It is neither allegorical nor topical. . . . I think that many confuse 'applicability' with 'allegory'" (Tolkien 1994a, xiv–x). This same distinction between applicability and allegory could be made with regards to *TLWW*.

If we can agree that the biblical parallels in *TLWW* do not make it an allegory, we still might ask, Do these biblical parallels make it a lesser work? A better work? While readers fall on both sides of this argument, perhaps the best way to evaluate the novel is simply to let the story stand on its own merits, neither adding to nor subtracting from our evaluation of it because of any parallels it has with the Bible or with any other work for that matter.

Finally, we may also want to ask just how much importance we should give to Lewis's own statements—typically made years after he had written *TLWW*—about what he believed he was doing in the novel. Interestingly, in his essay "On Criticism" Lewis himself made clear that we should not automatically take what an author says about his own work as being accurate. He writes, "Of a book's meaning, . . . its author is not necessarily the best, and is never a perfect, judge. One of his intentions usually was that it should have a certain meaning: he cannot be sure that it has. He cannot even be sure that the meaning he intended it to have was in every way, or even at all, better than the meaning which readers find in it" (1982c, 140).

In the end, *TLWW* is what it is—not what critics or even Lewis himself may have said it is. While the issue of the biblical parallels in the Narnia books is one that has generated, and will continue to generate, some widely divergent opinions, perhaps a final word from Lewis himself may be allowed to conclude our discussion here. In his essay "The Genesis of a Medieval Book," Lewis wrote about the problem of judging a work on the parallels it may or may not have to other works. Lewis argues, "The text before us, however it came into existence, must be allowed to work on us in its own way, and must be judged on its own merits. . . . Within a given story any object, person, or place is neither more nor less nor other than what that story effectively shows it to be" (1989, 39–40).

Returning to the story in *TLWW*, we discover that the Stone Table has cracked, but what precisely the cracking indicates is not made clear. Perhaps the cracking simply means that in the future, traitors will not be sacrificed there anymore. Perhaps it means that the blood which was previously a requirement for treachery in Narnia will no longer be required. Perhaps the cracking means that death has worked backwards in this one case, Aslan's case, and his return to life has cracked the table. What is clear is that this is another of the places where Lewis intended to suggest possible meanings, not fully explain them.

Lucy's first question for Aslan is to ask if he is dead. His response is "Not now" (162), and the implication is that just as we are meant to think Aslan is a real lion, we are also meant to understand that he was really dead. Susan's first reaction is to ask "in a shaky voice" if Aslan is a ghost. Susan stammers, "You're not—not a—?" Lewis will later give Eustace a similar reaction upon seeing Caspian when the old friend first reappears after dying in *The Silver Chair*. Referring to Caspian, Eustace will ask, "But, hasn't he—er—died?" (1994f, 239). Aslan replies, "Yes, he has died. Most people have, you know. Even I have." The resurrected Caspian will interject, "Oh, I see what's bothering you. You think I'm a ghost or some nonsense" (239–40). In *TLWW* Susan, in halting words like Eustace's, can not bring herself to say the word *ghost*. In response, Aslan simply licks Susan's forehead and lets her feel the warmth of his breath and smell the rich fragrance of his hair, then asks, "Do I look it?" (163). Lewis will reprise this scene in *The Horse and His Boy* where Aslan breathes on Shasta, saying, "There, that is not the breath of a ghost" (1994a, 163).

In a short time Lucy and Susan are convinced that Aslan is truly alive once more, and just as readers earlier shared their grief, they now share the sisters' joy as the girls fling themselves upon Aslan, covering him with kisses. Other than his being "larger," nothing indicates that the resurrected Aslan is any different than his earlier self. Certainly if he had wanted to, Lewis could have given the resurrected Aslan a different sort of physical body, as was true for the resurrected Christ and as Tolkien did with Gandalf (1994d, 484). The only visible difference in Aslan now is that he is "larger than they had seen him before" (162), a trait which may be intended to say more about Lucy and Susan than about Aslan (Lewis 1994e, 141).

In response to Susan's question "But what does it all mean?" (163), Aslan offers a somewhat lengthy explanation which both does and does not help to clear things up. He explains to the girls that there was "a magic deeper" than the Deep Magic, one which was created "before Time dawned" and hence before the Witch's knowledge. According to this Deeper Magic, "when a willing victim who had committed no treachery was killed in a traitor's stead, the Table would crack and Death itself would start working backward." This is all the explanation readers will get, and here Lewis once more intends that we somewhat understand but also that this issue remains somewhat a mystery.

Among the questions Aslan's reply might raise are two funda-mental ones. What exactly does "Death itself would start working backward" mean here? We must conclude it refers to Death in just this one particular instance of Aslan's death, as opposed to Death in general, because just a few pages later at the Battle of Beruna "most of the enemy" will be killed (178), and Edmund and many of Aslan's other forces will clearly be near death themselves (179). Secondly, given the exact wording of Aslan's explanation, we might ask, could *anyone* who had "committed no treachery" have died in Edmund's place? And if so, would they then have been resurrected in just the same way as Aslan, since they had fulfilled the two re-quirements of the Deeper Magic? Whether or not this was Lewis's intention here, Aslan's account of the Deeper Magic seems to leave open this possibility, and if true, would be another way that Aslan's sacrifice for Edmund is different from Christ's. Alternatively, it may be argued that except for Aslan no completely innocent person exists. While there are no other characters besides Edmund in *TLWW* who have risen to the level of being classified as a traitor, so too there are no other characters besides Aslan who are free of some form of treachery. And thus, Aslan alone can offer his life for Edmund.

After Aslan's explanation, Lucy and Susan have "such a romp" in celebration with Aslan "as no one has ever had except in Narnia" (164). Paul Ford has observed, "The ecstatic romp of the Lion and the girls has no equal in Lewis and perhaps none in any words of Christian imagination" (1994, 21). Lewis will revisit this scene in *The Last Battle*, where the humans and animals in the new Narnia will run faster and faster and readers will be told "no one got hot or tired or out of breath" (1994b, 197). In *TLWW* we read that after the romp "the girls no longer felt in the least tired or hungry or thirsty" (164), a condition which is only temporary, thus fore-shadowing the permanent condition in *The Last Battle*.

As readers have seen, feasting, celebrating, and romping are integral ingredients in what makes Narnia, Narnia. Aslan's resur-rection inaugurates a permanent return to those times before the Witch's interference when "the whole forest would give itself up to jollification for weeks on end" (16). The romp Lucy and Susan take here in *TLWW* will be reprised in *Prince Caspian*. There Bacchus will arrive with Silenus and ask, "Is it a Romp, Aslan?" (Lewis 1994e, 158), and then we are told that everyone begins playing a game like tag. The romp will end, as it does here in *TLWW*, with everyone "flopped down breathless on the ground" (160). In a further similarity, Lucy and Susan's romp in *Prince Caspian* is followed by a ride on Aslan (197), just as it will be here in *TLWW*.

In keeping with his dual nature of being good but not safe (80), "good and terrible at the same time" (126), after the playful romp with the sisters, Aslan lets out a great roar which bends the trees like grass in a meadow, and we are told his face becomes "so terrible that they did not dare to look at it" (164). In the prophecy Mr. Beaver related earlier, the children were told, "At the sound of his roar, sorrows will be no more" (79). This is the second time we have heard the sound of Aslan's roar in *TLWW*; the first was after the Witch questioned Aslan about keeping his promise (144). After that first roar, sorrows did not cease; if anything, they increased. So if we take the prophecy entirely literally (though it is probable we are not supposed to), after this second roar is when sorrows begin to be no more.

Lewis makes a curious statement about the ride which the girls take on Aslan's back at this point in the story, calling it "perhaps the most wonderful thing that happened to them in Narnia" (165). Possibly we are supposed to think that meeting Aslan for the first time was the most *marvelous* thing and that seeing him alive after his resurrection was the most *joyous* thing. Otherwise, readers may wonder if Lewis truly meant the ride to overshadow these other two events. Besides Lucy and Susan, the only other character in the Chronicles to be offered a ride on Aslan will be Caspian's old nurse (Lewis 1994e, 204).

Soon Aslan and the girls arrive at the Witch's castle with its "pointed towers" (166). Earlier the castle had seemed to Edmund to be "all towers; little towers with long pointed spires on them, sharp as needles" (92). If readers compare Baynes's drawing of the Witch's castle (93) with her drawing of Cair Paravel (180), they will see that while both structures are full of towers, the Witch's castle is much more perpendicular, narrow, and pointed. Aslan chooses to leap over the wall, although he certainly could have broken down the locked gate, and in the next chapter this will allow him the opportunity to request Giant Rumblebuffin's assistance. In the great leap, Lewis hints that one of Aslan's many unexplained powers may be the ability to fly, as he describes how the lion "jumped—or you may call it flying rather than jumping—right over the castle wall" (166). The trio lands safely inside, and as the chapter ends, the girls find themselves "tumbling off his back in the middle of a wide stone courtyard full of statues."

SIXTEEN

What Happened about the Statues

Early in *TLWW*, Mr. Tumnus was worried that the Witch would find out he had not reported Lucy and that then he would be turned into a statue of a faun "in her horrible house" (20). As chapter sixteen opens, Susan and Lucy find themselves tumbling off Aslan's back in this very place. Earlier Lewis mentioned that Edmund was "afraid of the House" (92), but perhaps because Aslan is there with them and the Witch is not, Lucy does not find the Witch's castle horrible or a source of fear. She says to Susan, "What an extraordinary place. . . . It's—it's like a museum" (167). In *The Magician's Nephew* when Digory and Polly first arrive at the Witch's palace, it too will be filled with frozen statues, which will be described as being "like the most wonderful waxworks you ever saw" (Lewis 1994d, 50). While both places are initially described in somewhat positive terms, the creatures in both locations are prisoners under the spell of the same evil magic.

Years later, Lewis may have had the following scene in *TLWW* where Aslan breathes life into the statues in his mind as he wrote the scene in *The Magician's Nephew* where Aslan sings life into Narnia. In *TLWW* we find the following passage when Susan asks for quiet so she can watch Aslan change the stones back to life:

> "Hush," said Susan, "Aslan's doing something."
> He was indeed. (167)

In *The Magician's Nephew*, Lewis would create a very similar passage as Frank the Cabby asks Uncle Andrew to be quiet so he can listen to Aslan's song of creation:

> "Oh stow it, Guv'nor, do stow it," said the Cabby. "Watchin' and listenin' 's the thing at present; not talking."
> There was certainly plenty to watch and to listen to. (1994d, 114)

The parallel between the two scenes is made even clearer when in *TLWW* the former statues come to life with a collection of "roarings, brayings, yelpings, barkings, squealings, cooings, neighings, stampings, shouts, hurrahs, songs and laughter" (169). The creation scene in *The Magician's Nephew* concludes with a similar catalogue of "cawing, cooing, crowing, braying, neighing, baying, barking, lowing, bleating, and trumpeting" (Lewis 1994d, 123).

Donald Glover has called the transformation of the stone lion back into a living, breathing lion "one of Lewis's finest descriptive touches" (1981, 143). Here again readers see the motif of gradualness which has been woven into the story from its beginning. Like many other times in *TLWW* when Lewis wants to interject the sense of something special happening, he switches to the first person voice of the narrator who blends the marvelous with the ordinary, saying, "I expect you've seen someone put a lighted match to a bit of newspaper which is propped up in a grate against an unlit fire. And for a second nothing seems to have happened; and then you notice a tiny streak of flame creeping along the edge of the newspaper. It was like that now" (167–8).

A streak of gold begins to run down the lion's stone-white back and then gradually spreads like a flame over paper, like spring gradually spread over Narnia earlier. When Lewis wrote this description, he envisioned his readers as being familiar with a fire "in a grate" or a fireplace made with paper and wood or coal. Modern readers, if they have fireplaces at all, may have ones which burn gas rather than wood and so may have to imagine both the literal and the figurative elements in Lewis's simile. Of course, most readers will still know what a fire started with paper looks like from their experiences with campfires and bonfires.

Everywhere that Lucy and Susan look, the statues are "coming to life" (168). Paul Ford has suggested a parallel here to what is known as the Harrowing of Hell from the Christian tradition (1994, 21, 102)—the story of Christ's visit to Hades to release the captives there. As with the other Christian parallels in *TLWW*, some aspects are dissimilar and some are similar. In the Harrowing of Hell, Christ visited Hades during the time between his death and his resurrection—not after his resurrection. Those he sets free have died and after his visit go to live in heaven. Here in *TLWW* the captives at the Witch's castle are not there because they have done something wrong but presumably because they, like Mr. Tumnus, have done something right in standing up to the Witch. After the battle, unlike the captives released from Hades, the former statues go back to their normal lives in Narnia and, we assume, eventually die a normal death.

In the previous chapter Aslan had breathed on Susan to reassure her that he was not a ghost (162). Here Aslan breathes on the statues to return them to life. Aslan's breath will have special powers throughout the Chronicles. In *Prince Caspian* Aslan will tell Susan, "Come, let me breathe on you" (Lewis 1994e, 154), and she is able to forget her fears. In that story, readers will also be told of the effect that Aslan's breath has on Edmund: "Aslan had breathed on him at their meeting and a kind of greatness hung about him" (179). At the end of *Prince Caspian*, Aslan will breathe on the first

Telmarine to go through the door back to Earth, and "a new look" will come into the man's eyes (219). In *The Last Battle* Emeth, in telling the others of his encounter with Aslan, will say, "Then he breathed upon me and took away the trembling from my limbs" (Lewis 1994b, 189).

Some critics, among them Walter Hooper, see Aslan's breath as a representation of the Holy Spirit, the third member of the Christian Trinity, although as Hooper admits, the association is "vague" as it rests on connections which come from outside the story rather than inside (1996, 440). Hooper suggests that when reading the passages about Aslan's breath, "The Christian will recall Jesus's appearance to the Disciples and His resurrection," in particular, the encounter recorded in John 20:22 where Jesus "breathed on them and said, 'Receive the Holy Spirit.'" He points out that the word *spirit* in both Hebrew and Greek is the same word that means *breath*. Paul Ford, citing the same Scripture, argues that "Aslan's breath (with its sometimes emphasized fragrance) is the chief symbol of the Spirit's activity in the Chronicles" (1994, 230).

After the transformation of the lion, dwarf, dryad, rabbit, and centaurs, Lewis uses another of the catalogue-style listings that have appeared earlier as he further describes the process. Instead of "that deadly white" (168), the courtyard is now "a blaze of colors" with "glossy chestnut sides of centaurs, indigo horns of unicorns, dazzling plumage of birds, reddy-brown of foxes, dogs and satyrs, yellow stockings and crimson hoods of dwarfs; and the birch-girls in silver, and the beech-girls in fresh, transparent green, and the larch-girls in green so bright it was almost yellow" (168–9). Soon the silence of the castle is replaced with a raucous celebration causing Susan to worry, as she often has, "Is it safe?" (169).

After all the stone creatures outside have been transformed back into living creatures, Aslan asks everyone to help him find all the "poor prisoners" who are statues inside (171), and at this point Lewis has Aslan speak a line from what today is a somewhat obscure nursery rhyme titled "Goosey, Goosey, Gander." The entire poem is

> Goosey, goosey, gander,
> Whither shall I wander?
> Upstairs, and downstairs,
> And in my lady's chamber.
> There I met an old man
> Who wouldn't say his prayers!
> I took him by the left leg
> And threw him down the stairs.

In calling his forces to search everywhere, Aslan recites the poem's third and fourth lines. As mentioned earlier in connection with the Father Christmas issue, Lewis, in giving advice on writing fairy tales, wrote, "In a fantasy every precaution must be taken never to break the spell, to do nothing which will wake the reader and bring him back with a bump to the common earth" (1993, 468). Here by having Aslan recite lines from a nursery rhyme which comes from England, Lewis may briefly break the spell for some readers, as its use may seem out of place in Narnia.

Even if readers do not have a problem with the use of a British nursery rhyme in Narnia, they may have a problem with the events it originally referenced. Like many nursery rhymes, this verse has a historical background which most people are unaware of. The first line may refer to the goosestep march of the special squads of soldiers sent out by the Puritan dictator Oliver Cromwell to look for Catholic priests who would often hide in "priest holes" that were frequently located behind bedrooms ("my lady's chamber"). After finding a priest, a man "who wouldn't say his prayers" using the newly adopted Protestant Book of Common Prayer, the Puritan forces would often torture him ("I took him by the left leg / And threw him down the stairs"). We have no indication that Lewis knew the background behind the origins of the verse. In fact, we must assume that he did not, because if he had known its origins, he likely would not have chosen to include the lines in *TLWW*.

When Lucy finds Mr. Tumnus, Lewis makes a somewhat surprising choice not to fully describe Lucy finding the faun frozen in stone and Mr. Tumnus's subsequent revitalization by Aslan. Instead

Lewis has these events, for the most part, take place off stage out of sight (171). Given the fears that Mr. Tumnus had expressed about being made into a statue and the pathos that readers felt at seeing his devastated cave (57), this moment seems to be a missed opportunity for Lewis to genuinely evoke the joy that characterizes the last quarter of the novel, especially since during Edmund's visit to the Witch's castle, Lewis went to the trouble of showing us "a little faun with a very sad expression on its face" inside "a long gloomy hall" (98).

Finally all the statues have been "liberated" (171) and the castle stands open to the light. The spell of winter once cast over Narnia by the White Witch is at last fully broken as "the sweet spring air" floods in. Certainly Aslan could have shattered the castle gates himself, as later in *The Silver Chair* he will knock down "thirty feet" of the school wall with his roar (Lewis 1994f, 241). But here rather than doing this himself, Aslan asks the giant to knock them down. This is likely the figure with the fierce face, shaggy beard, and great club which Edmund had seen earlier (97). However, since Aslan later refers to *giants* in the plural as he prepares to leave (174), more than one statue giant seem to have been found—although only one will be named as entering the battle (177).

After Giant Rumblebuffin finishes, Lewis provides another contrast between the lifeless control of the Witch and the endless freedom and release Aslan has brought. Those standing in the "dry, grim, stony yard" can look through the gap to see "grass and waving trees and sparkling streams of the forest, and the blue hills beyond that and beyond them the sky" (172).

The giant has worked up a sweat, and for the second time in the story, Lewis has Lucy offer someone her handkerchief, something which most readers, unlike Lucy, might not always seem to be carrying around with them. In the comment made by the narrator that "it was only about the same size to him that a saccharine tablet would be to you" (173), Lewis takes another step which, like Aslan's use of the nursery rhyme discussed earlier, is uncharacteristic of his typically highly skilled writing. Here Lewis makes a comparison which may not be universal enough to be effective. Some modern readers, especially younger ones, will probably guess from context how big a saccharine tablet might be but may never have seen one. For them Lewis's comparison has to work backwards. Instead of knowing what a saccharine tablet is and imagining how small Lucy's handkerchief must seem to the giant, some readers may visualize how small Lucy's handkerchief must seem and so be able to imagine how little a saccharine tablet would be. Perhaps Lewis never foresaw a day when saccharine tablets, widely used during his time, would not be familiar to everyone.

Surely Aslan could have found out himself where the battle was, just as he could have knocked down the gates himself, but instead he asks "those who are good with their noses" to help him (174). Those who "can't keep up" are to ride on the backs of "those who can," and so here at the castle we see a continuation of the idea, discussed earlier in connection with the Christmas presents, that in Narnia each individual is to help out in whatever way he or she is best suited. In Aslan's use of the first person plural in the statements "Our day's work is not yet over" and "we must find the battle at once," he further emphasizes this point of a communal effort. On the following page, readers will learn that a sheepdog helps Aslan to sort his forces.

One of the hounds picks up the scent, and readers are told, "Soon all the dogs and lions and wolves and other hunting animals were going at full speed. . . . The noise was like an English fox-hunt only better" (175). Two issues are raised in this short description. First, though they do not play any further role in *TLWW*, good wolves live in Narnia as well as wolves which have chosen to serve the Witch. Second, in Lewis's description of the noise of the animals tracking the scent of the Witch, we find a simile that some readers today might find surprising or even out of place in a story where animals are portrayed with such sympathy: a positive comparison to a fox hunt.

While to kill a talking beast in Narnia is the equivalent of murder, no negative connotations are associated with catching, killing, eating, or hunting nontalking animals. Earlier at the Beavers' house readers were told "there's nothing to beat good freshwater fish if you eat it when it has been alive half an hour ago" (74). On the trek to the Stone Table, Mrs. Beaver brought along a ham (100), presumably cut from a nontalking pig. In the final chapter, the Great Hall of Cair Paravel will be described as having one wall "hung with peacock feathers" (181). The distinction between talking and nontalking animals is further clarified in *Prince Caspian* where Nikabrik will accuse Caspian of hunting beasts "for sport" (Lewis 1994e, 71). Caspian admits he has but points out they were not Talking Beasts. When Nikabrik tries to argue that "it's all the same thing," Trufflehunter replies, "No, no, no, you know it isn't." In addition, in *The Voyage of the* Dawn Treader, Lewis will seem to cast vegetarians in an unflattering light (1994g, 3).

Green and Hooper note that during the process of writing *TLWW*, Lewis was persuaded to remove "bird's nesting" from his original list of activities that the Pevensie children engage in while at the Professor's house (1994, 242). As they point out, Lewis was apparently unaware of the revolution against "egg-collectors" which the books of Arthur Ransome had sparked. Given changing perspectives on the treatment of animals—from fox hunting to wearing fur and feathers to eating meat—it will be interesting to see to what extent Lewis's attitudes toward nontalking beasts in Narnia may or may not produce a break in the spell, or a least a "bump," for future readers.

At the same time one must also note that although Lewis saw no problem in killing the dumb beasts in Narnia for food, as Paul Ford has observed, they are still "to be respected" (1994, 155). Ford explains that for Lewis, who was "an animal lover himself" (436), cruelty to animals of any sort was "a grave moral fault" (435). In *The Magician's Nephew*, Digory's immoral Uncle Andrew will be portrayed as experimenting with guinea-pigs, causing some of them to die and others to explode "like little bombs" (Lewis 1994d, 24). In *The Voyage of the* Dawn Treader, Lewis will also be critical of the actions of Eustace who, before the change he undergoes in Narnia, likes animals if they are "dead and pinned on a card" (1994g, 3). In *The Silver Chair* evidence of Eustace's changed character will be seen when he stands up to a classmate named Cater who is mistreating a rabbit (Lewis 1994f, 5).

As the group travels on, the scent becomes "easier and easier to follow" (175), and before too long Lucy hears a noise which gives her "a queer feeling" inside, the sound of "shouts and shrieks and the clashing of metal against metal." Lewis gives few clues about where the upcoming battle takes place. Has the Witch surprised Peter's forces near their camp at the Fords of Beruna? If so, readers may wonder if Peter's plan to camp on the far side might have, in fact, proven helpful. Earlier the fords were described as "a place where the river valley had widened out and the river was broad and shallow" (146). Here Aslan's forces come "to the last curve in a narrow, winding valley," and then leaving this "narrow valley" they see the fighting (175). Not until *Prince Caspian* will the fighting seen here in *TLWW* be referred to as "the Battle of Beruna" (Lewis 1994e, 103).

Lewis depicts the battle scene, as he has many others, from Lucy's perspective. She sees Peter, Edmund, and the rest of Aslan's forces fighting "desperately" against a crowd of "horrible" creatures (175). While Lucy is not aware of it, at this point in the battle Edmund has been "terribly wounded" during his successful attempt to smash the Witch's wand (179). Lucy sees Peter fighting against the Witch—her wand now destroyed, she uses her Stone Knife against his sword.

Peter's army looks to be "terribly few" against "far more" of the Witch's forces, and here Lewis includes a surprising detail: the members of Peter's army have their backs to Lucy (176). If Aslan's reinforcements have been following the trail taken by the Witch's army, this position is somewhat counterintuitive. We might expect Lucy to see the backs of the Witch's troops. Perhaps Lewis simply wanted to give a sense that Peter's army was being forced backwards, but more likely, perhaps, Lewis turned the forces around so that the Witch would see Aslan coming rather than having him jump on her from behind. Also, with the Witch facing Lucy, we are able to see through Lucy the Witch's expression of "terror and amazement" as Aslan, whom she thought was dead, flings himself upon her.

In the drawing of the battle, Baynes depicts the Witch raising the knife that had killed Aslan the night before against him once again (176), this time in vain. Although Aslan kills the Witch, he does not win the battle all by himself. Here, as elsewhere, those with the appropriate skills will participate. We are told that "at the same moment" Aslan attacks the Witch, all the "war-like creatures" he has led from the castle also rush into battle (177).

In *Prince Caspian* Trumpkin will try to tactfully explain his disappointment in finding the children as the answer to the horn's call for help, telling them, "They'd been imagining you as great warriors" (Lewis 1994e, 103). Edmund will counter, "I suppose you don't believe we won the Battle of Beruna?" Edmund's use of *we* as referring to himself and Peter may be seen as a possible inconsistency since Peter and Edmund in fact appear to be losing the Battle of Beruna until Aslan shows up. In *Prince Caspian* Lucy will comment on the role Aslan played on their first trip to Narnia, telling him wistfully, "I thought you'd come roaring in and frighten all the enemies away—like last time" (Lewis 1994e, 143). Having mentioned this, it should be noted that despite the fact that they seem to be on the verge of being defeated, Edmund's own courage and performance in the battle here certainly would put him in the ranks of "great warriors."

In Baynes's illustration which closes the chapter, we can see the graphic representations of some of the participants which Lewis describes in the text: four dwarfs with their battleaxes (one behind the giant), several dogs with teeth, the giant with his club and feet, one of the unicorns with its horn, and one of the centaurs armed with swords and hoofs (177). One cannot tell exactly which of the figures Baynes intended to represent the stone statues created on the battlefield, but just to the right of center stands a dwarf who seems to be frozen with his ax raised to strike at nothing. And Edmund, who at this point would be among the fallen wounded, does not appear to be included in the drawing.

SEVENTEEN

The Hunting of the White Stag

For a book challenged in the Howard County, Maryland, school system for depicting "graphic violence, mysticism, and gore," *TLWW* offers readers relatively few details of the climactic battle. In addition to the few sentences at the end of the previous chapter, Lewis adds two more here at the start of chapter seventeen, simply telling readers that the battle "was all over in a few minutes" (178), most of the enemy was "killed in the first charge," and those not killed "gave themselves up or took to flight." Surely if Lewis had wanted to include graphic violence and gore, this would have been the place to do it. Except for the brief details of Peter's encounter with the Witch and the attack led by Aslan, the rest of the Battle of Beruna is given in summary. If violent action was his goal, at the very least Lewis would have provided a full, real-time description of Edmund's dramatic attack on the Witch, not the short synopsis we receive after the fact.

As has been discussed earlier, the Witch's army had two distinct types of creatures: those inherently bad, such as the ghouls and hags, and those capable of both bad and good, such as the dwarfs and wolves, the kind of creatures that are found fighting on both sides. Lewis is not explicit here about which creatures surrender or about what happens to those who do, but readers might wonder how, or if, a Cruel, Hag, Incubus, Wraith, or Horror might be rehabilitated.

In *The Lord of the Rings*, Tolkien is less ambiguous about the issue of surrender and clemency. While men who have been fighting for Sauron may surrender and be spared, orcs never do and never are. After the battle at Helm's Deep, readers are told, "No Orcs remained alive; their bodies were uncounted. But a great many of the hill-men had given themselves up; and they were afraid, and cried for mercy. The Men of the Mark took their weapons from them, and set them to work" (Tolkien 1994d, 532). Later Gandalf will offer mercy to his fellow-wizard Saruman and will invite him to surrender and join the forces of good (Tolkien 1994d, 568), but this choice never seems appropriate for the Witch, at least not at this point in her evildoing. Like Sauron, the White Witch is "bad all through" (81) and is never presented as capable of redemption.

In *Perelandra*, the second volume of Lewis's space trilogy, the protagonist, Elwin Ransom, encounters a counterpart to the Witch. The Un-man is a creature who was once a scientist named Weston but in the end becomes nothing but a conduit for evil—like the Witch, "bad all through" (81). As Ransom engages in physical combat with the Un-man, he is suddenly strengthened by the fact that he need have no sympathy for his enemy. As Lewis writes:

> Then an experience that perhaps no good man can ever have in our world came over him—a torrent of perfectly unmixed and lawful hatred. The energy of hating never before felt without some guilt, without some dim knowledge that he was failing fully to distinguish the sinner from the sin, rose into his arms and legs till he felt that they were pillars of burning blood. . . . The joy came from finding at last what hatred was made for. (1996g, 132)

Perhaps Peter and Edmund felt similar feelings as they fought the Witch. Certainly their experience was very different from the one Sam has in *The Two Towers* when he sees his first man killed. Earlier Sam had slain orcs with no remorse, but now as he and Frodo hide in the brush with two of Faramir's troops, they watch as one of the enemy Southrons is killed right in front of them. Tolkien tells readers: "It was Sam's first view of a battle of Men against Men, and he did not like it much. He was glad that he could not see the dead face. He wondered what the man's name was and where he came from; and if he was really evil of heart, or what lies had led him on the long march from his home; and if he would not really rather have stayed there in peace" (Tolkien 1994d, 646). Lewis's depiction of the White Witch's demise has none of this type of regret, for she has been a very different type of foe, the type found only in fairy tales.

Lucy sees Peter shaking hands with Aslan and notes that her brother seems "so much older" (178). Certainly the trials of the battlefield would have aged Peter psychologically, but how much physically older Peter is supposed to have become in the one day since Lucy last saw him remains unclear. Like many authors for young people, Lewis sometimes has his children acquire skills faster than would be plausible in the real world, but perhaps this is simply part of the magic of Narnia. Later, in *Prince Caspian* when Edmund will have his "little fencing match" with Trumpkin, Lewis's narrator will comment, "I don't think Edmund would have had a chance if he had fought Trumpkin twenty-four hours earlier. But the air of Narnia had been working upon him ever since they arrived on the island, and all his old battles came back to him, and his arms and fingers remembered their old skill" (Lewis 1994e, 105).

At this point in *TLWW* Peter does not have any "old skill" to remember; however, the air of Narnia seems to have changed him a good deal since the battle with the wolf left him "shaky" and "crying" (132). Now just two days later, without any practice that we have witnessed, he has been able to use his sword so effectively against the Witch that it looked like "three swords" (176). Edmund too has seemed to develop quicker than would be possible in England.

We learn that he "fought his way through three ogres" in order to smash the Witch's wand (178).

After the battle Peter tells Aslan, "It was all Edmund's doing. We'd have been beaten if it hadn't been for him" (179). While Peter's first assertion is somewhat of a generous overstatement, his second claim is true in the sense that Edmund's heroic action has allowed them to hold on long enough for Aslan to arrive. Here in his first undertaking since having his talk with Aslan, Edmund acts in an entirely different manner than seen earlier. Readers are told that "nothing would stop him" as he battled through to the Witch and destroyed her wand. In making Edmund, not Peter, the one who turns the tide in battle, Lewis interjects the theme that the worst sinners often make the most valiant saints, a theme which he will revisit in later Chronicles with Eustace.

Mrs. Beaver is caring for Edmund, who has been critically wounded. Lucy has forgotten about her cordial, but Aslan knows about it, just as he knew about Susan's horn, and tells her that she is to use it on her brother and afterwards on the others who also have been injured (179). Here Lewis interjects a minor defect in Lucy's otherwise unflawed character, making her a more realistic figure: she speaks crossly to Aslan, although possibly more out of worry than real impatience.

Lucy has never seen the actions of the healing cordial and so perhaps may be excused for wanting to see what effect it has on her brother. Aslan calls her away, and readers are told that "for the next half-hour they were busy—she attending to the wounded while he restored those who had been turned into stone" (179). Again we have an instance where Aslan could undoubtedly have performed both tasks, healing the wounded as well as returning the newly made statues back to life. But as before, each character, including Lucy, is called upon to help out in whatever ways are appropriate.

Lucy does not return until she has finished tending all the wounded. When she comes back, she finds her younger brother restored to his "real old self again" (180), to the person he was not just before being wounded but before "his first term at that horrid school," the place where "he had begun to go wrong." Readers are told that once more he "could look you in the face," a condition that contrasts with that of the Witch, and raising the question of why Edmund's talk with Aslan earlier had not accomplished this inner healing. Perhaps Lewis's point here is that just as Edmund's descent happened over a good deal of time and in a number of stages, so too does his recovery. While he was fully repentant and fully reconciled with his siblings after his apology at the Stone Table, perhaps Edmund needed, in addition to Lucy's cordial, to give his service in the battle before he was completely restored, as his way of making up for the great wrong that he had committed.

Eustace, whose transformation in *The Voyage of the* Dawn Treader mirrors Edmund's in many ways, will also show a gradual improvement, not an instantaneous one. Lewis will write, "It would be nice and fairly nearly true, to say that 'from that time forth Eustace was a different boy.' To be strictly accurate, he began to be a different boy" (1994g, 112). Lewis finishes his description of Eustace with a specific word that matches the healing seen in Edmund, stating that the "cure" had begun.

Lucy and Susan debate whether they should tell Edmund "what the arrangement with the Witch really was" (180). Susan is against this, Lucy for it. Paul Ford suggests, "It is possible that Lucy won her argument with Susan and told Edmund what Aslan did for him, for he grows up to be a graver and quieter man than Peter" (1994, 162). In *TLWW* Lewis leaves it unclear whether Edmund ever finds out, but later in *The Voyage of the* Dawn Treader Edmund will explain to Eustace who Aslan is, telling him, "He is the great Lion, the son of the Emperor over Sea, who saved me and saved Narnia" (Lewis 1994g, 111), clearly indicating that by this point in time he has learned about the "arrangement" Aslan made to die in his place. In *Prince Caspian* no specific mention of Aslan's sacrifice for Edmund is made, but the stone reliefs of Aslan carved in the tunnels surrounding the Stone Table imply that the knowledge of what Aslan did there is widespread (Lewis 1994e, 92), and may suggest that Edmund too is aware of what took place.

Readers who are undecided about whether Aslan is better seen as an allegory for Christ or as a Christ-figure might note that in

Lucy and Susan's comments here we find another way Lewis chose to make his character somewhat different from Christ. As Peter Schakel has argued, "There is no Narnian equivalent for the orthodox Christian belief that salvation is gained by awareness of what Christ has done and 'acceptance' of him as savior" (1979, 132). Although Edmund does seem to learn about Aslan's sacrifice for him much later, he clearly comes to a right relationship with Aslan long before he has any knowledge about or acceptance of the event.

Now time in the novel begins to speed up. After "a fine high tea" on the grass which Aslan provides in the same unexplained way as Father Christmas did earlier (181), three days quickly pass as the four children travel with Aslan's troops to the coast and Cair Paravel, where Aslan crowns them. They ascend the empty thrones which have been waiting for them, fulfilling the prophecy first alluded to by Mr. Tumnus what now seems a long time ago (20).

In his last words in the novel, Aslan makes a somewhat vague proclamation, declaring, "Once a king or queen in Narnia, always a king or queen" (182). How should this statement be interpreted? Some readers might take this to mean that even if sent back to England, the children are guaranteed someday to return to Narnia. This is certainly the meaning that the Professor suggests when he inexplicably seems to know this proverb at the end of the book and repeats it to them as proof of his claim, "Of course you'll get back to Narnia again someday" (188).

With this interpretation, Aslan's use of the term *always* might hold special significance for Susan, the only one not to return to Narnia permanently in *The Last Battle* (154). Since she is still alive as the final book closes, Aslan's statement here in *TLWW* may imply hope for her, although if she returns, she will have to return as a queen in the new Narnia. In a letter written in 1957, shortly after the series was completed, Lewis himself would hint at the possibility for Susan's return, writing: "The books don't tell us what happened to Susan. She is left alive in this world at the end, having by then turned into a rather silly, conceited young woman. But there is plenty of time for her to mend, and perhaps she will get to Aslan's country in the end—in her own way" (Lewis 1995, 67).

Paul Ford offers a different reading of "Once a king or queen in Narnia, always a king or queen." He interprets it as meaning "Even though they are children in England, when they return to Narnia, they are still Kings and Queens in that country" (1994, 254), and as being Lewis's version of Pope Leo the Great's dictum, "Recognize, O Christian, your dignity" (22).

The music provided by the mermen and mermaids here in honor of the new kings and queens will be one of the "lovely times" which Susan remembers in *Prince Caspian* (Lewis 1994e, 19). Compared to the Narnian music which is played at the feast that night, the Sea People's music is described as "stranger, sweeter, and more piercing" (182). Later when Lucy sees the Sea People during *The Voyage of the* Dawn Treader, she will mistakenly claim that they are the same race that "came to the surface and sang at our coronation" (Lewis 1994g, 226). Edmund will correct her, saying, "I think that must have been a different kind, Lu. They could live in the air as well as under water."

After the children are crowned, their first action is to give "rewards and honors" to "all their friends" (182). The list which Lewis provides here is not meant to be complete for it omits the sheepdog, eagles, dogs, and unicorns who had helped out earlier at the Witch's castle and in the battle (174–7). The wording in the list also raises an additional question. When we read that rewards were given to "the good dwarfs" (182), the adjective seems needed to distinguish them from the dwarfs who fought on the Witch's side. If we accept this line of thinking, what might Lewis have meant by the similar phrase "the good centaurs"? Although all the centaurs mentioned in the Chronicles are good, perhaps the implication here is that evil centaurs were also in Narnia at the time.

When Aslan slips away during the festivities, the children are not alarmed because they have been warned by Mr. Beaver that Aslan's nature is not to like "being tied down" (182). His prediction that Aslan will "often" drop in may or may not be accurate and may seem inconsistent with his earlier statement that Aslan is "not often" in Narnia (78). As far as Lewis records in the rest of the Chronicles, Aslan seems to make very infrequent visits to Narnia.

However, perhaps not all of his visits are included, and maybe some of his appearances will be in the kind of dreams and visions which are seen in the later books. Additionally, as mentioned earlier, in later books we find the implication that Aslan is always present in Narnia even when he is not visible.

Mr. Beaver explains that Aslan "has other countries to attend to" (182), and Lewis will have Aslan appear in one of these other countries in *The Horse and His Boy*. Mr. Beaver's use of other *countries* rather than other *worlds* might seem to refer to countries in the world that Narnia is part of. However, at the end of *The Voyage of the* Dawn Treader, Aslan will tell Edmund and Lucy that he is present in their world also, though is known there by another name (Lewis 1994g, 247). Edmund's exact question, "Are you there too?" and Aslan's answer, "I am," will emphasize his presence rather than just his visible appearance.

In the years which follow, the children grow into adult kings and queens who govern Narnia well. We are told that by their efforts all the remnants of the Witch's army are "stamped out" (183). Among the specific tasks which Lewis lists is the fact that they liberate "young dwarfs and young satyrs from being sent to school," possibly a further nod to Lewis's own unhappy schooldays. Two of the statements about the monarchs' activities will be picked up by Lewis in future books. The giants which are described as being driven back to the North will appear again during the quest which Jill and Eustace undertake with Puddleglum in *The Silver Chair*. In *The Horse and His Boy*, readers will be told about one of the "visits of state" mentioned here, a trip which Edmund, Susan, and Mr. Tumnus make to the country of Calormen.

As the children grow up, each continues to be characterized by one or two dominant traits, much as they were at the start of the story. We are told that Peter becomes a "great warrior" (183), though when Peter and his siblings return to Narnia, Lewis will portray him more as a great leader than a great warrior.

Susan becomes a "tall and gracious woman" who is sought after by foreign kings (183), a quality which will serve as the basis for a major conflict in *The Horse and His Boy* (Lewis 1994a, 64–73). In

The Last Battle her fixation on being seen as attractive will cause her to lose interest in Narnia, at least temporarily (Lewis 1994b, 154). Readers may wonder exactly why she comes to be known as "Susan the Gentle" (184). Perhaps the fears she has experienced herself in *TLWW* will be the source of her gentleness toward others. Susan's reluctance to tell Edmund about Aslan's sacrifice because "it would be too awful for him" (180) certainly could be seen as a demonstration of her gentleness. In *Prince Caspian* she will be called "tender-hearted" (108) and will be afraid to shoot an attacking bear for fear it is a talking bear. Susan calls the animal "poor old Bruin" (121), and readers will be told then that "she hated killing things."

Presumably because of his treachery, repentance, redemption, and forgiveness, Edmund grows into a "graver and quieter" man than Peter (184). Called Edmund the Just, he gives valued council and judgment. In *The Horse and His Boy*, after Shasta confesses to accidentally overhearing the royal plans, readers will be given an illustration of King Edmund's quiet and compassionate brand of wisdom. Edmund will tell Shasta, "I know now that you were no traitor, boy. But if you would not be taken for one, another time try not to hear what's meant for other ears" (Lewis 1994a, 178).

Lucy, in contrast to Edmund, remains lighthearted. In contrast to Susan, she is wooed by "all Princes in those parts" rather than by "the Kings of the countries beyond the sea" (184). Lewis gives no explanation in *TLWW* as to whom these princes might be, but presumably they are humans from nearby regions. In *The Horse and His Boy*, readers will learn that during this time humans live in the nearby kingdom of Archenland. Lucy's title complements her gaiety. She is called Lucy the Valiant, signaling that she continues to demonstrate the courage which has characterized her as a young girl. Lucy's two dominant traits are exhibited when she appears as an adult in *The Horse and His Boy* and is described on her way to battle as "a fair-haired lady with a very merry face who wore a helmet and a mail shirt and carried a bow across her shoulder and a quiver full of arrows at her side" (Lewis 1994a, 176).

Finally all that remains for Lewis seems to be to get the four Pevensies back through the wardrobe. But why must they go back? In many stories the hero-cycle ends with a return home, but not in all. Lewis provides little by way of a direct answer to this question in *TLWW*. Certainly one reason they must return is the fact that the children's parents are in England and certainly would miss them. Additionally, one could argue that Peter, Susan, Edmund, and Lucy have an unspoken wish to go back to England, their parents, and their home because the return will come about through hunting the White Stag, a magical animal who grants wishes.

Tolkien followed the cycle of there and back again in both his narratives, but each time with a twist. Bilbo Baggins returns to Bag End at the end of *The Hobbit* only to leave again at the start of *The Fellowship of the Ring*. Frodo comes back to the Shire after his quest but less than two years later departs over the sea. Lewis uses this same pattern both in his space trilogy and in the Narnia books. Ransom comes back to Earth at the end of the first two space books, but at the end of the series he is taken to Perelandra. The Pevensies return to the Professor's in *TLWW* but, except for Susan, will return to Narnia for good in *The Last Battle*.

We also might raise the reverse question of why the children are brought to Narnia. Of course they are brought to provide help, but what effect do the journeys have on them? In some of the Chronicles, the adventures can be seen as a corrective. Edmund and Eustace will be turned away from their tendencies toward selfishness and bullying, and Susan will have the chance to conquer her fears. A second effect is seen in *The Silver Chair*, where Jill and Eustace will return with a curative power to right the injustices at their school. In *The Voyage of the* Dawn Treader, Aslan will offer an additional explanation, telling Lucy and Edmund, "This was the very reason why you were brought to Narnia, that by knowing me here for a little, you may know me better there" (Lewis 1994g, 247).

In accomplishing the return home through the hunting of the White Stag, Lewis skillfully ties together the novel's beginning and end, for as readers may recall, Mr. Tumnus had earlier told Lucy about "long hunting parties after the milk-white stag who could give you wishes if you caught him" (16). The return of the White Stag here can be seen as Lewis's way of indicating that Narnia is finally back to normal, as it was before the Witch. By reminding us of the novel's start, Lewis also wants us to see a series of events which, like those at the beginning of the story, come about not by chance but through the hand of Providence. First comes the news that the White Stag has "once more appeared" (184). Then, as the hunting party gives pursuit, we learn that "the horses of all the courtiers were tired out and only these four were still following." Finally the Stag just happens to disappear into the thicket where the lamp-post is located. As mentioned, the Stag's connection with granting wishes seems to suggest that the children have an unspoken desire to return to their own world, a wish fulfilled in the book's final pages.

According to Lewis's Outline of Narnian History, the Pevensies reign in Narnia from Narnian year 1000 to year 1015, a fifteen-year period later referred to as the Golden Age (1994e, 54; 1994f, 47). Peter, who entered Narnia when he was thirteen, would have been twenty-eight as they set out to hunt the White Stag. Susan, who entered Narnia at age twelve, would have been twenty-seven at the end. Edmund, ten at the start, would have been twenty-five by the time the last scene takes place. And Lucy would have been eight at the start and twenty-three by the time they return through the wardrobe.

In the final scene in Narnia, readers hear the courtly language that the four children use as adult monarchs, language which is spoken to a lesser degree in adult scenes in *The Horse and His Boy* but not in the children's later returns to Narnia. *TLWW* will be the only one of the Chronicles in which Lewis has his protagonists grow up. If readers are somewhat less captivated by the adult versions of Peter, Susan, Edmund, and Lucy here, we can perhaps conclude that Lewis was too, as he will always keep them young in further tales.

As the four arrive at the lamp-post, Edmund has a feeling he has seen it before, and Lucy voices the premonition that if they continue on, they will either find "strange adventures" or "some great change of our fortunes" (186). Edmund, Peter, and Susan share this premonition, but Susan, even now still concerned about safety, concludes, "Wherefore by my counsel we shall lightly return to our horses and follow this White Stag no further."

Peter asks to be excused from any turning back since during their reigns they have never before done so once they had set their hands "to any high matter" (186). Lucy the Valiant agrees with Peter, telling her older sister, "We should be shamed if for any fearing or foreboding we turned back from following so noble a beast as now we have in chase" (186–7). To her credit, Susan responds to her siblings' correction and declares herself ready "to take the adventure that shall fall to us" (187). In *The Silver Chair* Lewis will have Rilian voice similar thoughts as he, Puddleglum, Jill, and Eustace are about to set out on a similar journey back to the surface world. The Prince will tell his companions, "Let us descend into the city and take the adventure that is sent us" (Lewis 1994f, 191). Tirian will use similar words in *The Last Battle* when he agrees to allow Eustace and Jill to come with him and take "the adventure that Aslan would send them" (Lewis 1994b, 106). There Lewis will point out that this phrase does not mean the same thing as taking "their chance" but has clear providential overtones.

The four monarchs enter the thicket. Just as he had not earlier explicitly described their entrance into Narnia, here Lewis does not fully explain the means by which they return to the Professor's. Before they have gone twenty steps, they remember what the lamp-post is. Before twenty more, they are passing through coats, not branches. The next moment they tumble out of the wardrobe restored to their former ages and wearing the clothes in which they had left.

Five of the seven Narnia books will end with the human characters returning to England—the exceptions being *The Horse and His Boy*, where Shasta and Aravis journey from Calormen to Narnia, and *The Last Battle*, where the Seven Friends of Narnia leave the old Narnia and enter the new. The challenge for Lewis was how, in five returns, to not end up repeating himself. Earlier, when writing the first two books of his space trilogy, Lewis faced the same challenge when Ransom travels first to Mars and then to Venus. In the first journey, Ransom is transported in a spherical spaceship built by a human scientist. In the second, he travels in a white coffinlike structure propelled by an angelic being called an Oyarsa. In an interview Lewis alluded to the need to make each trip different, stating, "It's only the first journey to a new planet that is of any interest to imaginative people" (1982h, 145).

In the Chronicles, each of the five returns and subsequent changes of clothing will be staged somewhat differently. In *TLWW*, the children are somehow magically returned in their original clothes, a mechanism which is necessary since the old school clothes were presumably outgrown, worn out, or simply discarded many years previously. In the second return, described in *Prince Caspian*, the children must "take off their royal clothes" and put on "their school things" before walking through a doorway which Aslan has set up (Lewis 1994e, 222).

Perhaps we are meant to believe that before the four Pevensies departed on the hunt for the White Stag, they had left Peter's sword and shield, Susan's bow and arrows, and Lucy's cordial behind at Cair Paravel, because in *Prince Caspian* these objects are found still preserved in the treasure chamber, but Susan's horn is not. About her horn Susan will explain, "I took it with me the last day of all, the day we went hunting the White Stag. It must have got lost when we blundered back into that other place" (Lewis 1994e, 27). In *Prince Caspian* Doctor Cornelius will present the horn to Caspian with this explanation: "That is the greatest and most sacred treasure of Narnia. Many terrors I endured, many spells did I utter, to find it, when I was still young. It is the magic horn of Queen Susan herself which she left behind her when she vanished from Narnia at the end of the Golden Age" (61–2). When he declares Susan's horn to be Narnia's "greatest and most sacred treasure," Doctor Cornelius is seemingly unaware that the other gifts are still in existence.

Back at the Professor's, the children return to the same day and same hour that they left, but not the same moment. When a person is in Narnia, time does pass in England, but much more slowly. The fur coats left behind in Narnia long ago as the weather warmed become the reason the children feel they must tell the Professor about their adventure. Mysteriously, he seems to somehow know that the wardrobe, after allowing the three previous passages described in *TLWW*, will not serve again as a means of transport to Narnia—a prediction which holds true throughout the Chronicles. Exactly why the children will not enter Narnia through the wardrobe again is never explained, but in *Prince Caspian* Lewis will offer a clue. Toward the middle of the book when Lucy tells Aslan that she thought he would come roaring in and frighten all the enemies away, as he did on their first adventure, he will answer, "Things never happen the same way twice" (1994e, 143). This is a statement which perhaps should not be taken too literally, since Lucy was able to enter into Narnia not only twice but three times in the same way and Edmund was able to use the wardrobe passageway twice.

Not only does the Professor know that the children will not use the wardrobe again, he also knows that they will return to Narnia someday. His mysterious power of intuition is also never explained but will be seen again in *The Last Battle*. There Eustace will tell Tirian, "The Professor had a feeling that we were somehow wanted over here" (Lewis 1994b, 58).

The Professor further tells the children that they should not "*try* to get there at all" (188), a somewhat interesting bit of advice in light of what takes place in two later stories. In *The Silver Chair* Eustace and Jill could be said to "try" to get to Narnia. They stand with their arms in front of them with the palms down and call, "Aslan, Aslan, Aslan" (Lewis 1994f, 10), although Eustace makes it clear this is a request to Aslan and not "as if we thought we could make him do things" (9). In what seems to be an even clearer attempt to try to get to Narnia, later the Professor himself will send Peter and Edmund to retrieve the magic travel rings he and Polly had used earlier (Lewis 1994b, 58). Perhaps worth noting, this later attempt is not successful.

Finally, the Professor tells the children, "Don't mention it to anyone else unless you find that they've had adventures of the same sort themselves" (188). This recommendation turns out to be a good one, for in *The Voyage of the* Dawn Treader, while Eustace is staying with the Pevensies, he will accidentally overhear them talking about Narnia and then will love "teasing them about it" (Lewis 1994g, 7). Lewis will also revisit this bit of advice in the final book of the series when Jill will tell Tirian, "The Professor and Aunt Polly had got all us friends of Narnia together . . . so that we could all have a good jaw about Narnia (for of course there's no one else we can ever talk to about things like that)" (Lewis 1994b, 57–8). Eustace is not present in *TLWW* when the children are given this injunction, so perhaps we should not be surprised when he makes an exception to this principle by telling Jill about Narnia at the start of *The Silver Chair* (Lewis 1994f, 7).

How will the children know if someone else has had "adventures of the same sort"? The Professor tells them that "odd things they say" and even their looks will "let the secret out" (189). Careful readers will remember that the Professor himself said one of the oddest things in the story in his response to Peter and Susan: "How do you know that your sister's story is not true?" (47). His looks too were described as odd (3). So perhaps this is his way of hinting to the children that he has been to Narnia himself.

Lewis uses the Professor's declaration, "Bless me, what *do* they teach them at these schools?" (189) to end the novel with a laugh. Lewis will turn to the same device in the next book, as *Prince Caspian* will close with Edmund's complaint, "Bother! I've left my new torch in Narnia" (1994e, 223). A comical quip from Uncle Andrew will be the last line in *The Magician's Nephew* (Lewis 1994d, 202).

And so after 189 pages of adventure, Lewis closes the door on the wardrobe but ends with the door open to Narnia. In the Professor's promise, "Of course you'll get back to Narnia again someday," we have the possibility though not the necessity for a sequel. The final sentence in the story is, "But if the Professor was right it was only the beginning of the adventures of Narnia" (189), and in his use of *if* here, Lewis himself emphasizes the point that further stories are certainly a possibility but not more than this.

Earlier the question was raised, "Why do the children have to leave Narnia?" One additional answer might be *because we do*. The book *The Lion, the Witch and the Wardrobe* is like a magical wardrobe itself, taking us—along with Peter, Susan, Edmund, and Lucy—to an enchanted land. When we finish the last page and close the cover, we too are returned to the place we started. What effect does the journey have on us? While each reader will answer this question in a somewhat different way, perhaps three general effects might be briefly mentioned.

First, we are certainly meant to identify with the children, to learn what they learn, and to be challenged and encouraged by their example. In Edmund we might see our own selfishness and self-deception, and through his story we may be able to begin confronting these faults in ourselves. The same could be said about the fearfulness Susan must prevail over. Like her, we may become more ready to "take the adventure that shall fall to us." Like Peter, we might learn we can do more than we imagine if we will only try. Our admiration of Lucy's sensitivity and compassion toward others may lead us to nurture these qualities in our own encounters.

Second, whether readers see Aslan as a Christ-figure or simply as Aslan, by the end of the story readers come to share the trust he engenders. The children learn through their encounters with him not only to trust him but also to believe in themselves and in the abilities of those around them. After meeting Aslan we, like the children, come to have a greater faith that things will work out, though sometimes with great difficulty and sacrifice and often in ways unforeseen.

Finally, I mentioned in the introduction that Lewis once classified two types of books for young people based on their effect. One kind makes us less contented with our ordinary world; the other helps us return to our world with newfound wonder and admiration. Tolkien recognized this second effect as a quality of the fairy tale, with its ability to "clean our windows" from "the drab blur of triteness and familiarity" (1966, 77). This type of story, Tolkien argued, helps us recover a way of "seeing things as we are (or were) meant to see them." After closing the cover to *The Lion, the Witch and the Wardrobe*, to paraphrase Lewis (1982e, 38), we do not despise the real lions, woods, wardrobes, lamp-posts, or beavers in our world because we have read of enchanted ones. The reading makes all real things a little enchanted.

In a letter written in 1951, just one year after *The Lion, the Witch and the Wardrobe* was published and before the rest of the series was finished or even fully conceived, Lewis wrote to a friend, "I am going to be (if I live long enough) one of those men who *was* a famous writer in his forties and dies unknown. . . . One thing is certain: much better to begin (at least) learning humility on this side of the grave than to have it all as a fresh problem on the other" (Lewis 1993, 415). Here we have one of the more obvious instances where Lewis was wrong about something—completely wrong. After the seven stories about the land of Narnia were published in his fifties, C. S. Lewis went on to become more famous than ever. And given the huge success that the Chronicles had during Lewis's own lifetime, not to mention afterwards, they were highly unlikely to be very helpful in teaching him much humility.

Ten years after he finished *TLWW*, Lewis wrote another letter, this one to a schoolgirl in America who had written requesting advice on writing. Lewis gave her a number of practical tips, and among them were reading "all the good books you can," turning off the radio (today he might also have mentioned the television and the computer), and taking "great pains to be clear" (1993, 485). Near the end of his list, Lewis included the following recommendation: "When you give up a bit of work don't (unless it is hopelessly bad) throw it away. Put it in a drawer. It may come in useful later. Much of my best work, or what I think my best, is the rewriting of things begun and abandoned years earlier."

In this final suggestion, Lewis claimed to be speaking from his own experience. Begun in 1940 on the back of another manuscript, the opening paragraph for a new story about four children named Ann, Martin, Rose, and Peter was quickly abandoned and seemingly forgotten. Taken out of its drawer, completed, and published ten years later, *The Lion, the Witch and the Wardrobe* would go on to become, as readers and even Lewis himself seem to agree, among the "best work" he ever did.

Reference List

Andersen, Hans Christian. 1984. "The Snow Queen." *The Complete Hans Christian Andersen Fairy Tales*. Ed. Lily Owens. New York: Gramercy Books, 53–75.

Auden, W. H. 1976. "The Hero Quest." *Tolkien and the Critics*. Notre Dame, IN: University of Notre Dame Press, 40–61.

Bremer, John. 1998. "Clive Staples Lewis 1898–1963: A Brief Biography." *The C. S. Lewis Readers' Encyclopedia*. Eds. Jeffrey D. Schultz and John G. West Jr. Grand Rapids: Zondervan, 9–65.

Campbell, Joseph. 1968. *The Hero with a Thousand Faces*. Princeton, NJ: Princeton University Press.

Carroll, Lewis. 1998. *Alice's Adventures in Wonderland and Through the Looking Glass*. Oxford: Oxford University Press.

Chesterton, G. K. 1994. *Orthodoxy*. Wheaton: Harold Shaw.

Christopher, Joe. 1987. *C. S. Lewis*. Boston: Twayne Publishers.

Duriez, Colin. 2000. *The C. S. Lewis Encyclopedia*. Wheaton: Crossway.

Filmer, Kath. 1993. *The Fiction of C. S. Lewis: Mask and Mirror*. New York: St. Martin's Press.

Ford, Paul F. 1994. *Companion to Narnia*. 4th ed. New York: HarperSanFrancisco.

Gibson, Evan. 1980. *C. S. Lewis: Spinner of Tales*. Grand Rapids: Christian University Press.

Glover, Donald. 1981. *C. S. Lewis: The Art of Enchantment*. Athens, OH: Ohio University Press.

Green, Roger Lancelyn, and Walter Hooper. 1994. *C. S. Lewis: A Biography*. New York: Harvest.

Hein, Rolland. 1998. *Christian Mythmakers*. Chicago: Cornerstone.

Hooper, Walter. 1980. *Past Watchful Dragons: A Guide to C. S. Lewis's Chronicles of Narnia*. London: Fount.

———. 1996. *C. S. Lewis: A Companion and Guide*. New York: HarperCollins.

Howard, Thomas. 1980. *The Achievement of C. S. Lewis*. Wheaton: Harold Shaw.

Hunt, Peter. 2001. *Children's Literature*. Oxford: Blackwell.

Karkainen, Paul A. 1979. *Narnia Explored*. Old Tappan, NJ: Fleming H. Revell.

Kilby, Clyde. 1964. *The Christian World of C. S. Lewis*. Grand Rapids: Eerdmans.

King, Don. 1984. "Narnia and the Seven Deadly Sins." *Mythlore* 10:14–19.

———. 1986. "The Childlike in George MacDonald and C. S. Lewis." *Mythlore* 12:17–22, 26.

———. 1987. "The Wardrobe as Christian Metaphor." *Mythlore* 14:25–27, 33.

———. 1998. "Chanson D'Aventure." *The C. S. Lewis Reader's Encyclopedia*. Ed. Jeffrey D. Schultz and John G. West Jr. Grand Rapids: Zondervan, 112.

Kocher, Paul. 1972. *Master of Middle-Earth: The Fiction of J. R. R. Tolkien*. New York: Ballantine.

Kort, Wesley. 2001. *C. S. Lewis: Then and Now*. Oxford: Oxford University Press.

Lewis, C. S. 1955. *Surprised by Joy*. New York: Harvest.

———. 1961a. *A Grief Observed*. New York: HarperSanFrancisco.

———. 1961b. *A Preface to Paradise Lost*. Oxford: Oxford University Press.

———. 1962. "The Literary Impact of the Authorized Version." *They Asked for a Paper*. London: Geoffrey Bles, 26–50.

———. 1964. *Poems*. New York: Harvest.

———. 1967. *Letters to an American Lady*. Grand Rapids: Eerdmans.

———. 1974. *The Great Divorce*. New York: Touchstone.

———. 1979. *The Letters of C. S. Lewis to Arthur Greeves*. Ed. Walter Hooper. New York: Collier.

———. 1982a. "It All Began with a Picture. . . ." *On Stories and Other Essays on Literature*. Ed. Walter Hooper. New York: Harvest, 53–54.

———. 1982b. "The Novels of Charles Williams." *On Stories and Other Essays on Literature*. Ed. Walter Hooper. New York: Harvest, 21–7.

———. 1982c. "On Criticism." *On Stories and Other Essays on Literature*. Ed. Walter Hooper. New York: Harvest, 127–141.

———. 1982d. "On Stories." *On Stories and Other Essays on Literature*. Ed. Walter Hooper. New York: Harvest, 3–20.

———. 1982e. "On Three Ways of Writing for Children." *On Stories and Other Essays on Literature*. Ed. Walter Hooper. New York: Harvest, 31–43.

———. 1982f. "Sometimes Fairy Stories May Say Best What's to Be Said." *On Stories and Other Essays on Literature*. Ed. Walter Hooper. New York: Harvest, 45–8.

———. 1982g. "Tolkien's *The Lord of the Rings*." *On Stories and Other Essays on Literature*. Ed. Walter Hooper. New York: Harvest, 83–90.

———. 1982h. "Unreal Estates." *On Stories and Other Essays on Literature*. Ed. Walter Hooper. New York: Harvest, 143–153.

———. 1986. *Reflections on the Psalms*. New York: Harvest.

———. 1988. *The Four Loves*. New York: Harvest.

———. 1989. "The Genesis of a Medieval Book." *Studies in Medieval and Renaissance Literature*. Ed. Walter Hooper. Cambridge, England: Cambridge University Press, 18–40.

———. 1992. *The Allegory of Love*. New York: Oxford University Press.

———. 1993. *Letters of C. S. Lewis*. Ed. W. H. Lewis and Walter Hooper. New York: Harvest.

———. 1994a. *The Horse and His Boy*. New York: Harper Trophy.

———. 1994b. *The Last Battle*. New York: Harper Trophy.

———. 1994c. *The Lion, the Witch and the Wardrobe*. New York: Harper Trophy.

———. 1994d. *The Magician's Nephew*. New York: Harper Trophy.

———. 1994e. *Prince Caspian*. New York: Harper Trophy.

———. 1994f. *The Silver Chair*. New York: Harper Trophy.

———. 1994g. *The Voyage of the Dawn Treader*. New York: Harper Trophy.

———. 1995. *C. S. Lewis' Letters to Children*. Ed. Lyle W. Dorsett and Marjorie Lamp Mead. New York: Touchstone.

———. 1996a. *An Experiment in Criticism*. Cambridge: Cambridge University Press.

———. 1996b. "First and Second Things." *God in the Dock*. Grand Rapids: Eerdmans, 278–81.

———. 1996c. *Mere Christianity*. New York: Touchstone.

———. 1996d. *Miracles*. New York: Touchstone.

———. 1996e. "Myth Became Fact." *God in the Dock*. Grand Rapids: Eerdmans, 63–7.

———. 1996f. *Out of the Silent Planet*. New York: Scribner.

———. 1996g. *Perelandra*. New York: Scribner.

————. 1996h. *The Problem of Pain*. New York: Touchstone.

————. 1996i. *The Screwtape Letters*. New York: Touchstone.

————. 2003. *That Hideous Strength*. New York: Scribner.

Lewis, Warren. 1988. *Brothers and Friends: The Diaries of Major Warren Hamilton Lewis*. Ed. Clyde S. Kilby and Marjorie Lamp Mead. New York: Ballantine.

————. 1993. "Memoir of C. S. Lewis." *Letters of C. S. Lewis*. Ed. W. H. Lewis and Walter Hooper. New York: Harvest, 21–46.

Lindskoog, Kathryn. 1998a. "Jill Flewett Freud." *The C. S. Lewis Reader's Encyclopedia*. Ed. Jeffrey D. Schultz and John G. West Jr. Grand Rapids: Zondervan, 175–6.

————. 1998b. *Journey into Narnia*. Pasadena, CA: Hope Publishing House.

————. 1998c. "Pauline Baynes." *The C. S. Lewis Reader's Encyclopedia*. Ed. Jeffery D. Schultz and John G. West Jr. Grand Rapids: Zondervan, 93.

MacDonald, George. 1996. *George MacDonald: An Anthology*. Ed. C. S. Lewis. New York: Touchstone, xxi–xxxiv.

Manlove, Colin. 1987. *C. S. Lewis: His Literary Achievement*. New York: St. Martin's.

————. 1993. *The Chronicles of Narnia: The Patterning of a Fantastic World*. New York: Twayne Publishers.

Meilaender, Gilbert. 1998. *The Taste for the Other: The Social and Ethical Thought of C. S. Lewis*. Grand Rapids: Eerdmans.

Mills, David. 2002. "The Writer of Our Story: Divine Providence in *The Lord of the Rings*." *Touchstone* 15.1:22–28.

Milton, John. 1969. *Paradise Lost*. Ed. William G. Madsen. New York: Modern Library Edition.

Muir, Edwin. 1954. "Strange Epic." *The Observer*. August 22, 1954. 7.

Myers, Doris T. 1994. *C. S. Lewis in Context*. Kent, OH: Kent State University Press.

Nesbit, E. 1994. "The Aunt and Amabel." *The Magic World*. New York: Puffin, 191–203.

Sammons, Martha. 1979. *A Guide Through Narnia*. Wheaton: Harold Shaw.

Sayer, George. 1994. *Jack: A Life of C. S. Lewis*. Wheaton: Crossway.

Schakel, Peter. 1979. *Reading with the Heart: The Way into Narnia*. Grand Rapids: Eerdmans.

————. 2002. *Imagination and the Arts in C. S. Lewis*. Columbia, MO: University of Missouri Press.

Shippey, Tom. 2000. *J. R. R. Tolkien: Author of the Century*. New York: Houghton Mifflin.

Tolkien, J. R. R. 1966. "On Fairy-Stories." *The Tolkien Reader*. New York: Ballantine, 33–99.

————. 1994a. *The Fellowship of the Ring*. Boston: Houghton Mifflin.

————. 1994b. *The Hobbit*. Boston: Houghton Mifflin.

————. 1994c. *The Return of the King*. Boston: Houghton Mifflin.

————. 1994d. *The Two Towers*. Boston: Houghton Mifflin.

————. 2000. *The Letters of J. R. R. Tolkien*. Ed. Humphrey Carpenter. Boston: Houghton Mifflin.

Walsh, Chad. 1979. *The Literary Legacy of C. S. Lewis*. New York: Harcourt Brace Jovanovich.

Wilson, A. N. 1991. *C. S. Lewis: A Biography*. London: Flamingo.

Devin Brown has been writing and speaking about C. S. Lewis for over ten years. He is a professor of English at Asbury College, where he teaches a class on C. S. Lewis's fiction. He and his wife live in Lexington, Kentucky.